BEING BODIES

BEING BODIES

BUDDHIST WOMEN
ON THE PARADOX
OF
EMBODIMENT

Edited by
LENORE FRIEDMAN
and SUSAN MOON

SHAMBHALA
Boston & London
1997

SHAMBHALA PUBLICATIONS, INC.
Horticultural Hall
300 Massachusetts Avenue
Boston, MA 02115
http://www.shambhala.com

9 8 7 6 5 4 3 2 1

First Edition

Printed in the United States of America

♾ This edition is printed on acid-free paper that meets the American National Standards Institute Z39.48 Standard.

Distributed in the United States by Random House, Inc., and in Canada by Random House of Canada Ltd

Library of Congress Cataloging-in-Publication Data

Being bodies: Buddhist women on the paradox of embodiment/edited by Lenore Friedman and Susan Moon.
    p. cm.
  ISBN 1-57062-324-4 (pbk.: alk. paper)
  1. Women (Buddhism) 2. Body, Human—Religious aspects—Buddhism. 3. Women in Buddhism. I. Friedman, Lenore. II. Moon, Susan Ichi Su, 1942– .
BQ4570.W6B45 1997
294.3′422—DC21   97-10188
                         CIP

CONTENTS

॰७৫॰

Part Four: Body as Vehicle

Part Five: Body as Self

ACKNOWLEDGMENTS

FIRST, WE WOULD LIKE TO THANK our contributors, without whom, needless to say, there would be no book. And we thank our editor at Shambhala Publications, Emily Hilburn Sell, who proposed the book in the first place, and provided help along the way.

We thank the staff at Hedgebrook, including Denise Anderson, Kristen Birchett, Linda Bowers, Sandy Menashe, Jennifer Rose, and all the gardeners, for the gift of space, time, and fresh raspberries. We thank the other writers who shared our time there, especially Cynthia Anderson, Jan Clausen, Kia Corthron, Sharon Hashimoto, and Jeannie McCabe, for their companionship and good jokes.

Thanks to Scott Catrette, Tom Desmond, Amy Duncan, and Sonja Gardenswartz, for their meticulous transcriptions of talks and interviews.

Thanks to all the people who shared their ideas about bodies with us, including Susan Aposhyan, Bernd Bender, Angie Boissevain, Sandy Boucher, Jean Courtney, Rosalind Diamond, Thaisa Frank, Susan Griffin, Jane Hirshfield, Fanny Howe, Paula Kimbro, Rosie King-Smyth, Joanna Macy, Kathleen Meagher, Wendy Palmer, Vicki Pollard, Loie Rosenkrantz, Donald Rothberg, Judith Smith, Teah Strozer, Nancy Wakeman, and Lin Zenke.

Sue thanks Jordan Thorn for his kindness. She thanks the members of her writing group for their helpful feedback: Mary Barrett, Melody Ermachild Chavis, Ann Elliot, Kitty Hughes, Karen Payne, and Barbara Selfridge.

Lenore thanks Mimi Sternberg, Anita Barrows, Connie Batten, and Martha Boesing for being there at all the right moments, for hard questions, for laughter.

And most of all, we thank each other for the joyful experience of working together. We've both weathered rough periods while the book took shape, but our collaboration has always warmed our hearts and minds.

INTRODUCTION

✺

ONE FOGGY DAY WE WENT FOR A
walk at the Berkeley Marina, Lenore and Sue and Lenore's dog Molly.
Old friends, we hadn't seen each other for some time. We asked about
each other's writing projects—Sue was working on fiction, Lenore was
doing research for a possible book on hatred. Somewhat offhandedly,
though sincerely, we agreed that it would be fun to collaborate on a
project together.

Two days later, the thought became reality. Emily Hilburn Sell,
editor at Shambhala Publications, called Lenore to propose an anthology of writing by Buddhist women, the theme remaining open. Lenore
was intrigued and asked if it might be a collaboration with Sue Moon.
Emily said yes, and then Sue said yes—and the project was born.

But what would the theme of the anthology be? Over the next couple of months we let it simmer, passing postcards and phone messages
back and forth, until we knew: Bodies! Not the bodies themselves,
without us in them, but *embodiment*.

We wrote a proposal for Shambhala and signed a contract. We sent
out a letter inviting submissions, and slowly at first, then faster, the
manuscripts began coming in. We sifted and sorted and edited, we
talked with each other and with the contributors. We left manuscripts

on each other's front porches. All of this was fitted into the cracks of
our very busy lives.

As the collection began to take final shape, we went together to
Hedgebrook, a women's writing retreat on Puget Sound, where we had
a few weeks to work together on the book with no distractions.

There we continued the editing process, and each wrote our own
essay for the book. Over cups of tea in front of the fire it became plainer
and plainer why we were doing this work: we both love bodies. We
love our own and other people's, the body of the planet and all its
creatures. We love the beauty of form, however transitory.

But why write about women's bodies from a Buddhist perspective?

First, we are women. In unmistakably female bodies we practice
the Dharma. Our bodies define and delight us, and they torment and
betray us. From birth to death we are never without them. Menstrua-
tion, sexual union, childbirth, nursing, menopause, aging, dying—each
is a huge, embodied experience. Each links us to the physical world, to
the moon and tides, to our fellow mammals, to creatureliness in all its
myriad forms.

More and more now, we hear the Dharma from women, although,
as Rita Gross points out, this has been a hard-won battle in mainstream
Buddhism. Feminism and the women's movement have encouraged us
to speak the truth, to value ourselves, and to take charge of our bodies.
But our perspective in this book goes beyond the idea that we have
bodies for which we are entitled to make our own choices. We move
from *having* bodies to *being* bodies. And from that place of inhabiting
ourselves completely, we confront the paradox of embodiment.

We spend our lives in bodies, and if we realize anything we care to
call "enlightenment," it's in our bodies. In this book we wanted to
address a tendency we've both observed for spiritual seekers to leave
the body behind. From our study of the Dharma we are clear that the
body is not the ultimate truth, and that attachment to it causes suffering. But still, we don't simply leap into the realm of the Absolute. The
Absolute is here, we say, in each embodied moment—when we breathe,
when we sweat, when we bleed, when we feel desire. Even then? Even
then, we say. No other time.

Yet daily our bodies confirm for us our separation: my intact, en-
closing skin bumps up against yours. Our sense perceptions embellish
the obvious with elaborate details of how you're like me or not like me.

Whether we become enemies or friends we remain separate, looking out at each other from behind separate eyes.

But then there's the mystery: if we stay very still, inhabiting our bodies with the finest degree of awareness, if we don't move away from *anything*, we may find our edges dissolving into the everything that includes no-body. Or, as Joan Tollifson says, we "actually experience the body as permeable, borderless, empty space."

These "little" bodies, then, are what we're given in this lifetime to get to the "big body" that our conceptual minds obscure.

The body is vast; it contains multitudes, to borrow (and bend) a few words of Walt Whitman's. Everything we do, have done, will do, is in our body, from its most basic physical functions to the far reaches of acute pain to the few moments we are granted of ecstasy. Confronted with such vastness, we worked to shape and focus our theme.

The Buddha said that life is suffering, and that is where our book begins. Among the issues we invited contributors to explore were sickness, disability, pain, and death. The essays we received in return blink at nothing. The authors look at the assaults that life has thrown them with eyes as clear as water (and sometimes, in the process, they are startled by joy). In Part One, Body as Suffering, Katherine Thanas discovers her body to be her teacher as, by means of steady, exquisite attention, she allows it to slowly reveal its secrets.

We also wanted to consider our bodies as nature, as part of the body of the earth. The mountains and rivers inside us, we say, match the mountains and rivers of the earth. We trek into the wilderness to free the wildness inside us. In Part Two, Body as Nature, Kuya Minogue, in the snowy bush country of northern British Columbia, speaks of that experience.

We were curious about our ideas about our bodies: how do we perceive, construct, imagine them? What does it mean to be female, to be gay, to be old, to have bodies of different shapes and sizes and colors? And what do others think about us in these disguises? How do they define us? These issues arise throughout our book but especially in Part Three, Body as Gender, where, for example, Fran Tribe speaks about the beauty myth, and Jisho Warner about her experience as a lesbian Buddhist priest.

What about the devotional body, the body as vehicle for the divine, for the Absolute, for the nonself? We thought about devotional practices in Tibetan Buddhism (Anne Klein, Pema Chödrön, and others respond here), as well as the devotion of nonviolent civil disobedience described by Casey Hayden, and the dance/theater work of Ruth Zaporah in which movement passes beyond itself into stillness. These and other authors write about Body as Vehicle in Part Four.

What we probably discussed most, from beginning to end, was the timeless conundrum of the body and the self. Initially we both thought our own essays would explore this theme, and perhaps in the end they have. At bottom, every essay in the book probably touches upon it. But those in Part Five seem to do so most directly.

Of course despite whatever we originally planned for the book, in the end it was shaped by what each author was inspired to write. Although we suggested topics we ourselves were interested in, we gave writers freedom to choose. When all the pieces were in, they covered a lot of territory, but there were a few gaps—most notably sex! And we regret that only two pieces, Phyllis Pay's and Casey Hayden's, touch on the issue of race. Furthermore, although we invited some women of color to contribute, the book includes no ethnic Asian Buddhists (despite their significant numbers in the United States) and no African American Buddhists (still a relatively small group). We acknowledge this absence with regret. Our book reflects the lack of diversity in the *sangha* of American converts to Buddhism: it also reflects the invisible structures of racism in our lives.

So we do not pretend that our book is a comprehensive collection of everything that Buddhist women in the West have to say about the body. But it's a rich brew and we are part of a larger dialogue which includes, for example, Marianne Dresser's fine anthology, *Buddhist Women on the Edge*. We hope our collection will further the conversation.

Some of the contributors to our book live around the corner from us in Berkeley, California; some live as far away as Alaska or Ladakh. We have been immensely grateful for their honesty and willingness to talk in print about sensitive issues like disability, chronic illness, chronic pain, and eating disorders. The very subject of meditation practice and how we experience it personally is, according to some traditions, not to be spoken of. Some women in our book feel bound by these constraints, concerned with genuine dangers of ego-inflation and the possibility of confusing the psychological with the spiritual. Others dare to "speak the unspeakable," as Julie Henderson says, with trepidation and with care.

Our process of working together has been a joy. We've gotten to know each other well, and to trust each other's judgment. We complement each other with our different offerings of intuitive and analytical, hard and soft, patient and eager, looking out far, looking in deep.

As we've worked, our relationships with our own bodies have been cast into relief. We haven't turned away from each other's bodily struggles, as is so easy to do, but have together gently considered our headaches and sore hips and insomnia. We've been able to attend to each other's pain instead of feeling trapped inside our separate bodies.

At Hedgebrook, as we wrote our individual essays, they too became collaborations. The subjects we chose—aging and loneliness—particularly frighten us (that's partly why we chose them). Sometimes one of us, sometimes the other, felt she was stumbling in the dark, with no visible exit. But it was never completely dark; we always heard the other's voice saying that all was well. We honed our thinking, talking at length about what it means to us to be "old," what it means to be "alone." In the evenings we took long walks, sometimes in the rain, sometimes in the company of Mount Rainier on the southern horizon; and we talked about difficult ideas like "no fixed self" and the possibility of unconditional love.

Entering the final stages of the book together, we were struck by how much it felt like a conversation of overlapping voices, revelations, and perceptions among these many diverse women—a conversation in which we take courage from each other, a conversation that we hope now includes you. We are not alone here, after all.

Today it is hard to imagine either one of us doing the book without the other. In fact it couldn't have happened. We've done what we hoped to do when we first began: to go to the edge of what we knew, and then to go further, together. Our process has matched our content. Collaboration has moved us beyond our separate selves.

PART ONE

◎◎

Body as Suffering

Body of Radiant Knots
HEALING AS REMEMBERING

JOAN ITEN SUTHERLAND

THE TWO THINGS THAT HAVE shaped my adult life more than anything else are meditation and being sick. I know this is true because I cry as I write it. They are so tightly braided that I can no longer imagine what either would be without the other. Meditation helped me to make it through years of illness; illness forced my meditation to be deep and strong and real. Because of their unyielding collaboration, the dark colors of the open wound and the experience of bearing the unbearable are known to me.

Also known is the experience of healing. Healing not as the elimination of disease, but as a falling in love with the poignancy of being alive: taking the great injured heart of the world for my own and coming to respect the essential mystery of life, so that my answer to many questions is "I don't know," and this not knowing is a form of generosity.

A Zen koan says, "The buddha made of wood won't pass through the fire. If she does, she will surely burn." What does it mean to burn in this way? What does it mean to become smoke and ash, and where does that buddha go?

Since 1979 I've experienced neurological and immunological problems arising from accidental exposure to a toxic chemical. Several times I was pretty sure I might die; mostly, long stretches of being bedridden have alternated with periods when I've struggled to live as normal a life as possible. For most of this time, to the extent I could, I practiced Soto Zen meditation, which meant counting my breaths or sitting in *shikantaza*, a state of still attention.

Through illness, I was conscripted into an experience of the Dharma. At times my haywire nervous system caused moment-by-moment fluctuations in my perceptions, physical sensations, and mood that made it difficult to hold on to a sense of a continuing self, even when I desperately wanted to. As my immune system broke down in some areas—making me vulnerable to infections—and became overactive in others—so that I developed allergies and autoimmune reactions—my condition was constantly affected by subtle changes in my environment, making it difficult to pinpoint where self ended and other began.

Sometimes, when things were really difficult, focusing on my breath was a way of finding anchor in a sea of fear and distress, or of calling back the pieces of a rapidly fragmenting self. When I was feeling better the movement reversed, and breathing mindfully helped release the constrictions of illness, expanding and softening my edges as I opened back into the world.

With shikantaza, when I was relatively healthy and my body could be porous, I sank into the great hum of the world, my breath mixing with all the life around me. But when I was heavy with illness and couldn't feel my body's permeability, I stayed with heaviness. If I was stuck in pain or lightheadedness or hypersensitivity to sensory stimuli, I rested my attention there, and over time I developed an exquisite familiarity with my symptoms and emotional states.

I began to be able to call up this attention-without-comment throughout the day, and I tried to cultivate an attitude of curiosity to counterbalance the fear I often felt. I remember walking in my garden when my leg suddenly went out from under me, and I fell in a heap. A few hours later depression came on without warning, but I could see, with the awareness cultivated in meditation, that these two seemingly separate events were part of the same neurological storm system, and I was able to weather the depression without taking it personally. I remember coming out of a seizure once, filled not with terror for my loss of consciousness, but with awe at the vision I'd had of a woman in a beautifully decorated veil, who pulled it aside to sing to me.

Meditation enabled me to watch what was happening unflinchingly, and over time to deeply accept it as the fact of my life. It helped me to build a psychic container strong enough to hold experiences that otherwise might have overwhelmed me. It takes strength of soul to absorb the losses of chronic illness—losses of relationship, work, the simple pleasures of a body that simply works—and meditation does strengthen the soul. There's also an unanticipated sweetness that comes with including the hard stuff, an acceptance of all of myself that became easier to extend to others as well. Though illness limited my ability to practice in the traditional sense—I eventually stopped trying to be part of a sangha, and five minutes of lying-down *zazen* was as good as it got some days—it also brought me quickly, surely, and repeatedly to a confrontation with the Great Matter. We're all standing at the cliff edge of life and death all the time; it's just that, with chronic illness, you can never forget you're there.

In this mindful attention to my illness, though, I was also a little too ready to be okay with things as they were. Every practice has its shadow side, and I've come to see that this kind of Zen, at least the way I held it, had an aura of resignation about it. There is something noble about doing a hard thing gracefully, but there's something equally noble about seeking transformation with a white-hot desire and a willingness to risk everything.

A few years ago, through a network of friendships, I fell unexpectedly into the Lakota (Sioux) way of healing. The medicine man with whom I worked asked me two questions: Do you want to heal? Are you willing to ask for it with your whole heart and accept whatever comes? A Lakota prayer song goes, "Great Mystery, have pity on me; I want to live, this is why I do this." Shamanic tradition's straightforward expression of desire—the powerful act of naming what you want—brought me to a new relationship with both my illness and my practice. Could I, without reservation, put my faith in the possibility of transformative intervention? This felt really risky because it threatened my hard-won equanimity. Was I engaging in the very grasping and attachment that meditation practice is supposed to still? What if I rekindled my longing for health and it didn't work? In the end, it took a dream to make the way clear:

> I'm walking through a field with a Lakota friend of mine. A group
> of spirit-people are coming down a mountain in front of us. But

blocking our path is a lion attacking a wildebeest. I have to decide whether to intervene in this life and death struggle so that we can reach the spirit-people, or to let nature take its course. I decide to stop the lion, and I kick at it so hard I wake myself up.

And so for nine months I was doctored in the traditional Lakota way. I learned that people in grief are *wakan*, or sacred. It is this place of the broken heart, the broken spirit, the broken body, where we are, if we can see it, cracked open to the mystery. In this wakan moment, we are naked before the Great Matter. In the pitch-black of the sweat-lodge, sweat and snot and tears pouring from me, my face in the dirt as it got really hot, I sang and begged for mercy.

In ceremonies, dreams, and visions the spirits gave me many things to do. My life became a round of prayer, purification, and sacrifice. A Lakota prayer begins by acknowledging one's humility and asking for help; it ends with a dedication of the prayer to all one's relations. I came to see that my illness was a tear in the fabric of not just my life, but in life-as-a-whole, and that my relations—human, spirit, plant, animal—were more than willing to help stitch it back up. In return, I undertook to continue circulating the gift through the sangha of all beings in whatever ways I am able.

When the ceremonial cycle was complete, a radical change in my condition had occurred. This is not to say that I am without physical problems, though they are vastly fewer and farther between. It's more that I've experienced how life-as-a-whole is dealing with them, and I feel lighter. In Buddhism we talk about raising one's *bodhicitta*, one's intention toward enlightenment for the benefit of all beings. It was shamanic practice that showed me how this worked in all directions: how all beings desired my healing, which enabled me to desire it for myself.

Shamanic practice brings in the wild. It cracks things open, turns them on their head, throws the broken bricks of ruined structures up into the air to fall back to earth in a rain of flowers. In that vivid space I could see that the truest acceptance of my circumstances was not the same as resignation to my fate. Acceptance can be dynamic; it can include the possible as well as the actual. This new openness, and my increasing health, led me to begin practicing in a different Zen tradition, which in some important ways integrated my meditative and shamanic experiences. I started sitting with the Diamond Sangha, who practice a combination of Rinzai and Soto that includes koan study. This involves meditation on a series of questions that can lead to direct insight into the nature of reality, and then deepens and broadens that understanding.

In the experience of insight, body and mind fall away. The distinctions we make between the two, and the distinctions between self and other, disappear. The question of living or dying falls away, too. I've experienced this, with great wonder, as "nothing to stand on, nowhere to fall." And yet at the same time there is a profound sense of location: I am right here, sitting in the *dokusan* line before dawn, one candle burning, incense smoke hanging in the air. When the landscape is lit from within, the body is no longer something alive, but life itself, pure and clear.

There's an essential mystery here. From the perspective of emptiness, living or dying doesn't matter, sick or well doesn't matter. This is not indifference, but an affirmation that life shines everywhere equally, without distinction or preference. It's all holy. In the same moment, without separation, it does matter whether my head hurts or my energy is good today. This is also holiness. Both are buddha-nature: empty buddha, sick buddha. Body of radiance, body of knots. Body of radiant knots. Just perfect, this crankiness; completely frustrating, this perfection. At night it all tumbles into sleep together.

This is an act of remembering. This is Zen's direct transmission outside the scriptures. In koan practice you return the gift by presenting your insight, embodying it. You can't explain a koan; you can't keep it at a distance. You have to become intimate with it, let it enter you as you enter the moment of eternity it opens before you. It's physical and visceral as well as intuitive. Sometimes the answer to a koan comes in a flash of insight, where I suddenly know that I know. At other times, when I don't understand a koan, I act it out, and the answer becomes apparent through a kind of kinetic intelligence. When I truly *am* the old Chinese monk or the oak tree in the garden or the young woman sitting in meditation, when the koan is embodied in me, then I've answered it.

Through years of illness my body was the dark engine of my practice. Now this same body is itself a locus of wisdom. As I learn to trust this, the uninhibited presentation of koan practice can be a challenge.

At some point, though, I stopped worrying about making a fool of myself and *became* the fool. This is the process of remembering my buddha-nature in my bones and sinews. There's nothing more delightful than hearing gusts of laughter or big thumps on the floor coming from the dokusan interview room and knowing that someone else is being exquisitely foolish too. I love that this practice allows for, asks for, playfulness: the ground note for me these days is a kind of idiot joy. I appreciate our great Chinese ancestor Pang Lingzhao, who, when she saw her father trip and fall, threw herself down beside him. He asked her what she was doing, and she replied, "I saw you fall to the ground, so I'm helping."

A few years ago I moved to this cottage out in the country, not sure if I'd come here to live or to die. My intuition was true, if not literal: here in the woods, at the edge of the ocean, I've let illness kill me, let meditation kill me, so that I might live. These are lovers who ask everything and promise nothing. Like the wooden buddha in the fire, I've had to burn for it. Because of the intensity of my experience, the heroic qualities of the traditional Zen path are in some ways attractive to me. But in the end my healing has been a different kind of story: the dragon once slain doesn't stay dead, the grail once gotten winks in and out of view. In the hero's tale, illness would be a test—you triumph over it to win the prize, but in real life the initiation goes on and on, simultaneous with the grace of small healings. All of it arising all the time, always getting better, always falling ill.

Having no choice in the matter, I've decided to be grateful for the insoluble problem of chronic illness, which keeps things close to the bone. At the same time, I can't really see it as a gift; considering how most people live, with malnutrition and disease and too much hard work, it seems more like the common condition of being human. Having known pain, it's pretty hard to be indifferent to the sufferings of others. What the experience of emptiness provides is a kind of buoyancy that makes me less likely to drown in the sea of life; I'm able to respond to suffering without being overwhelmed or paralyzed by it. A helpful compassion can be born here, I think.

So healing, for me, has been a kind of ripening. It's learning to suffer in an authentic way so that I can begin to stop suffering. It's seeing illness as an event within the body of the community that needs attending to. It's always having one ear open to the ground note of joy that comes from the experience of emptiness, a sound that's underneath both happiness and sorrow. As I become simultaneously more transparent and more vivid, as more life comes through, I revel in the delights of being a body. As Hakuin Zenji wrote, "This very place is the Lotus Land, this very body, the Buddha."

We focus so much on the enlightened mind, but what is an enlightened body? Some clues might be found in the idea of the *trikaya*, the three bodies of the buddha. The *nirmanakaya* is the transformation body, the unique form each thing takes. It's what makes conifers different from broadleaf trees. For me, shikantaza built a strong platform for my practice and opened me, through an exploration of my own particularity, to intimacy with this world of form. In my shamanic journey into *sambhogakaya*, the body of interbeing in which each thing contains all things, I came to know the spirits and my relations in the natural world as sangha. The cultivation of insight through koan practice led me directly to experience the third body, the *dharmakaya*, the absolute reality of pure and complete emptiness.

Perhaps the enlightened body, then, is all three of these: the physical body, intimate with itself as substance, matter, flesh and blood; the spirit body, intimate with other spirit bodies; the empty body, intimate with its own buddha-nature. All sick, all well, all alive, and all dead. All held in the great shining body of the world, and already true, if we can just remember it.

⊚⁄⊚

The Only Way I Know of to Alleviate Suffering

DARLENE COHEN

SELF-HEALING IS AN AREA I'VE explored intensely because I have had rheumatoid arthritis, a very painful and crippling disease, for eighteen years. It began in my seventh year of Zen practice, while I was living at Green Gulch Farm in Marin County, California. I think the idea of self-healing is especially appealing to people who have some sort of practice because we tend to use our illness and the healing process as a mode of penetration into the true nature of things and the self.

In *The Blue Cliff Record*, Yun-men said, "Medicine and sickness mutually correspond. The whole universe is our medicine. What is the self?"

When I was first very ill, and other Zen students took care of me, I actually didn't have any place to turn for healing outside of myself. When I went to the doctor, I found out there is no cure for rheumatoid arthritis. There are palliatives, drugs that lessen pain and stiffness, but there is no long-lasting remedy.

When you're in a situation like this, people give you lots of advice. My doctor, with all of society's authority behind him, told me to take toxic drugs. My friends suggested a great variety of treatments: I was given rice bread to eat instead of wheat; I was wrapped in comfrey-soaked sheets; I must have been given extracts from every benevolent plant that grows in northern California and China. But I got worse Despite all this loving care. My mobility became so impaired that people at the Zen center began cleaning my room, doing my laundry, and washing my hair. As my body got weaker and my pain got greater, I had to figure out: What is the most important thing to pay attention to here? Is the salvation I need inside or outside of me?

As it turned out, my Zen meditation training was a very great help. I had been taught to study the objects of consciousness: feelings, perceptions, sensations, and thoughts. In long periods of zazen, such as *sesshin*, I even had been able to watch my perceptions as they were being formed. This is, of course, the business of Zen meditation, to observe all these things. You simply focus your attention on what is happening now, the stream of your consciousness. There is no goal involved. The business of self-healing, on the other hand, is manipulating those objects of consciousness to increase your health.

Because of my pain I lived in a world of continual intrusive sensation. It was very much in my self-interest to notice what circumstances increased or decreased my pain and then to alter my pain level by manipulating those circumstances. Before becoming so ill, I had trouble interrupting my discursive mind to make the observations necessary to begin a mindfulness practice. On a Sunday I would vow to notice all my postural changes, determined to say to myself when I went from sitting to standing to lying: "Now I'm standing." "Now I'm lying." Then the next time I remembered, Thursday, say, I would suddenly cry, "Oh! I'm standing!" After becoming ill, I was highly motivated to make these observations. Changing my posture was a dramatic event in my life. I needed to heed every little sensation in my legs and feet in order to go from sitting to standing.

I lived a half-block from the San Francisco Zen Center and used to try to go to dinner there once a week as a treat to myself. I would walk down the hill, which brought me to the bottom of a number of steps to the front door. Going up the steps would be the second leg of a laborious journey. Sometimes I would make it all the way to the steps and not be able to go up them. So I would have to strain all the way back up the hill to my apartment. I asked myself, what is it about my walking that is so tiring? What I called "walking" was the part of the step when my foot met the sidewalk. From the point of view of the joints, that is the most stressful component of walking. The joints get a rest when the foot is in the air, just before it strikes the pavement. I found that when I focused on the foot that was in the air instead of the foot that was striking the pavement, my stamina increased enormously. After making this observation, I never again failed to climb the steps to knock on the front door of the Zen center.

I was struck that the focus of my attention could make that much difference in my physical ability. I began to search out the times my brain was clumping together many disparate motions into an idea which would prevent me from overcoming an obstacle, and then I concentrated on breaking down these aggregates of ideas into discrete units of smaller experience that I could master. Sick or well, we all do this all the time. We get into the idea of something, the clump, the heap, the pile, rather than the actual experience. Someone says, "I can't practice because I haven't been to the *zendo* in three weeks" instead of just going to the zendo when she can. During the arthritis workshops I give, I haul out the carrots and the cutting board, and everybody immediately groans: "I can't cut carrots with my arthritic hands!" But when you actually hold the knife in your hands, feeling its wooden handle and sharp, solid blade and you touch the vulnerable flesh of the carrot on the cutting board, your wrist goes up and down, up and down, and the orange cylinders of carrot begin to pile up on the board, and you realize: "I *can* cut carrots." Tears come to people's eyes.

Most importantly I learned from my study of Zen to be less attached to things. This is an important aspect of healing yourself as well: diminishing your clinging to something that was before but is no longer. It is very difficult for us to have a strong functional body displaced by a painful helpless one. It shakes us to our very identity. In order to heal, people in this situation have to give up their past, to grieve for their former bodies and then turn away, to learn to see their present bodies as real and their current lives as demanding all the creativity and energy they can summon.

Injured or not, we all have to face this situation as we age. Most people, the "temporarily abled," get to face it a little at a time rather than in one swift irreparable blow. But if you live long enough, you will know this suffering. We all have to give up our bodies someday. The sick among us get in practice.

So it's true that you can use mindfulness practice to achieve your health goals. You may even get rid of your disease or injury. But if you practice mainly to get rid of your suffering or restore an ailing body to function rather than to express your life and your nature, it is a very narrow and vulnerable achievement. Just as a clay buddha cannot go through the water or a wood buddha cannot go through the fire, a goal-oriented healing practice cannot permeate deeply enough. We must penetrate our anguish and pain so thoroughly that illness and health lose their distinction, allowing us to just live our lives. Our relief from pain and our healing have to be given up again and again to set us free of the desire to be well. Otherwise, getting well is just another hindrance to us, just another robber of the time we have to live, just another idea that enslaves us, like enlightenment. Fortunately for our way-seeking mind, recurring illness is like a villain stomping on our fingertips as we cling desperately to our healthy, functioning bodies.

The problem with being preoccupied with your health is that you get into this illusion of progress: Am I getting better? Am I getting worse? The reality is that illness and wellness are opposites on a continuum of preoccupation with health, and as opposites they have the same nature, like life and death or love and hate. When we pluck wellness out of the void, illness always comes with it. There is no essential difference between sickness and wellness; form is emptiness, emptiness is form. If you are preoccupied with how well you are, you will also notice how ill you are. This leads to despair and discouragement alternating with euphoria and encouragement, and condemns you to a life of disappointing setbacks alternating with happy swells of improvement. You become discouraged with your health when you still have some gaining idea, or some ideal you are measuring yourself against, like how you used to feel, or how someone as sick as you healed himself or herself. Your health habits can be more reliably based in daily practices which do not change with feelings about your body. You can decide how to best take care of your body, your life, and you can do it dispassionately.

Healing yourself is just like living your life. It is not a preparation for anything else, nor a journey to another situation called wellness. It is its own self; it has its own value. It is each thing as it is. Form is form; emptiness is emptiness. You live your life to express your own sincerity, your own nature. You take care of your body because it yearns to be taken care of and you feel generous toward it. You are aware of wanting to rest, wanting to eat, needing stimulation. When you feel impatient with your body or disappointed with its range of function, you can use that restlessness to express its yearning to move.

Ironically, my body was nearly immobile before I ever appreciated it. I had had a very strong, healthy body. Like a slave, it obeyed my commands. It sat through hours of pain in sesshin but I always thought, why won't it get into full lotus? I used to run with the wind along the hills above Green Gulch Farm but I always thought, why can't I run farther? Then lying in bed unable to stand up alone, I thought, thank God for one part, *any* part, that still goes up and down. Even if your body is weak or painful, it's still your home, it's how you're manifesting this life. From the practice point of view, it's also your penetration into reality. Your body is the only way that you can experience the transparency of all things and their interrelationships.

In my body therapy practice, I had a client who was in a wheelchair with a diagnosis of severe arthritis of the hips and spine. She came to me to learn how to spend some time out of the wheelchair, to walk around her house. I taught her many stretching and strengthening exercises so that her weak body could begin to support itself. For a long time she did her exercises like taking medicine—she didn't actually live through them. I could tell that by her uninspired questions: how many of each exercise should she do and what order should she do them in?

Then one session she greeted me with a big grin. She said with the tenor of real delight in her voice, "I found out everything that happens to me is information about my body. Hurting or getting tired or not feeling like exercising. I'm noticing everything!" And I knew she had gone from mechanical movement into the timeless realm of sensation itself. The whole universe was her medicine.

How do we develop this appreciation of things just as they are, the spacious and bountiful spirit of letting everything be, especially if we are sick and in pain? Our teachers tell us to look into ordinary things. Thich Nhat Hanh says that combing your hair or washing the dishes gets you in contact with reality. It is an expression of sanity to be so intimately connected to your activity itself that you can allow a broom to sweep you just as you sweep the broom. After having arthritis for several years, I spent a summer on the staff of a resort in Big Sur. Since I was spending most of the day in meetings, I wanted to make certain I had a period of vigorous exercise in the mornings. I requested the job of cabin-cleaning, a daily three-hour stint of preparing cabins for new guests. Usually only teenagers were assigned to cabin-cleaning because of the prevalent belief that the job required youth and stamina. The duties were clear-cut: replace the sheets, blankets, and bedspreads on every bed; sweep the floor; scour the sink and toilet; empty the trash; and wash the windows and mirrors. The tasks were performed at high speed because anywhere from fifteen to twenty-five cabins needed to be done by lunchtime.

Because there was no conceptual thinking required on this job, I spent the entire work period every day as an exercise session, interweaving my movements and the contact I had with inanimate objects. It required particular intimacy between my body and my task. I did back-bends and stretches while changing the bed linen; I twisted my body rhythmically to sweep floors; I hung sequentially from each vertebra in my back to scour the toilet; I squeezed the Windex bottle with all five fingers, alternating my hands, to wash the windows. I breathed fully and deeply to set a rhythm for my body movements. After a few weeks of this activity I was exhilarated and bursting with energy. My posture had improved dramatically as a result of changing between twenty and forty beds each morning. In contrast, by lunchtime every day almost all of my co-workers (no one over twenty-five years old and most of them in their teens) would be complaining about their backaches from making so many beds and scouring all those sinks. I still marvel at the efficacy of my exercises—not only the physicality of them, but the difference it made in my sense of well-being and my stamina, to be so intimately connected with my activity.

It works on a purely somatic level as well. If you slowly turn a sore leg in bed or feel your bones accept your weight, you are connected with real stuff. For some of us, being sick is the first time we slow down enough to notice our ordinary lives. Going to the bathroom and rising from the toilet seat. Listening intently to sounds we once considered background noise: children playing outside, cars passing, the sudden flash of irritation when a pen rolls off the table. Of course, these events happen to all of us all the time, sick or well, but usually we ignore them as mundane.

When Chögyam Trungpa Rinpoche wrote in *Shambhala: The Sacred Path of the Warrior* that "the human potential for intelligence and dignity is attuned to experiencing the objects around us, the brilliance of the bright blue sky, the freshness of green fields, and the beauty of the trees and mountains," I think he was suggesting that our intelligence and dignity themselves are developed by our being alive for the mundane chaos of our lives. If we cultivate awareness of our actual experience, without reference to any preconceived idea, then we don't prefer any particular state of mind. Intimacy with our activity and the objects around us connects us deeply to our lives. This connection—to the earth, our bodies, our sense impressions, our creative energies, our feelings, other people—is the only way I know of to alleviate suffering. To me our awareness of these things without preference is a meditation that synchronizes body and mind. This synchronization, the experience of deep integrity, of being all of a piece, is a very deep healing. It is unconventional to value such a subtle experience. It is not encouraged in our culture. We're much more apt to strive to feel special, uniquely talented, particularly loved. It's extraordinary to be willing to live an ordinary life, to be fully alive for the laundry, to be present for the dishes. We overlook these everyday connections to our lives, waiting for The Event.

A client of mine was very annoyed and scolded her husband for coming in and telling me a joke while I was massaging her at her house. When I asked her why she minded so much, she said to me, "He was using up my time with you." She was not in a state of mind that could be satisfied by simply listening to the sound of her husband's voice as he told a joke, of feeling my fingers on her body, of sensing the animal presence of the three of us sharing the room. She didn't even examine the starved, jealous mind that resented his brief interruption.

Paradoxically, noticing this kind of small-mindedness can actually add rich texture to the weave of your life. When you include the shadow in your perceptions, your conscious life begins to be shaded and textured by your anguish and your petty little snits. Sanitizing your thoughts and your preoccupations not only squanders vital energy that would be better spent in your creative endeavors, but your not-so-presentable life can be enormously enriching and provide the compost for the development of compassion. If you have never given in to temptation of any kind, how can you ever understand—or embrace—the sinner? I pointed out some of these things to my client. When I next saw her she told me that after our session she had begun to be flooded with perceptions. She had noticed how much pain her tense relationship with her teenage son was causing her. Being numb had enabled her to tolerate their friction, but now it was clear to her that she couldn't live with those hard feelings. She had to engage him and discuss their problems.

People sometimes ask me where my own healing energy comes from. How in the midst of this pain, this implacable slow crippling, can I encourage myself and other people? My answer is that my healing comes from my bitterness itself, my despair, my terror. It comes from the shadow. I dip down into that muck again and again and am flooded with its healing energy. Despite the renewal and vitality it gives me to face my deepest fears, I don't go willingly when they call. I've been around that wheel a million times: first I feel the despair, but I deny it for a few days; then its tugs become more insistent in proportion to my resistance; and finally it overwhelms me and pulls me down, kicking and screaming all the way. It's clear I am caught, so at last I give up to this reunion with the dark aspect of my adjustment to pain and loss. Immediately the release begins: first peace and then the flood of vitality and healing energy. I can never just give up to it when I first feel it stir. You'd think after a million times with a happy ending, I could give up right away and just say, "Take me, I'm yours," but I never can. I always resist. I guess that's why it's called despair. If you went willingly, it would be called something else, like purification or renewal or something hopeful. It's staring defeat and annihilation in the face that's so terrifying; I must resist until it overwhelms me. But I've come to trust it deeply. It's enriched my life, informed my work, and taught me not to fear the dark.

It seems to me that when we fall ill, we have an opportunity we may not have noticed when we were well, to literally in-corp-orate the wisdom of the buddhas, and to present it as our own body.

Enjoying the Perfection of Imperfection

JOAN TOLLIFSON

Meditation is so very simple. Reality is always right here, immediate. But the mind creates a web of complications that come to seem more real than the actual sounds and sensations and listening presence that *is* this moment. Apparent embodiment in a particular perishable form, with a complex brain, is undoubtedly at the root of our illusory sense of separation from the totality, and all our subsequent human problems, for it is in thinking about and identifying with the body that we seem to be vulnerable and alone. Paradoxically, the body also offers the way home, for it is in fully meeting whatever appears as pure sensation (without interpretation) that we discover the emptiness of form—the undivided wholeness of being that has no solidity, no boundaries, no limits—that which no word or image can capture, in which every thing is included. By going into the very core of whatever appears, we begin to turn our attention from the particular objects to the seeing. In that, no obstacles or problems remain.

The appearance of the body has been a koan for me throughout my life. I was born without a right hand, so from early on I have been dealing with myriad reactions, internal and external, to ideas of "imperfection" and "abnormality." When I was a toddler, people would stop my mother on the street and tell her we were being punished by God.

Children would stare and point and ask questions. Adults would hush them up. In high school, I was not a hot item with the boys. Growing up, the only cultural images I saw of disabled people were negative: Captain Hook or the Easter Seal poster children seemed to be my choices. Understandably, I did not want to think of myself as disabled.

As a young adult, I drank excessively, smoked cigarettes, took drugs, lived recklessly on the edge, and nearly died. I cultivated a kind of wild, rebellious, belligerent, tough identity. I understand, as a result of my own experience, that people don't willfully choose to commit crimes or become addicts and abusers. And I understand from my own life the healing power of love, acceptance, and caring attention.

Waking up, I went into therapy and began to discover that being disabled didn't have to mean that you were ugly, incompetent, pitiful, evil, or better off dead. I didn't have to be Captain Hook. I got involved in the disability rights movement, worked with other disabled people, and began to see my identity as a disabled person in a positive light. In the same vein, I became a proud lesbian-feminist. Certainly this was an improvement over self-hatred and self-destruction, and perhaps a very necessary step. But who am I really?

Delving seriously into Zen meditation several years later was another turn because Zen is the end of all identification. I resisted this emptiness tooth and nail. I clung to my identities, to the stories constructed by life-saving progressive politics: stories about the strength of the feminine, the virtues of being gay, the revolutionary potential of lesbianism, the righteousness of this or that cause, the suffering and oppression I'd been through. These were better than the old stories in which women were inferior, gays were mentally ill, and whatever troubles we had were the result of our own personal failures. However, these new stories were still fictitious abstractions. They had their usefulness, but many of us held on to them as reality itself. I didn't want to question this new picture of how the world was that made me feel righteous and superior. I was afraid that if I did, maybe I'd be back where I was before therapy, before women's liberation, before disability rights, back in the old story of worthlessness, the one that culminated in alcoholism and rage and near-death.

It was (and is) a slow, lifelong (yet always instantaneous) process, discovering that there can be a letting go into a deeper truth where there is no story at all, no identity, no "me" to protect, no "other" to blame, no history to cherish. In this new perspective, I don't know anymore why I became a drunk or why I sobered up. All stories, including the one I've just told, are recognized as fiction. Fiction and imagination are wonderful. We can enjoy stories, but we don't need to become entranced by them in ways that cause suffering to ourselves and others. That's what waking up is all about, as I see it. Not knowing anything. Then anything is possible.

This awakening is about coming alive to what is actually happening right now. In this aliveness, the body and the whole world of form is more vibrant and present than ever before, but it isn't solid anymore. Concepts and images don't stick. The stories (and the people we apply them to) are no longer fixed. In this openness that no longer knows what everything is, there is freedom. This not knowing is love. In this open being, every moment is devotion.

Flower, car horn, rain, contraction, headache, person, word, thought, wheelchair. What is it? Zen invited me to listen to each moment and wonder. The mind divides and evaluates. It provides answers. It imagines bondage and liberation, desirable and undesirable. In sitting quietly and listening without explanations or ideas, I discovered that there is no body. If there is just listening and experiencing, what is the body? Where is it? Where does it begin and end? Meditation reveals that the body is a painting that appears and disappears in imagination. It seems solid when we think about it, or if we look into a mirror (and think), or look at another person (and think), but in quiet sitting we can actually experience the body as permeable, borderless, empty space. And we can experience how nothing is separate from this space.

We can also see clearly how different bodies arise at every moment, not just physiologically or sub-atomically, but psychologically, image-wise. One moment I feel athletic, strong, beautiful, flexible. Another moment I feel clumsy, weak, unattractive, stiff. Whatever body image or sensation appears, there is always the possibility to see it, experience it, and not identify it as "me," not take it too seriously.

In high school I took a class in filmmaking. In the first class, I remember the teacher had us look at our thumbs. We sat there in silence, gazing at our thumbs. Minutes ticked by. We shifted restlessly in our seats. Three minutes. Five minutes. Ten minutes. Finally the teacher asked how many of us were bored. A lot of us raised our hands. He told us that if we were really seeing, we wouldn't get bored. He gave us homework assignments that involved sitting in front of trees and looking at small sections of bark for an hour, or watching grass blow in the wind.

One night I was lying on the floor in our dining room in the dark, watching shadows move on the wall. My mother came in, a bit upset, and asked me if I had finished my homework. I told her I was *doing* it. Lucky for me I could honestly say that. Otherwise I would have been told to get up and get to work. I'm not criticizing my mother; it was her job to do that. That's part of what parents and teachers have to do, they have to socialize little open beings into functional members of society. But in the process, we come to believe that the imaginary constructions of convention are reality.

Meditation is returning to that original seeing that is playful and interested in exploring. We turn from mental fantasy and story line and trying to figure things out, and open to this exact moment as unconceptualized sensate experience (smells, sounds, sensations, just as they are, without analysis or labels, without judgment). As we experience what is actually happening, we find that nothing is solid, nothing is bound or limited. By turning our attention to what is apparently most concrete, we discover that it is actually empty, spacious, and not even there. In the mental stories, we appear to exist as substantial, discrete, continuous individuals, heroines or victims of our narratives, struggling with problems that seem very tangible and real. In simple, direct experiencing, we are not there anymore as separate entities. The drama is gone, our problems dissolve into thin air because only thought kept them going. There is pure listening, without meaning or purpose. The mind is uneasy with this lack of identity and drama, and we may discover a surprising reluctance to let our troubles go. Thought quickly begins weaving another story. But there is always, in every moment, the possibility of seeing the story for what it is, and of waking up to bare presence, to just what is. This is very simple. It requires no particular body position, no especially quiet setting, no special costumes or decor, no years of grueling work. It is available every moment, everywhere.

But when spirituality gets institutionalized, often what tends to happen is that people begin inventing and sanctifying special costumes and correct postures to be in while "doing" it. I have no objections to formal meditation, nor to robes and rituals, but I wonder if these complicated systems may sometimes create an atmosphere where people who are different begin to feel that they are less than fully authentic. People with disabilities can't always get into the official costumes or the correct postures. Certainly if we imagine that waking up requires *any* particular circumstance we are missing the point.

I've lived for several years now at a meditation retreat center where all the traditional forms have been dropped, where sitting in an armchair is perfectly acceptable for anyone, where there are no particular postures or costumes to get into. I've learned here beyond any shadow of a doubt that real meditation can happen in any clothing, in any position, in any place, in any body. Even calling it "meditation" can be a step away. For me, this has been enormously freeing. It has helped me to see that meditation is every moment, not just something I do in a special place, in a particular form. It is simply being here.

Babies and animals automatically live this way. They approach my arm, the one that ends just below the elbow, without ideas. They aren't frightened or repulsed by it. They don't feel sorry for me. They don't think I'm heroic or amazing. They see the actual shape of what's in front of them without concepts and labels. They don't see it this way because they're practicing meditation or trying to be enlightened. It just happens. And the same simple seeing happens for us, too, every moment. The only problem is that for us it tends to get obscured by our belief in the reality of all the thoughts that arise, and particularly by our belief in the central thought of "me" as somebody separate from the totality, somebody who is somehow incomplete, not quite right, and in need of fixing.

Disability is a problem if we want to fix it, if we think we should be other than how we are. It ceases to be a problem as soon as we see it simply, the way the baby sees it. The physical difficulties and discomforts may still be there, the social injustices and all the rest. But none of this has to be a problem. We do what we can to relieve pain, to improve physical functioning, to change oppressive social conditions: aspirin, acupuncture, surgery, wheelchair ramps, legislation, consciousness raising, whatever. But perhaps it can be done without expectations, without attachment to our personal ideas of how everything should be, without idealism and blame, with more openness and compassion. As we rest in what's actually happening, we discover the complete perfection of imperfect existence. Physical imperfections and limitations lose their sting, and the imperfections of society (the prejudices and bad attitudes, the flawed responses) become less bothersome as well. We do what it makes sense to do, but we don't feel personally attacked and victimized by life's injustices in the way we once did. We come to realize the impersonal nature of the whole thing. In meditation we quickly discover that all the behaviors and attitudes we hate "outside" of us are there in our minds as well; the same reactive, defensive, conditioned processes are going on in all of us. There is no "other" to blame. Everything is happening on its own.

Living with disability (like all forms of upset and disappointment) is a gift if we work with it intelligently, as an opportunity to see and question our images, ideals, expectations—our basic desire to be different than we are. As these mental constructions become more transparent and begin to unravel, beauty reveals itself right here and now where we least expected to find it. Meditation teaches me that perfection is life as it actually is from moment to moment. Asymmetrical. Messy. Unresolved. Out of control. Imperfect. Terrible. And miraculous.

A Mama Raccoon
in the Net of Indra

BARBARA GATES

THIS PAST WINTER the diagnosis that I had breast cancer catapulted me out of a dark time in which I had often felt closed and disconnected. Panicked by the possibility of early death, of leaving behind a motherless five-year-old, I am challenged to heal. Each day now I nap on the grass beneath the feathery boughs of our dawn redwood, my daughter's climbing tree. Recovering from surgery and radiation, I sink gratefully into a bed of clover and dandelions. Dozing on and off I scribble in my journal and reflect back over these past months.

AS I STRUGGLED over my first treatment decision—whether to get a mastectomy (have the breast removed) or a lumpectomy (excise the tumor), I heard from deep inside myself a strict and bold voice. It might have been the voice of a Theravadan nun, I imagined, perhaps from long ago. Simple and direct in her saffron robe, she spoke, "Who needs hair? Who needs breasts?" This nun has influenced my decisions over the years to keep my grey hair undyed, my clothes and possessions simple. Here the verdict was absolute: On some vast and fundamental scale, it doesn't matter whether I have two breasts or one, or none, whether, in fact, I live in this earthly form or not.

◎◎ As I lie here well over a month since I completed radiation, I still experience exhaustion, an ache as if inside my bones. I don't know how much I am weakened by the radiation, how much I am depleted by anxiety or even the cancer itself, which we all are hoping to be gone. Again and again I wonder: What angle of mind should I take to heal? Shouldn't I visualize myself getting well, imprint my immune system with vitality, my whole body with strength? Yet, I wonder, in such a practice, is there a danger of denial? Am I fully acknowledging the reality of change? Isn't my practice now to learn to embrace life with all its thistles and stink?

As MY THOUGHTS ricocheted back and forth over this decision—breast or no breast—I felt as if I were wrestling with the whole question of what it meant to be embodied. I kept asking myself: What is this body? If I am not my body, can't I simply let the body go and take to the mind as refuge? A memory surfaced of an image I'd worked with on a three-month meditation retreat many years before. As I did the walking meditation, I would imagine my body as dead meat, a moving corpse. Then I would ever so subtly begin to distinguish the consciousness, a separate strand, interwoven, yet somehow not the body. I would experience this sometimes in an eerie way, an ongoing process of body with a parallel process of mind. But after learning of the cancer, in thrashing out a way to view my body, I found that I was repelled by this image.

◎◎ Often, hours before I begin my nap in the grass, I find relief from tangled thoughts by opening the back door to the garden. From our landing on the second floor, I can see the yards of our neighbors. Opening the door, I find the sky and the sunshine and our climbing tree. I can see Amy in back, or John in the house to our right, putting out bowls for the neighborhood cats, and I imagine Steve, down the block, putting out his bowls. I wave and Amy waves back. Our dog Cleo dashes out to chase the cats nimbly parading on the fence before they leap down on the other side toward their food. I feel somehow expanded, more permeable.

A FEW DAYS before the appointed surgery, still undecided as to whether I would keep the breast, I fled to the garden. I spent a few feverish hours digging narcissus and anemone bulbs into the hard February soil. As I dug my fingers into the ground, I felt less afraid. After this planting, I began to hear in myself a gentler voice, an invitation to tend the earth in its various forms, to help bring out its loveliness. Is gardening, then, any different, I asked myself, from honoring my body? It was then that I told the surgeon to save the breast unless he saw signs that the cancer was spreading. But to honor this physical body felt scary. Instead of simply telling the surgeons to cut the breast out of my awareness, I wanted to be present with what I might lose. And so I remembered. I conjured up the delicate nipples of adolescence like tender pink stars, the new breasts, velvet to my touch under my nightie, the erotic breasts caressed by my husband, Patrick, and past lovers over these many years, the milk-filled mother's breasts which suckled my daughter Caitlin. Cautiously, I wanted to experience the history of this embodiment, at the same time seeing the impermanence. It is much easier to be absolute, drastic, than it is to be open, uncertain. Could I learn to honor the body without insisting that it stay young or healthy or never die? Caitlin chided me the other day, "Mommy, hold me in your arms, but don't grip me."

∞ As I am napping in the grass, my neighbor Amy calls through the fence. "Barbara, come quick, you'll never believe this!" When I look through the door in the fence, I see the usual line of cats at their bowls in front of the garage, and then at the far end, in broad daylight, a raccoon feeding at the farthest bowl. "It's a female," whispers Amy. Indeed, this mama raccoon, her teats distended and red, clearly ravenous after days of nursing her babies, has risked to forage side by side with the cats, in view of us people. I imagine her to be exhausted, starving. Challenged to survive, she has felt compelled to leave her cubs in their nest under the deck of some overgrown yard and, without the protection of night, to brave this territory. Now, seemingly oblivious to the cats, she moves from bowl to bowl. Suddenly, one cat, defending his food, arches and hisses. The mama raccoon rears, bares her teeth, and flattens her ears. Darting at her, Amy shouts, "Git!" And the raccoon flees.

I keep thinking about this mama raccoon. I feel a kinship with her that I don't understand. On this first encounter, she inspires me. How brazen she is! What courage she has to claim her place among the cats in full daylight.

ON THE NIGHT before I had surgery, I invited friends to come to a meditation circle at my house. It was from the surgery that we would learn how serious this cancer was, whether or not it had spread to the lymph system. I had invited my yoga teacher, Saraswati, and friends whom I have known over years of Buddhist practice. I had asked others who live far away to sit in their own homes and join us in meditation. At first I didn't feel comfortable asking my mother, who had come from New York, and Patrick— neither of whom are meditators. So often in the past I had felt wrenched between my spiritual practice and my loyalty to these two, neither of whom was drawn to Buddhism. But each in their turn approached me. Please, might I join the circle?

After Caitlin had gone to sleep, we gathered quietly in the living room. As we settled on our cushions, my hands trembled. But with the potency of the meditation, I became deeply still. I could hear Patrick, on one side of me, and my mother, on the other, both weeping. It was then that I felt a shift, a deep feeling of relief. The poles of my spiritual and secular life were aligned, at least for this moment. And when, at the close, my friend Wes asked everyone to send me their healing thoughts, I felt my whole being burst into light, as if the very cells were illuminated, like so many candles on a solstice tree. I was full with this circle, lit with the energy of our pooled attention. I could sense Caitlin dreaming in the next room, my friends sitting in faraway places, also lit, the very meridians of the planet brightening.

As I rest, I breathe in the scent of wet rosemary, listen to the water sprinkling the calla lilies. Last night, up to comfort away Caitlin's nightmare, I had so little sleep. How early this morning did she start bouncing on the bed? Why wouldn't she stop? I hated the way I grabbed her arms, screamed for her to give me peace. On a day such as this I feel so fragile, crave comfort myself. When I take Caitlin to school, I interrupt the teachers at their prep to demand my hellos and good-byes. Then I am swept with shame at my neediness. How can I cut through this? Should I consider *chöd* practice: each day imagining the moment of death, working actively with impermanence? I question what practice is right for me at this time. If done unskillfully, couldn't these death-awareness practices hasten death?

Even though the news from the surgery was hopeful and I was able to keep the breast, I found it impossible to sustain the feeling of luminosity I experienced through the meditation circle. After ten days of having cooked us every meal, my mother went back to New York, and my old friends, Marie and Peter, began to attend to their own jobs and families. As I became exhausted from the radiation, I saw my intense need for attention and help. To my relief one morning I found a letter in my mailbox from someone dear to me, my only relative who lives here in Berkeley. A love note, a letter of support? I was stunned to read his angry letter, to find out that he was enraged with me about something that had happened before the cancer. I was aghast. In my own initial burst of venom, I saw my insecurity, my lack of self-control, my vindictiveness. I had imagined that with "death over my left shoulder" my most mature and forgiving potential would blossom. When I saw how I was even tempted to use my sickness against him, I became, as an overlay, furious at myself.

I was ashamed to notice on several occasions how I looked forward to telling people that I had cancer, as if that would trick out of them their hidden love for me, their feelings of guilt for having ignored or jilted me. At times, the prospect of becoming seriously ill, or even possibly dying—just to get a break from my own constriction—felt exhilarating. There had been an excitement about all the attention and expressions of love I was getting from friends and relatives at the time of the surgery. I would catch myself imagining my memorial service, people meditating, reading aloud from my journals. And seeing this, I was scared. If I failed to embrace life now, would I prevent myself from healing?

∞ I think again of that mama raccoon and I am shaken by opposing feelings. In her black mask, I see her now, coming as a thief to steal from the bowls set up for the cats. Does the ferocity of her hunger serve her? No. She scares Amy, who, instead of offering her food, chases her away. I am distraught as I feel myself in this raccoon mama. I think of the ceremony I attended the other night as a guest at a Zen center. As I reflect on the formality and intimacy of this gathering, I am consumed with worry. Did I intrude? So often when I look back on my daily encounters, I am swept with embarrassment or guilt. As I review an incident, I see myself driven by my needs, ignoring the boundaries set by others, crashing in where I am not wanted. As a child of divorced parents, I felt like an intruder in both my father's and my mother's homes; now in Berkeley I often feel like a gate-crashing New Yorker, and in New York like an infiltrating Californian.

WHEN I BEGAN radiation, I descended into dread. Perhaps, most of all, this was a dread of loss of contact. I dreaded walking through the corridors of Alta Bates Hospital each day, trying to win a smile from the receptionist. I dreaded waiting in the hall in my green gown, watching some of the other cancer patients rolled in on gurneys. I dreaded listening to the technicians carry on their conversations over and through me, arranging my limbs as if they belonged to a corpse or were some extension of the equipment. Most of all, I dreaded hearing the door click shut in the treatment room and being left alone with the Star Wars equipment gliding over me and the high-pitched yammer of the machine.

To counterbalance the touch of the radiation, the machines, and the technicians—touch without awareness—I bought myself a weekly massage. Surprised when one masseuse introduced herself as a beginner, I commented on her strong hands, her sure sense in rooting for knots. She told me that before she worked on humans, for many years she had massaged horses. Hearing this, I felt unexpectedly moved. As her fingers worked the braided muscles of my back, that back became the tight flank of a mare, contracted from hours of work in the ring. Through the touch of this horse masseuse and her story, I felt the animality of my body, I felt sister to the horse, the dog, the tree.

As I lie here under the wide arms of the redwood, I recognize the pain of feeling like an "intruder." Into the grass, I weep for the mama raccoon driven by her ravenousness to break in, and I weep for myself, driven by my hunger to belong. I bite my lip, tasting the salt-tang. This sense of being an intruder feels more fundamental than my particular psychology and history. Isn't this a basic human malady? To feel like a visitor on the planet who needs to steal from life, rather than partake in it. To fear that after a brief stint of a lifetime on stolen turf, I will die and leave no trace.

At my cancer support group, I talked about the rift with my relative and about my reluctance to ask for more help from the close friends who had given me so much of their time when I had the surgery. I cried as I remembered that the teachers and families at Caitlin's nursery school had offered to provide us dinners. "I am just barely learning the names of some of the women who are offering to cook for me. How can I ask?" One of the longtime group members, the mother of a woman with cancer, urged me, "I have been approached by several people whom I barely know, asking if it would be okay if their prayer groups prayed for my daughter. Even as strangers, it has been satisfying for them to provide this support. Let these women cook for your family, Barbara." So I did.

The nourishment I experienced through this cooking went far beyond the meals themselves. Laurie, who made one of the first dinners, said, "I thought about you as I was cooking this and imagined what good foods would make you strong." Later that evening, as I ate her soup, I brought Laurie into my awareness. As I discovered the lentils and chickpeas, the tomatoes and carrots, I remembered Laurie remembering me. Robert, my acupuncturist, tells me, "Kind attention, meditation, and food are all energy. In the dinners these families cook, they are offering energy to you from all over the world. Take it in as love." As our family ate each meal: lasagnas, corn soups, and chile rellenos— old family formulas and favorite recipes passed from friend to friend—I experienced the energy moving in my body, and the channels lighting up between myself and these people.

◉◉ Through the fence, I can hear Steve from down the street talking to Amy. He will be gone for a week, so could she be sure to put out extra food for the wandering cats? As I listen, I am moved and my imagination stirs. It occurs to me that there are kind people who put out bowls for feral cats in the backyards throughout this neighborhood, throughout Berkeley, Oakland, Albany, Richmond, and beyond. Who knows how far? I find this thought comforting. I think of my sister, the raccoon. It occurs to me now that, in feeding at the cat bowls, she is able to tap in to a great network which was already there. Somehow, I sense that I am too. As I listen to Amy pouring the dry food into the many bowls, I am resting in this vast net of connectedness that is always there, yet needs to be illuminated through awareness.

SEVERAL MONTHS into my treatment, my friend Pat drove me to meet with a local healer, an acupuncturist and herbalist who is also knowledgeable in Western medicine. "Cancer is a chronic disease," Michael said. "It cannot be cured. But it can be contained." I hated hearing this. Yet I sensed its truth. He invited me to open to this uncertainty. After several hours of questions from me, he then took my pulses. He described the imbalances in the flow of energy through my body. Then he told me: "Take more risks. That's a prescription!"

I was aghast. "Do you say this to everyone?" "No," he said, "I read your pulses. I'm saying it to you." "What do you mean, risks? Bungee jumping? Camping I could imagine, backpacking maybe. But if you mean rock climbing, spelunking—No!" He continued, "More risks in your thinking and in your actions. You'll have to figure out what is appropriate for you. But," he laughed, "once you've gotten used to something, then it won't qualify as a risk anymore, and you'll have to find something else. At some point in camping there may be nothing else to do but to try rock climbing. . . ."

I was scared, confused, even outraged by this prescription which I didn't understand. Yet something resonated. It was the next day that I turned from my usual morning walk along the streets bordering on Tilden Park into the meadow. Afraid of possible murderers or rapists, I had never before ventured into the park on my own. But now I could hear Michael's voice, "Consider the imagined dangers next to the danger of this disease you're facing. . . ." So I kept right on walking through the trees, along the stream, into the park itself—our own Bay Area patch of wilderness.

As I strode, breath deepening, arms swinging, I enjoyed the spring—the lupine and poppies—the tart smell of eucalyptus and bay, the call of birds along the stream. After an hour's walk, rounding a bend, I was startled to meet the liquid eyes of a doe. She was so close, I could see the quivering of her nostrils and the pink glow where the sun shone through her cocked ears. Unwittingly, I must have made a tiny movement. With a tremble, she bolted and a fawn, hidden until that moment in the grass, flashed after her. The two deer leapt up an almost imperceptible path which I then saw wound up the slope of the hill. As I watched them bounding to the crest, the boundaries of my awareness broadened up the hills toward clear June sky.

◎◎   I imagine the mama raccoon returning to her nest. Strengthened after feeding from bowl to bowl, she nurses her cubs. As they grow older she can perhaps lead them on foraging expeditions, showing them the yards of the neighborhood almsgivers. But what if on her rounds she is trapped in a broken fence, hit by a car? What if she doesn't make it back? Often I come to my nap worried about Caitlin. (Is she sturdy? Am I passing on my upset, my fragility?) What if I become ill again, what motherly soul will help Patrick to protect and nurture her? Will Caitlin know to look for the bowls that are out there? My friend Marie once said, "I have to believe that if I weren't there, the universe would take care of my children." I find it a great challenge to keep such trust.

ONE MORNING AS spring was turning to summer, I left the paved path and headed up the hills on the deer trail. Feeling weakened from lack of sleep, I hoped to revive myself on this walk. I mustered a brisk pace through the pine grove and began to climb a series of brown hills toward the peak. As I gained momentum, the blood flowing and oxygen circulating woke up my awareness. Consciously then, I applied this awakened awareness to my limbs. I could feel the streaming in my arms, the tingling in my feet and fingertips, the stirring in my belly. I recognized how in risking to follow these deer paths, I was at the same time opening up all of the subtle channels through my being. I sensed the channels of energy extending through my body and beyond—out through the world.

◎◎   Today I want to notice everything, the Mexican primroses with their soft pink faces and yellow tongues, the dead rat shriveled by the tomato patch. Day after day I am more and more sure that mindfulness—bringing my awareness to whatever is there—is the most healing practice for me. And the danger here? Perhaps sometimes a distance or coldness. In our bath together, Caitlin takes the soap dish and pours water on my raw radiated breast, over the hard contour of the hematoma left from surgery. How I love this bathtub blessing. Can I permeate awareness with a wash of tenderness?

OVER THE SPRING and summer our family spent many hours in the vegetable garden. As Caitlin pulled red threads of radish roots, I pinched the suckers off the tomato plants, Patrick seeded new grass, I felt our intimate collaboration with rain, sun, earthworms. One August afternoon, as I weeded the lettuce, I remembered a call I'd had that morning from the East Coast. A friend who had been precious to me twenty-five years back was also being treated for breast cancer. As I gardened, I thought about all of the women in my generation—dear friends from Cambridge to San Francisco—who now have breast cancer or who have died from it. To what degree, I wondered, is this epidemic due to the toxicity of the vegetables that we grew up on, poisoned by pesticides and herbicides? I thought about the danger when we on this planet lose our intimacy with the larger web of life. Hidden by the scarlet runner vines, I sat in the dirt that afternoon crying for my friends and for all the women I didn't know who would suffer from this profound carelessness.

Late into the night, intertwined with Patrick, I absorb the heat and heartiness of his sleeping body into mine. Through the slope of my chest and belly, the curve of my thighs and knees, I pass him back my thanks.
When Caitlin climbs onto my lap and molds her form to mine, something mysterious passes each to each.
As I nap on the grass, the earth passes me its aliveness. And I pass back mine.

ONE DAY AS I followed the deer trail up toward the crest, I imagined the mama raccoon following these same paths down the hill. For the first time, I saw the reciprocity. I come from the city into the woods to be nourished, and the mama raccoon comes from the woods into the city to feast in our backyards. We crisscross and exchange.

෧෧ Sometimes when I hike, if I feel a surge of fear (Will the cancer recur? Will I die young?), I remember to draw the vast landscape into my awareness. Welcoming the eucalyptus grove, the brown hills, the meadow of dry grass and thistles, I open the field of who or what I perceive myself to be. I begin to sense that the narrow self within this particular package of mortal flesh is an expression of the ongoing exchange of life. When I experience this exchange, I am, for a moment, more fully alive and also not so afraid to die.

No Eye, Ear, Nose . . .

BARBARA BRODSKY

No eye, ear, nose, tongue, body, mind;
No form, sound, smell, taste, touch, or objects of mind . . .

—PRAJNAPARAMITA HRIDAYA SUTRA

No EAR; NO SOUND; NO REALM OF hearing. In 1972 I lost my hearing and all the inner ear nerves which affect balance. This loss has been my life's greatest burden and greatest gift.

I dealt with this loss the way I'd always dealt with difficulties, which was to put my energy into the coping, and not allow myself any self-pity. I was the mother of an infant, and although I felt vulnerable and sick, my upbringing didn't allow me to be needy. Coping "well" helped me to feel in control at a time of my life when my physical condition was so terribly out of control. I couldn't hear; I couldn't even stand, walk, read, or focus my eyes as the world reeled dizzily by my sickbed in nauseating spirals. I was encapsulated in a bubble that none of the world's voices could penetrate.

After a month I began to crawl like a baby, knees rubbing sore on the hardwood floors. Slowly I pulled myself to my feet and took my first steps, stumbling across the eternity between dresser and door, door and bookshelf, keeping my balance visually. Lipreading was not yet possible for me, but at last my eyes could focus enough to read.

The Buddha tells us to cultivate the body, but I abandoned the body like some discarded rag. I denied my pain and grief, denied the new limits of my body, pulled myself together and coped. I coped well on the surface. I had a loving husband and friends and fulfilling work as a sculptor and university teacher. I had two more beautiful children after I became deaf. I pushed away the anger and fear that threatened the safety of my life.

It is no surprise that I felt increasingly separate. One-to-one conversation was fine, but when several people were talking together, I felt like I was outside a window, looking in at a group gathered in warmth around a feast-laden table. I could only sit outside in the cold and watch them with longing. Always this glass pane of silence divided us.

Of course friends tried to include me. They spoke slowly. Many learned to finger spell. Someone would fill me in on others' conversations. Soon I saw that it wasn't their thoughtlessness but my longing and anger that caused me to suffer. That realization was almost worse, because then I began to criticize myself for not appreciating the loving concern of those around me.

It became clear that I needed to investigate my sense of separation. Indeed, my suffering forced such practice on me. But how to do the needed work? I was young. I had not yet met Buddhist practice. My Quaker devotional practice of many years nurtured me, but gave me no tools to be more fully present.

To attend the pain of daily life became my practice. I was a sculptor. Part of the work of a sculptor is creative, but there are also hours of drudgery, polishing or filing huge pieces of bronze, for example. Before I became deaf I used to play music in my studio as entertainment during the noncreative times. Suddenly there was no entertainment, nothing but the echo of my own thoughts. For the first nine months I memorized songs and sang to myself, but finally this wore thin. Each day in the studio brought deeper discomfort.

What follows are excerpts from my journal, written as I began to attend to that which cried for healing—not the deafness, but the illusion of separate self.

    ☞ *March 1.* Last week in my class we were talking about the joy of creativity, and some students commented that they loved that part of art but found much of the work boring. A student asked me what I do all day in my studio, am I always focused on my work? I felt some embarrassment as I told him about memorizing songs and singing to myself to combat the boredom.

Why was there embarrassment? Later, I realized that I'm losing a big chunk of each day by labeling it "boring." I'm also escaping from the pain of my deafness. Finally, I'm teaching my students that this pattern is okay. While meditating this morning I decided not to entertain myself for the next few weeks but just to watch the thoughts and emotions and see what I've been running from.

March 2. Not diverting myself while I work is the hardest thing I've ever done. I was cleaning the edges of a large piece with a power grinder and then with a file. After about an hour I felt so much restlessness and anger I had to stop and go for a walk.

March 3. This morning I tried to focus on my hands. Can I just watch their motion, knowing I'm filing when I'm filing?

Later: No! It doesn't work. It became a chant, "filing up, filing down," and had nothing to do with the experience of filing. There is such boredom with filing. Question: what is boredom?

March 4. I am so filled with anger, I don't know what's happening. I tried filing again, "up, down . . ." and again the words had nothing to do with the experience. I finally stopped and admitted to myself how much I hate this aspect of the work. There's nothing to do but file. A trained ape could do it. I'm feeling rage that my deafness has deprived me of the means to make this work bearable—listening to the radio and feeling connected to people.

I took a long walk and asked myself what I'm really angry at. I don't hate the filing; I hate the deafness! I hate the silence! Why do I hate the silence so much?

March 7. I walked around the meadow yesterday with Mike [my eleven-month-old son] on my back. He fell asleep so I walked around the marsh and through the woods. It's the longest I've walked since I got sick. While walking, I realized I'm deaf here, too, but there's no anger. My mind is very still when I walk, not asking for entertainment. What's the difference? I feel connected to the trees, the sky. There's nothing I'm pushing away; therefore I don't need diversion. The singing is diversion, not from the boredom of filing but from the anger and the pain of isolation.

March 8. While meditating this morning a wisdom deep within whispered, "Breathe. . . ."

Later: I started working with the piece that still needs seams bronzed, using the welding torch. I must pay attention or I get burned. Breathe? I realized that when I work with the torch and am paying close attention, breath is very present. I began to watch myself breathing as I worked; no, that's not quite right. I began to watch the breath moving in and out, the way I hold it with each circular motion of torch to rod, release when the bronze drips, hold it again as hand moves closer to the fire. It flowed all together, hands, fire, bronze, breath. I started to feel a great joy, like I was part of a dance. I don't understand it at all, but the morning's work flowed effortlessly, even joyfully, past.

March 11. Today I tried breathing while I filed. Attention shifted, almost imperceptibly, from breath to the movement of the hands, but the experience was different than last week when the noting of "up, down" was disconnected from the actual hands. Today I was just watching the hands, not forcing them, engaged in the same "dance" as with the breath and welding. I experienced something rather strange that I don't have words for, almost an intimate connection with the file and sculpture, a kind of lovemaking. It most definitely wasn't boring!

I still don't know what "boredom" is.

March 15. Today I found myself crying silently as I worked, just feeling sadness and letting tears run down my cheeks, not trying to push the reality of my deafness away. The sadness is clean. It's uncomfortable, but workable.

What changed the same filing from "boring" to deeply connected? It's continued that way for five days. With "boring" there was anger, not at the work but at the deafness which kept me from diverting myself from the work. I couldn't get away from "look what happened to me—not fair," and all of that. It burned. By ending "boring" I allowed some of that pain, without all the "stop feeling sorry for yourself" shit I've been spouting. Feeling sorry for myself doesn't solve anything, but maybe judging my feelings doesn't solve anything either. When I stay with the work, with my breath, with my hands, my mind stops trying to use thought to lead me to safety. I'm just there.

March 19. I can't control my mind with conscious will. Therefore, I can't keep myself safe and comfortable.

I don't know how to phrase this. I'm beginning to see that my deepest pain is not from what's happening or not happening in my life but from my relationship with it. My pain is not from the deafness but from how much I want to be rid of the deafness. But how can I ever make friends with this silence which so devastates me?

March 26. Non-boredom is connection! It doesn't *accompany* connection; it *is* connection, a mind state in which I'm totally connected! Boredom is separation. When I'm separate from myself (disallowing my thoughts and feelings), I'm separate from my family, from my work.

April 2. Has it really been just a month that I've been working this way? I find deep joy in it, am finding I very much look forward to being in the studio. It's become a time of deep focus and peacefulness. At one level mind is jumping around and at another level it's totally concentrated, just watching the jumping with much spaciousness and no obsession to control. It's the most peaceful thing I've ever done. I enjoy grinding seams! The bronze seems alive, responsive. Even "boredom" has become interesting!

It took me many years to really understand the nature of my suffering and even longer to understand and heal my relationship with my deafness. For all those years my day-long practice was just to breathe and create, breathe and file or weld, breathe and be. I spent hours a day, month after month, in this way for over a decade.

In those years my meditation practice changed and deepened. My suffering was less intense but still present, and increasingly, practice led me to investigate the nature of that suffering and to understand how it grew out of a sense of separation, an agony of aloneness. What was separate? How had I become ensnared in what my deepest meditations taught me was illusion?

At one point I began to have nighttime dreams of a giant surf, of wanting to swim but finding the waves huge and forbidding. Every morning when I sat to meditate, the question would arise of whether or not I wanted to go down to the beach in my meditation, to a non-physical but still wild sea. My answer was always "no." It became harder and harder to meditate. My back began to ache, first just while I was sitting, then in anticipation of it. I knew I was running from something, but I still wasn't clear what it was.

Finally, one morning during meditation I said "yes," and went to

the beach, opening to the experience of the waves while I sat. What
follows comes from my journals.

◎◎ *February 19.* The surf is huge, the waves dark. I understand that
I must submerge myself. I must take a single step into the unknown. A wave crashes down. I step into its ebb and see the next
wave tower above me, black belly, white foam, feel it slap me under,
roll me in its power. I am drowning. I can't breathe. Desperately I
force my eyes open. I breathe deeply, gasping breaths of cool air in
the safety of my room. I stop trembling. I close my eyes. I am back
on the same beach. I do the whole thing again. Over and over and
over. How much time goes by? My watch tells me later that it really
was hours.

I beg for help. No! Assurance that I can do it. Suddenly, in the
midst of a terrible wave, Barbara, the strong swimmer, takes over.
"Don't fight it," I hear my voice saying. "Be one with it." I start to
swim with the wave. I gather momentum, I dive down and come
up in the calmer swells beyond. I return to shore and do it again
and again, until I can enter the water, not without fear, but knowing how to harmonize with this previously overwhelming force. I
am complete. All that I need to bring to this wave is within me.

Coming out of the sitting, I began to reflect: death is not an
end but just another step. It is the step before birth. I need fear
neither. It is all part of the process. I began to do *metta* meditation.
"May I be healed; may I find peace; may all beings be healed and
find peace. . . ."

So I had accepted my deafness as a death, and I had learned that I
could survive that one step into the unknown, could allow myself to be
overwhelmed, but I still didn't know where this was going.

◎◎ *February 20.* This morning I felt like I'd never meditated before.
I couldn't sit still. I couldn't quiet my mind from its turmoil. My
back, which has continued to hurt through these weeks, ached hor-
ribly. My legs were cramped; my forehead itched; I was alternately
freezing and sweating. Most of all I felt so totally alone. "Sit with
it," I told myself. "Just watch it. Watch all the pain and anxiety
and see where it's going. Watch yourself wanting so desperately for

things to be different." After well over an hour I got up. I walked around for a few minutes. The aloneness, the agitation, came with me. I sat again.

The isolation became overwhelming. Searching for something that might help, I reached for the lines of the Twenty-third Psalm: "Yea though I walk through the valley of the shadow of death, I will fear no evil. . . ." Into the space I had opened through this small kindness to myself came the understanding: "You are never alone, but this is the isolation into which you've bound yourself. When do you remember feeling like this before? When do you last remember really needing that psalm?"

And with a rush the memories came back. I saw those first weeks of my illness. All sound was gone. I couldn't focus my eyes. To turn my head even a bit brought waves of dizziness. I felt help-less and alone. I realized, in this morning's instant of remembered pain, that in sixteen years I have never cried for my pain.

When I understood how I'd buried this pain, I sat there on the floor and cried, and cried. The remembering hurt, but not nearly as badly as burying it had hurt. I wept for the loss of my hearing, I wept for the aloneness, I wept for the fear, I wept for the one in a glass prison, seeing, but totally cut off from the world. All that week I re-membered and cried.

I had raged at my deafness but never allowed the pain into my heart. I simply buried it, and met any feelings of self-pity with con-tempt. I see that my deepest separation was from myself.

◉ *February 21.* Last night I shared this new awareness with Hal and cried with him and felt his love. Today I lay in bed before dawn, in the same bed where I was once so ill, and cried for the frightened young woman who had to cope with this illness. I reached out to my ears, gently searching for the nerves that were oxygen-starved and dead. They seemed to ask me for forgiveness for failing me. I touched my ears—that part of me that I've so often cursed—with love. Finally I reached out to myself, to the self I've so often criti-cized for feeling self-pity, for not "trying harder." "Barbara, I for-give you; Barbara, I love you."

Today I find I am no longer "deaf," only that I hear on a different level: I hear the silence! It is a wonderful gift! Yes, there's still pain when my children laugh and I know I've missed the beauty of that sound. No, there is no longer suffering. My deafness reminds me to keep my heart open to the ten thousand joys and sorrows of us all.

Hearing the Voice
of the Body

KATHERINE THANAS

Astudent recently said to me, "Now I understand why it's so important to sit still and not move. When you move, you don't find out what you are moving away from. When you sit still, you can experience what you want to move away from."

I thought that was pretty good. It sums up my personal practice of going to the body for answers when I do not understand what is arising in my life. It sounds obvious. When something arises in the body, you would naturally go to the body to inquire about it. Yet I have found that most of us do not know how to listen to our bodies. Long ago we turned off the voice of the body. The body obediently went silent as we agreed not to notice our emotional or feeling life. Although our bodies continue to hold in silence what was stuffed, there comes a time when the body finally needs to speak out, in its own voice, to catch our attention.

In my own experience, that speaking out has happened in practice through physical symptoms that could no longer be ignored. And the response that seems to work is to sit still, or lie still, and coax out what I have long excluded from awareness. This deep listening arises only through sitting still, with patience. It arises from bringing attention to the body without expectation, as one might attend a friend who is ill, as a kind of servant of the body.

I recently heard a longtime Buddhist teacher talk about her experiences of depression, terror, and helplessness that arose from a family history of abuse. Through her practice she learned to make space for those feelings. She learned that depression is just depression, and that when we are afraid of our feelings we make them as powerful as demons. It's just depression, she said. If we let it in, inhale it, feel it, and exhale it, it will naturally transform, like all phenomenal existence. The most important thing is not to deny or avoid the experience.

From my Buddhist practice I know that liberation arises in the midst of delusion. I do not remember where I saw this statement: "The true aspects arrive before the deluded aspects have departed." In the midst of confusion and pain, clarity arises.

Practice happens in the body. Paying attention to the body creates space around and inside the knots of tension. What has become compacted through being pushed down begins to expand, to claim its own space. As this part of us finds room to grow, it begins to draw energy from what is around.

I sometimes practice visualizing the space around tension as liquid, a pool of water. Seeing the space around hardness as water or air, as flow, modifies the hardness. Gradually hardness finds breathing space . . . the solidity softens just a bit.

The deep attending to hard knots of holding is a powerfully compassionate act, a turning toward rejected parts of our being. As this newly compassionate observing occurs, the object of observation, the body/self, is transformed, and we move from denial to acceptance, from rejection to inclusion. This is the beginning of metta practice, lovingkindness for the self.

My first experience of working intimately with the body to hear its voice happened a few months into practice, in 1967. In the midst of a rather confused life, seeking a graduate degree in painting (this would be my fourth college degree), I found myself in a graduate seminar where the painting style was quite different from the abstract expressionism I had learned as an undergraduate. At the new school I felt quite isolated and had a hard time defending my choices. My whole experience of painting was thrown into question. Why was I painting this way? Why did it matter what these people thought? And why was I so vulnerable to their questions and critiques?

In the midst of these questions one day, a terrible headache and stomachache seized me—I was ready for a deep meltdown. So I just collapsed in bed to wait for the pain to go away. But it didn't. Finally I just let myself experience the headache and the pain in my gut completely. I let it all come to awareness. I can still remember watching the strong sensations going round and round, and following them with my awareness. I had learned to do this a few months earlier in sesshin. But there was a place inside where my awareness did not want to go. I realized I was avoiding the center of the sensations. And as soon as I became aware of that I slowly, gently moved my awareness to the center of holding. Right away the energy began to break up and to circulate freely between stomach and head . . . and a deep thought arose as if from the bottom of my stomach-mind: "I don't have to paint." Painting, for me, had become the way to demonstrate my worthiness, lovableness, specialness. The activity was coming from a stuck place inside.

Even though I had already said to myself, you can stop painting any time, that message did not carry any conviction until I turned my awareness to the center of the knot, and the voice came forth from the body-mind itself.

After that experience, I found the courage to paint from my own experience rather than from the styles around me. Before long my canvases became lighter and brighter, pink and orange instead of black. I began to paint female figures for the first time and recognized them as my sister and myself. I felt I was "home," that I had walked through a dark passage into an open field.

Although painting then came with more confidence, I was also deeply involved with zazen and community life at the Zen center. Zazen filled an inner need that I had thought could be filled by painting. But it was not really a choice. Painting dropped off. My journey through art had brought me to what I now needed to do.

Some years later, a muscle spasm in my hip alerted me to an inner conflict between taking care of myself and taking care of someone else. I was sharing a living space and finding the arrangement not working. My housemate and I had different notions of how to live together. At that time I didn't trust my feelings and didn't know how to express them. I became withdrawn and irritable. After several weeks, a muscle spasm developed in my hip. When I was reduced to painful limping and then became bedridden, I was forced to look deeply into that area of my body. As I listened deeply to my hip, it spoke to my inability to protect my privacy and to a deep grief around my incapacity to allow myself to have personal needs. As with the stomachache and headache, this physical voice was totally convincing. It arose out of the body-mind; it was not a voice I anticipated, yet I recognized it when it spoke. I was able to make a clear, unambivalent decision to leave the housing arrangement.

Many years later during a sesshin I was leading I found myself in the novel situation of giving teachings and private interviews during the day and feeling like I was dying of heart palpitations, sleeplessness, tremendous anxiety, and dizziness at night. During the day I functioned well; at night I could not sleep and the steady hammering of my heart terrified me. Even when I realized I was enjoying the sesshin and was quite comfortable with my role, the night music continued. After waiting night after night for the palpitations to subside, I finally realized I was going to have to go into them with a kind and open awareness and not wish them away. I did this at night, in bed, when the palpitations were strongest. I put my attention into my heart's pounding and said something like "Welcome."

When I did this and stayed with it, a connection was gradually made with my abdomen. My breathing became heavy, and I started to cry. A "voice" that seemed two or three years old, maybe even younger, gradually came up. It was deeply hidden, almost incoherent. I had to listen carefully. It felt like a cry of grief and abandonment. I felt it as self-abandonment. Hearing its faint reach confirmed something I had known about myself but had been unable to experience. I knew I had a pattern of "stuffing" my most vulnerable feelings. I seemed to have done it one more time.

I had been conflicted about accepting the invitation to lead the sesshin, pleased to have been asked, yet uncertain about my energy to do it at that time. I did not know how to express the ambivalence, except to override it. At another time, such a conflict might not have produced a strong reaction. But on that occasion, feeling vulnerable about other things as well, my uncertainty was compounded. I could not touch the source of the anxiety, however, until that night when I consciously chose to attend to the palpitations.

What did I learn from this? To listen more carefully and respectfully when ambivalence arises, to trust it. Since that time I have on occasion declined invitations to teach even when I had "no reason" to do so, something I would not have felt permission to do earlier.

For me, practicing mindfulness of the body in this way requires solitude. Sometimes the symptoms may arise in the zendo, but the painful descent to early voices and to attitudes held at two or three years old is accomplished in the midst of such strong physical sensations that I can only do the work alone. Sometimes I lie down, maybe in the fetal position, maybe on my back. There is a deep effort to attend to physical symptoms which may be disgusting or frightening, to welcome them. To convert them from unwanted to welcome guests. To give them the attention that was not available in the past.

This deep listening takes sincere effort. Sometimes my stamina runs out. Sometimes the voice is so buried I despair of getting through to it. As I write this I imagine I am digging a tunnel with my bare hands, not knowing how deep is the dirt I must dig through or whether my hands will be strong enough to do it. It takes patience, stamina, a willingness to find nothing, to listen acutely with the ear of intuition, the ear of concentration. Is that Avalokitesvara listening?

In my experience, this recognition of the buried self is essential to the eventual release of emotional patterns that are no longer helpful.

About Death

NAOMI NEWMAN

I SAT BY MY MOTHER'S BED IN THE condominium of her widowed years, listening to her mumble over and over, "I'm doing just fine everything's coming along just fine." I didn't know if her mantra was meant to comfort me or to navigate her own dying. She wouldn't talk to me. "Can I read to you?" I asked. She shook her head, no. Can I sing to you? Another no. She didn't need me.

Once I was useful. I came into her room and found her on the floor, staring at the bathroom, as if the toilet were miles away. She'd slipped off the bed. There was shit on the sheets, shit on the carpet, shit on her white, white, still shapely legs. I washed her and cleaned up the mess while she apologized, "A real treat, a real treat I gave you."

She couldn't know what a treat it was. Better than the pot roasts, the gefilte fish, the Jell-O molds, even Bobie's special cookies. That smelly chocolate thickness from my mother's belly was her gift to me. Her last lesson of how the body does its journey, and not her will, or pride, or dignity, or passion for cleanliness could stop it.

"She's not dying," my sister said. "Months," nodded the doctor. Inside I knew, but I left her. I flew home to pick up my life, my career, the things I had to do. I didn't know how to just sit there. I didn't know how to rub her feet, or smooth the sheets over them, or lie down next to her, my fat warming her thin. I didn't know how to be with death.

It was only days before the dreaded call. Before the paramedics invaded her gentle going with poundings and machines, forcing air through her already surrendered lungs, so they would artificially pump until I got there.

June 14, 1989, my mother died of heart failure. I live with mine.

PART TWO

✺

Body as Nature

Running the Bush

KUYA MINOGUE

DARK GRAY AND LIGHT GRAY. MY world is changing from blue, green, yellow, red, and brown to dark gray and light gray. The spruce trees are dark gray; the snow, the sky, and the mountains are light gray. The only colors to be seen are in the skin, fur, and eyes of the handful of people who brave the outdoors, the dogs who dot the village paths, and the herd of free-running horses that appears and disappears out of the misty veil of falling snow. Everything else is dark gray and light gray.

I strap on my cross-country skis. The hot-pink fluorescent brand name painted on the top of them is soon covered with snow and ice. I glide through the gray and white. Whoosh. Whoosh. Whoosh. My rhythmic movements leave traces of sound in the empty air as I move deeper and deeper into the bush. I'm completely alert—watching for signs that the gathering packs of teenage wolves are stalking me. The voice of my seventy-year-old neighbor comes back to me, "Those wolves don't have any sense when they are teenagers. You have to be careful."

For a moment my mind takes me to inner-city Portland, where I had exactly the same problem with the two-legged teenage wolf packs who roam their territories looking for prey. I pull myself back to the present and bring that inner-city fear with me. The rhythm of my movement slows down. I'm thinking of turning back and hiding out in the safety of my room. My imagination turns a horse track into a grizzly track and I stop, heart pounding in my chest. Breathe in. Breathe out. I let the fear go and see that I am looking at the track of a horse's hoof and not that of a grizzly's paw. I reenter the rhythm of my movement. Whoosh. Whoosh. Whoosh.

I am not in inner-city Portland. I am in an isolated First Nations village of the Sekani people in British Columbia, where another big snowstorm has grounded the bush planes and prevented everyone from going in or out for several days. I've been alternating zazen and skiing in a monastic-style schedule since we got "socked in" here. Logging trucks have stopped carrying the trees away. Shiny red family trucks are sitting in driveways covered with snow and ice. Most people are inside their houses watching and re-watching video movies that are set in American cities and based on American violence. I'm out in the bush: a middle-aged, middle-class white woman trying to escape the cage of my conditioning and reenter the deep truth of the natural world. Whoosh. Whoosh. Whoosh.

The first time I experienced the bush was when Sarah and Ellie, two Sekani sisters, invited me to walk their ancestral family trap-line with them. Ellie drove us deep into the bush on a narrow gravel road in her four-wheel-drive truck. Christian country-western music blared through the supernova speakers. Ellie and I sang along. She was belting out praises to the Lord Jesus while I harmonized with Buddhist sutras in a Japanese chanting style. Sarah, the elder, made location reports to the logging trucks on the CB radio in her Sekani "Indian English" and chuckled at our silliness.

At the bottom of a long, slow hill, Ellie waved her arm around and said, "This has been our family's trap-line area from time immemorial."

We stopped at the side of the road and climbed out of the four-by-four laughing and talking. As Ellie led the way into a jumble of underbrush, the conversation became quiet and serious. At first I thought we were just walking randomly through the bush, but after a few minutes, we came across a snare that had caught a rabbit. There was one rabbit's foot left uneaten.

"Unlucky rabbit," Sarah said. She pointed to some bird shit on a nearby log. "Owl got it."

As we walked on, I began to see that we were on a trail—an "Indian Trail," as they say here. Every now and then we'd come across a broken red willow branch that marked the location of a snare. As we moved through the bush, Ellie and Sarah kept up a constant dialogue describing what they saw. "Fox passed here." "Snare is gone. Must be a big fox." Their attention was completely in the present. They had entered a perfect mindfulness meditation. I felt myself being pulled into it.

At one point Sarah gestured to the side of the trail and said, "Rabbit goes here." I stopped to look, and what had been a meaningless array of sticks, branches, and dead grass suddenly revealed itself as a clear trail—for rabbits. Sarah had made the invisible visible.

We stopped to set a new snare. Sarah stretched out a piece of brass wire that she'd been carrying in her pocket and chose a place where two seedling spruce trees grew on either side of the rabbit's trail. She tied her snare to one tree and hid the gold hoop within the branches of the other. Then she gently ran her finger around the inside of the circle and said, "Poor rabbit." We moved on.

As a woman who lives off the land, Sarah knows that she is one with Mother Earth. If the rabbits live, Sarah starves. If the rabbits die, Sarah lives. There is no place where the rabbit ends and Sarah begins. They are the same creature. As am I.

We finally came across one intact dead rabbit. Ellie untangled her from the snare and threw her at Sarah's feet. Sarah picked the rabbit up and cradled the lifeless mottled gray fur in her arms. Even though the rabbit was stiff with rigor mortis, Sarah gently stroked her and murmured some Sekani words over her. Perhaps she thanked and released her spirit. Perhaps it was the Sekani version of transference of consciousness at death. Whatever she did, it was a ritual so deep in Sarah's mind that she didn't even think of it as a ritual. It was simply her life and the rabbit's death.

After that brief moment of contact, Sarah took the rabbit by the foot and carried her with her head hanging down. She turned to me with a big smile and said, "Rabbit stew for dinner."

Later, when we found a dead squirrel, I cradled her, stroked her, murmured the *Enmei Jukku Kannon Gyo* over her, and carried her upside down back to the truck.

"I hope you didn't work too hard on your winter cache, Sister Squirrel," I said as I nestled her against the rabbit in the back of the truck. The women laughed. They too had been working hard on their winter caches. They too knew that even after months of hard work, they could become food for the larger and stronger meat-eating grizzly bear. It's the way of the bush.

After that trip into the bush with Sarah and Ellie, I began to walk through the bush along the edge of the Finlay River to visit their mother, Grandma Martha. One time on the way there, I came across a sprung leg-hold trap, its jaws biting down on the front paw and chest of a squirrel. She was lying very still, eyes glazed with the intensity of her suffering. When she sighted me, her eyes flashed with light and she began to struggle. It was clear that she was not trying to get away from me, but asking me to release her. I tried every way I could to pry open the leg-hold trap, but nothing worked. I wasn't strong enough. While I struggled to free her, she relaxed as if she knew I wouldn't hurt her. After about half an hour of pushing and prying and praying and crying, I finally admitted to myself that I would not be able to open the cold steel jaws that had caught my sister squirrel. I think she knew that I had given up, and her eyes asked for relief.

In the end, I picked up a nearby stick and hit her twice on the head while chanting *Homage to the Relics of the Buddha*, a sutra used in Soto Zen funeral services. Just before her body went limp, I felt her gratitude pass through me. I stayed with the squirrel after I had killed her, and did a brief Zen form of the *phowa* ceremony—transference of consciousness at death. I ended my ceremony with, "May you be reborn as a female buddha."

Woman as Nature. Life and death. My body was a vehicle to relieve the endless suffering of a small rodent caught in a leg-hold trap. The squirrel's small broken body taught me once again that every moment of my life I am making a spiritual decision.

I went on to visit Grandma Martha.

Grandma Martha is a ninety-three-year-old near-deaf Sekani woman who has lived through the slow death of her nomadic hunting and gathering lifestyle and now hobbles about in her propane-heated house with a high-tech aluminum walker. She spends a good part of each day worrying about whether the white nurse will come to care for her ingrown toenails. She seems to think I'm a nurse. I have been developing a sign language with her. She once knew the old trading signs, and I have a book on American Sign Language. The last time I visited her she had complained about aches and pains in her joints so I brought along some tiger balm.

As I rubbed her wrists, elbows, and shoulders my hands were alive with the energy of compassion that had been raised during my encounter with the squirrel. Grandma Martha's skin was so thin, her skeleton tiny, and her eyes bright with gratitude for my loving touch. She too was a squirrel in a leg-hold trap. Her bright, strong spirit was caught in her old shrinking bag of skin and bones. But she was not begging for release as the squirrel had done. There was a fierce determination to live in Grandma Martha, to enjoy every last spark of the vital energy in her woman's body. She loved her children, grandchildren, and great grandchildren. She had birthed them all, as midwife if not as mother.

When I finished massaging her, she advised me to start "running the bush."

I didn't have the courage to try running the bush until after the first snowfall left a light layer of snow on the ground. Grandma Martha had told me to go into the bush and run like a deer fleeing from a wolf pack. She hadn't told me why I should run the bush, and she had laughed when I tried to ask her what to do if I got lost. That was my biggest fear—that I'd be stuck in the bush with no way home. But snow on the ground makes it really difficult to get lost in the bush, so I finally did what Grandma Martha had told me to do. I ran until I was breathless and couldn't go anymore. I leapt over fallen trees, raced up the hills on all fours, took flying jumps off high rocks and then dropped to the earth in a crouch, panting, listening, looking, and smelling. Was any being out there talking to me in my first language? Motion. Light. Sound. I knew that the black bears had denned down, but the grizzlies could still have been wandering around.

I ran where there was no path—no human footprints to follow. I saw the tracks of wolves, coyotes, foxes, rabbits, mice, and wild chickens everywhere. I ignored fear and ran until I realized that I'd be lost if it weren't for my own tracks in the snow. I didn't carry a watch so I had to read time from the changing light patterns in the trees and on the forest floor. I was animal and my attention didn't wander one bit from eye, ear, nose, tongue, body, mind. If a grizzly arose in that emptiness, I wanted to see her before we engaged. They say you can taste the presence of a grizzly before you can see her, so I tasted the air and found only the sharp clear tang of the coming winter. Nevertheless, fear enveloped me.

Bitsy, a woman who still lives in the bush, taught me what to do if I meet a grizzly. "When you see that grizzly just stand there. Don't look her in the eye. She doesn't like that. If she stands up on her hind legs, crouch down and stay still. She'll stamp her feet before she attacks, so you'll know she's coming. Once she's attacked, there's only one way to get out alive. You have to bite her really hard. If you can hurt a grizzly, she'll run away." Then Bitsy paused and said, "We're all like that. We all run away from pain. It's our way of protecting ourselves."

I brought my attention back to the present, wondering where my run through the bush had taken me. My full attention rested in seeing, hearing, smelling, tasting, feeling, and understanding what was going on in the immediate moment. I entered a present tense that was both dynamic and timeless. Once again, the bush had taken me. Fear of imagined dangers was no longer meaningful. I let my footprints in the snow lead me home.

It's full winter now. The storms are intense. I'm grateful to Grandma Martha for encouraging me to confront my fear of the bush. I'm not imprisoned in my room. The snow is too deep to run through, but I go everywhere on skis. My fear hasn't stopped me from gliding between snow-laden balsam trees or following a set of wolf tracks that led me to a spectacular view of the mountains. Fear rises and passes as often as my thoughts. The snowfall is so heavy that my tracks disappear behind me. Dark gray and light gray. Whoosh. Whoosh. Whoosh.

Each time I come home from outings like these, I light some pine incense at my altar, make *gasshō*, take the Three Refuges and bow in a gesture of deep gratitude. Being here has transformed my altar from the traditional Soto Zen arrangement of candles, incense, water, and food offering. Now there is the rabbit's foot that was left by the owl, the owl's tail feather, the skull of a young wolf that I found in one of my flights through the bush, and a full set of bear claws that a friend gave to me. As the smell of the incense takes me back to the stillness of the temples and monasteries in which I have done Zen training, my heart of compassion reaches out and embraces both the hunter and the hunted. In this world, I am both.

Birth

LINDA CHRISMAN

EACH ONE OF US OWES OUR LIFE and breath to a woman. To create life on this earth some woman has opened and has cried. Whether by squatting, by standing, by dancing, on all fours, or on her back. Whether by scalpel, by breath, by prayer, by song, by grace, or by will. Whether at home, in the fields, beside a road, in a hospital, or in the water. Whether by cracking, by slicing, by oozing, by tearing, or by pushing. Some woman has opened, some woman has cried. This I know from my body. This I know from giving birth to my son.

I have always come to Buddhist teachings through my body. This is the only way I know and the only way which makes sense for me. It is through the searing pain of surrender in giving birth that I know of suffering and compassion. It is through the molten anguish of rage while birthing that I know of interdependence. It is through the sweet pause between my contractions that I know of emptiness. It is through abiding with the minutia of sensation that I have touched the limitless nature of our existence.

My labor began slowly. Each phase marked a surrender of control and a dissolving of form. I don't even know where to mark the beginning. The first contractions were weeks before my son was born. One night, as I got up to pee for the third time, my belly spontaneously began to contract. There was no pain, just intense waves of sensation. I felt like a boa constrictor, tightening and releasing to push the rat she had swallowed into her belly. When the contractions were over I was awestruck and relieved. It didn't matter that I had no experience and no idea about how to make a baby come out of me. I was a woman, so my body knew. As in my meditation practice, all I needed to do was relax and remain alert.

During the days before my son's birth I listened to requiems, over and over, for hours and hours. I listened and wept to Brahms and Berlioz and Fauré. I don't really know why, but I craved those requiems the way I had craved corn in the early months of my pregnancy. I was aware of death from the moment I knew that I was pregnant. As my baby grew in life inside of me, death grew as a presence beside me. Sometimes I was afraid my baby would die or I would die. Sometimes I was not fearful. The certainty of death, however, grew as my belly grew. I had understood the cycle of life into death and death into life, but now I felt this cycle. I could feel that in birthing this baby into life I was also birthing him into death.

In the beginning of my labor I tried everything I could think of not to feel the pain that was spreading through my abdomen. I danced. I undulated. I moaned. I changed my breathing. I even imagined I was a surfer riding on top of the waves of contractions. All of these activities helped a little, but my contractions seemed to have a life of their own. I felt a strange dissolving sensation along with each contraction, and for a moment I wondered if this is what it feels like to die. It was not the pain which brought dying to mind, but my inability to change the inevitability of a physical process. I understood then that birthing and dying were essentially the same process, and I felt a shiver of fear so deep that it startled me.

After several hours I called my midwife because my contractions were still irregular. I was afraid that I would have to go to the hospital and that I would have to have a cesarean. My midwife assured me that she was not alarmed and suggested I lie down and gently ask myself what I was afraid of. As soon as I asked, I knew the answer. I was afraid of pain. In the next moment, a contraction, a huge searing wave of pain, crashed over me. I lay very still and felt it pass through my uterus, my abdomen, and my diaphragm. I felt it begin to break me open and I knew then that there was no escape. There was nothing I could do except surrender. With each new wave of pain I kept repeating, "Break me, crack me open." These words sound harsh now as I write, but then they were filled with softness and love. Break me. Crack me open. Break me. I spent all afternoon lying on the sofa barely breathing, barely moving, feeling wave upon wave break over me, break through me.

Later, my midwife told me to eat a light supper and soak in a hot tub. The hot water would either speed up my labor or slow it down. If the contractions slowed down I was to drink half a glass of wine and go to bed. I would then probably wake up in three to four hours in active labor. I prayed for my labor to slow down. I wanted that half-glass of wine badly. I longed for bed and sleep and a respite from the contractions.

Instead, my labor sped up. There were no images to help me now. I just hurt, and I could feel something happening "down there." I wanted it to be over. I had had enough. I had done everything I knew, including surrender, and I still kept on hurting. I hurt and I wanted God or Buddha or whoever was out there to know I was finished. I couldn't take it anymore. This was my limit. But the contractions kept coming.

It was then, after I threw up my supper, while my husband dashed between making the bed, phoning our friends, pressing on my back, and timing the contractions, it was then that I began to vibrate with rage.

Every monk, every guru, every ascetic, every world leader, every corporate executive, every child, every man, and every woman is alive because a woman gave birth. A woman opened to suffering. And still this truth is not recognized. This truth is not respected. This truth is not honored. Women are not recognized. Women are not respected. Women are not honored. Instead of being recognized for birthing, women are beaten. Instead of being respected for birthing, women are raped. Instead of being honored for birthing, women are murdered. Women are killed.

No one was exempt from this rage. Not even our friend, a monk, who had called earlier and rejoiced in my labor. He had reminded my husband of the preciousness of human birth and the need to honor mothers. How sweet, I thought at the time. But in this birthing rage not even he was exempt. Even I was not exempt. I too had never recognized my mother for birthing my life or respected my mother for her suffering on my behalf. I too had never honored my mother for the gift of my breath.

My rage broke. My water broke. I entered into the final stage of pushing. I don't know how people endure ceaseless pain. I don't know how someone endures not knowing if pain will end. I knew this pain would end. This thought kept me willing to feel and to be present. To be honest, it was not the desire for my baby that sustained me. It was the desire to be free from pain. I was burning in hell and I wanted out. I was burning and my midwife kept telling me to push through the ring of fire. It was not enough to feel and be present; instead I needed to use every fiber of muscle and will to push into the pain. With each push my skin screamed that it was tearing. I was sure I was ripping open and I expected to see my bowels and guts oozing onto the floor between my legs. I didn't trust my midwife's assurances that I wouldn't split in two. I thought she would do anything to birth this baby, including lie to me. But I also knew that my friend Ruth wouldn't lie, and Ruth was sitting in my living room, holding my hand and telling me that she too had pushed into this fire and survived. So I pushed.

The pain of my contractions stripped me of everything that I thought I knew. I was left with raw sensation. There was no "I" in the usual way. As I pushed into the pain I remember hearing every word spoken by my midwife and friends. I remember a quality of precise awareness. And yet, when my husband asked, between contractions, if I was thirsty, I didn't know how to answer. I couldn't find the "I" that could detect thirst. I could hear. I could feel. But I couldn't discern something as particular or as personal as thirst. I couldn't formulate an answer. As my baby was slowly being birthed into air and earth, I was becoming more formless.

After what felt like an eternity of pushing, but was actually an hour and a half, my son's head appeared, wet and round and large. My joy was short-lived when I realized I still had to push out his shoulders. No one had told me about the shoulders! I thought when the head was birthed the rest of his body would slither out on its own. After another eternity of pushing, which probably lasted only a minute or two, I heard my midwife say that my baby was here. In one movement I sat up and without thinking reached down between my legs and pulled my half-born son out of my vagina and onto my chest as I lay back down to rest in my husband's arms. My baby was born and suddenly there was no pain.

The next day, as I nursed my baby and visited with my midwife, I realized that I felt I had failed. Even though my son was born at home with no complications and glowing with life, I had failed because I had experienced so much pain. Of course, I knew that childbirth was painful for most women, but I secretly believed that I was different. I had read stories of tribal women squatting in the fields birthing effortlessly and other accounts of women in ecstasy while giving birth. I knew that childbirth did not have to be painful. I knew from being Rolfed that the experience of pain is subjective, and before my son was born I privately believed that only repressed women who couldn't undulate their pelvis or moan or growl felt pain. I was certain that, because of my years of body awareness practices, childbirth would be relatively easy.

The feeling of having failed persisted for months, and I felt that my practices had failed me as well. I had spent fifteen years immersed in the study and practice of massage, Trager bodywork, Rosen method bodywork, continuum movement, mindfulness meditation, and Vajra-yana Buddhism. I understood and experienced my body to be an open, fluid, innovative organism, and I spent time daily attending to sensation through sound, breath, movement, and stillness. My basic meditation practice was to develop intimate awareness and compassion. But it was only after giving birth and feeling like a failure that I realized I had expected these practices to protect me from pain.

I was shocked by the depth of my feeling of failure. I kept asking myself: How can someone fail in birthing? Who fails? But no matter how I framed my questions, or what my midwife or teachers or friends said to me, the feeling persisted. Because I had felt so much pain and because the desire to stop the pain was stronger than the desire to hold my baby, I had failed.

Now as I write, I can feel another birth occurring. As I accept these feelings of failure, I sense a spacious strength, a flowering of compassion, and a deep knowing within myself. These are the gifts of my labor. I am aware of the strength that comes from feeling whatever occurs, moment to moment, whether fear or rage or surrender or pain.

I was humbled by the pain I felt. I know now that my practices could not have protected me. On the contrary, they were designed to make me feel. It was because of these practices that I was able to feel and be conscious of all the sensations of birthing, including pain. Pain is a part of life. I am not a failure for feeling pain. I am not a failure for being no different from any other woman who suffers in childbirth or any other person who cries out in agony. I am not a failure for wanting the pain to stop. It is through my body that I am challenged to feel the vastness of human suffering and to feel the truth that I am the same as every other being. I am challenged to feel whatever occurs with equanimity and openness. I am challenged to be intimate with life, with birth, and therefore with pain.

∅/∅

Midlife Sacrament

CONNIE BATTEN

THE SUN FELT COMFORTING ON MY
back as I knelt to remove an earthworm from a hole I was digging.
Something about this gesture reminded me of helping my mother with
garden work when I was a teenager. With the memory, a distant yet
familiar inner chill came over me, like a dark cloud moving across
the sun.

My mother had been the same age then that I was now, forty-five.
It was hard to go on thinking about this, but I allowed myself another
memory of an evening several years later, when the phone rang. By
then I was nineteen years old. I had moved several hundred miles away
from the confusing world of my mother's menopause and had been
trying to create a new life. The long-distance voice over the phone line
told me that my mother was near death and that I should come immediately. I was given the address of a hospital where they were trying to
revive her from a deep unconsciousness caused by an overdose of sleeping pills and the inhalation of gas from an open oven in a closed
kitchen.

I had kept these memories neatly locked out of my emotional
awareness. But now they were returning, full-blown phantoms, to in-
vade my life. As I moved the earthworm to a safer spot, I was in two
places at once—I was in that garden, age forty-five, feeling the sun on

my back—and I was driving through the night, age nineteen, feeling cold confusion all around me. While my mother's body was being resuscitated, some part of me went into hiding that night as I made that long, dark drive.

Twenty-six years later, it was my turn to pass through menopause. The time had come for me to regain consciousness of some wrenching disconnections which I had covered with the busy-ness of my early adulthood. My body was visibly aging after years of relative stability. Catching an unexpected glimpse of my reflection as I passed a store window, I would be startled by the stranger who was myself. Returning home after such an experience I would sometimes stare for long minutes into my bathroom mirror trying to identify with the aging image whose weakening eyes stared back at me. My inner chemistry was changing as my accustomed monthly cycles lost their regularity, and my inner equilibrium gave way to extremes of feeling. The cords of tolerance which had held me to my assigned role as wife and mother in this male-dominant culture thinned to threads and finally snapped, ending my marriage. I found myself living alone, older than I had ever expected to be, plunged into a period of internal darkness—redefining my relationship to almost everything.

Through the ancient practice of tending to seedlings, I was able to contain the emergence of painful memories. The crucible of menopause was transforming them, to be integrated at last, so that I became more whole. At times, when the memories were almost more than I could bear, I could feel myself being held by an inner sense of balance which took its source from the earth—the mirror of my embodiment and the receptacle which will receive its dissolution.

Respite came to me when there was nothing more in my consciousness than the wonder of being. Taking in the smells and sights, the general feeling of the season, the fresh earth, the early wild plum blossoms, the brooding sky gathering for a storm, the steadiness of an all-day rain, the gusts of wind, the clearing sky and changing light on the day after, with all the colors new and crisp, the luminosity of existence would astound me. The exquisite feeling of the air on my skin stripped me of thought, filling my senses, bringing me back to the shimmering boundary which both defined my separateness and dissolved to reveal that there is no separation.

Seven years have passed since menopause cut so abruptly across my life, changing me drastically. I've grown used to being unable to see clearly without glasses. The reflected image of the middle-aged woman with thinning hair and deepening wrinkles no longer looks to me like someone else. She and I are one. I no longer expect to be able to hike twenty miles in a day with a pack on my back. Nor do I wonder at the dry, tissue-papery skin of my legs and arms, thinking it looks more like my grandmother's than my own.

My inner journey during these years has required that I come to terms with my particular life story, working to heal wounds so painful that I had hidden them from my day-to-day awareness. Bringing them back to consciousness, I've felt isolated, at times to the point of despair.

I have mourned the loss of the dream that I would grow old within the comfort of a marriage kept vital by mutual commitment to common values and woven together by a shared interest in the growth of children and grandchildren. I am not just alone, but invisible: a middle-aged woman who has given up her identity as wife and mother, without having developed a career outside her home. The leaden fear of not knowing if I will find a way to survive financially has frozen me as I've filled out applications for entry-level jobs and been turned away.

It is from this dark place at the center of my own story that the seeds of compassion for my mother and for myself have begun to germinate. My fury at her for trying to kill herself, my guilt for being part of the context that made her want to die by her own hand, and the pain of abandonment in every direction can give way from time to time to a larger, more primal experience: just being upright on this planet, sensing the mystery of consciousness as it continues to unfold.

Last summer I hoisted a familiar pack onto my back, loaded with the supplies I would need to spend a week in the wilderness. My muscles responded out of age-old habit. As I started up the trail I thought of my mother and many of the women in her generation who had no access to the experiences which have sustained me. Any stirrings toward wholeness which my mother may have felt at menopause were progressively extinguished by the electroshock treatments that inevitably followed her repeated suicide attempts. She was divested, like so many of the women in her generation, of the inner source of direction which has guided me to sit still in silence on a *zafu*, or to fast for days in desert solitude—experiences which have allowed me to glimpse the paradox of my simultaneous separation from and union with the universe.

I realized, as I settled into a rhythm moving on up the trail, that my backpacking trips each summer have been an essential part of my spiritual path for many years. These journeys outside the numbing effect of modern culture have put me in touch most intensely with the implications of my embodiment. When I have put two days of steady hiking between me and the car I left parked at the trailhead, I know my personal insignificance relative to the forces and rhythms of nature. Primitive skills for dealing with the elements—earth, air, fire, and water—are essential to my survival. When I'm in the wilderness in this way, my personal impermanence is palpable.

As my boot prints stretched farther out behind me, the terrain shifted away from the sheltering presence of tall evergreens and thick forest loam. Scrubby sage, clinging tenaciously to unlikely crevices on granite slopes, began to define the landscape. By midday in arid surroundings, I pricked up my ears for the faintest sound of flowing water. I stood still for a moment to increase the silence. Yes, there was a stream off to the west. I stashed my heavy pack, removed my water bottle, took out the small stuff sack with lunch food, and started off toward the magical sound. Within ten minutes I had come to a ledge dropping off some ten feet toward moss-covered rocks and lush stream-side vegetation. Scrambling down the steep slope took no time at all, and I was suddenly in another world where the rich smell of water and wet earth filled the green shade.

I washed away the trail dust with my bandana, returning it again and again to the clear running water, and finally tied it, soaking and cool, around my neck to refresh me when I returned to the hot trail. But meanwhile there was time for a leisurely lunch of sunflower seeds, raisins, my ration for the day of one slice of bread spread with sharp mustard, and finally, the sweet sections of an orange to be savored slowly, one by one. Such simple joy in elemental existence, breath after breath, brought a pang of sorrow that my mother had never dared to venture into the wilderness in this way, though she had habitually taken long walks close to home. I would have loved to have shared such a timeless moment with her, but my life remains a frightening mystery to her. Our paths diverge, further and further it seems, as she approaches her eightieth birthday, while modern mood-altering medications have mitigated the desperation which once made her life seem intolerable.

I finished my lunch, refilled my water bottle, and returned to my backpack and the trail I would follow until I found a spot to set up a base camp.

Late the following afternoon I came upon a granite basin which held a small lake and I knew I would stay a while. There was simple pleasure in the unfolding of rituals which create a temporary home in the wilderness—the search for a flat tent site, the scavenging for firewood, the creation of a cooking area, the checking for good places to view the change of light, sunset, moonrise, stars, and sunrise.

On the afternoon of my second day in this camp, I sat on a granite slab overlooking the lake, watching the reflections of changing cloud patterns move across its surface. The sun was warm, the air was pleasant, there was no urgency that anything in particular should happen or not happen. The only justification I needed for my bodily existence was this moment of unencumbered witnessing. I remembered the story of the Buddha's enlightenment as he sat beneath the Bodhi tree, himself a clear lens through which the universe could see and delight in itself. Buddha recognizing and enjoying Buddha.

As I sat there beside that particular lake on that particular afternoon, one being among numberless beings, one afternoon among eons of afternoons stretching back and forward into infinity, I could feel my edges beginning to dissolve. There was no separation. And then the light shifted as a cloud's shadow crossed through the sun's warmth, hinting of approaching rain. The firewood supply, the location of my tent if a storm were coming in. . . .

Suddenly my attention crystalized around survival. Instincts designed to preserve this particular being leapt into prominence, unfurling the line that defines duality.

Scraping a trench in the earth to carry runoff around the edges of my tent, sheltering a small pile of dry kindling for the first fire after the rain, preparing to separate myself from the oncoming storm, to ride it out inside the tenuous protection provided by my camping gear and my wilderness know-how, I could hear in my head the words of the Heart Sutra, rumbling like thunder:

> . . . all things are essentially empty—not born, not destroyed;
> not stained, not pure; without loss, without gain.
> Therefore in emptiness there is no form, no sensation, perception,
> formulation, consciousness;

no eye, ear, nose, tongue, body, mind,
no color, sound, scent, taste, touch, thought. . . .

If I am one of the prisms through which the universe perceives itself, it is part of my purpose to maintain a distinct and separate position made up of personal history, desire for safety, and fear of extinction. And as a temporary bubble afloat on the stream of universal flux, I am sometimes given the gift of knowing in utter effortlessness that there are also no distinctions.

Aging as a Russian Doll

LENORE FRIEDMAN

I AM OLD. I START SIMPLY, LEAVING complexities aside. For now, I want only to look, without pretense or hope or lack of hope. I want to touch my aging self with tender fingers and speak to you (sitting in your armchair, or hunched over your kitchen table) as I go.

"Time chops at us all with an iron hoe," Mary Oliver writes. In the shower this morning, my flesh inescapably sagging, belly, thighs, my mind turned away, didn't *want* simply to look: this is my body now.

Everything outside the window looks young. Early summer. Vibrant greens and startling purple-pinks, pulsing with life. Fir fronds stretch their bright ends toward me, toward each other. On this still chilly morning, the flames bursting out of the logs in the woodstove are fiercely orange and impetuous.

How old *am* I, this body that has lived sixty-seven years, this discrepant mind? At the moment I feel confusingly young: eighteen or nineteen mixed up with forty-five. Behind my eyes, looking out at the green, reaching fronds, I feel foolishly girl-like, startled by the extravagance of it all. Green behind green behind green. Now a bird calls, and another. Immediately I feel happier. They continue and I am smiling. They remind me of the rest of the grand, mysterious confusion. Mysterious order.

Yesterday was the solstice. Lying in bed, I felt the orderly turning of the solar system and galaxies, the regularities that hold us, that we cannot fall out of. We are that, and we are the falling into entropy, the chaos as well. When I feel both, I feel young—no, I feel timeless. My body and your body coexist, exist together everlastingly. We are made of the same stuff, we have evolved together, have been cells in one great body since the beginning of time.

Which means, so what? So what if I'm right now older than you? If you and I are you/I, and the dance goes on and on?

Still, here I am, an elder, toward the end of the millennium, without a clan or tribe to hold a place for me. There are no porches or huts where the old ones sit, where the younger ones gather to hear the ancient stories, the good and bad news. What this means, often, is to not even be perceived. On the street in front of my house last week, three sauntering teenage boys would have pushed me aside and kept right on moving if I hadn't swerved out of the way in time. Except with our intimates, we older ones sometimes exist in a parallel universe, on downtown streets, in computer class, at the auto mechanic's, in any crowd. Still, invisible, we do what we like, smile with unspoken knowledge at each other, can have secret wild lives.

"In old age I will grow leaner and meaner," an unknown woman proclaimed on a poster I saw years ago. In our invisibility we become unfettered and free, careless of convention, closer to our bone.

A blue flower is dying in a vase in front of my eyes. My first response is to discard it, but instead I'm just looking. Crumpled blue flower, your petals hang like my flesh does. Except for a few still fresh at the top, they have dried out, like my skin. But the heart of you is full of lavender filaments that poke out undaunted from your silvery green center. And from behind your dying petals, six spikey green leaflets stretch out like the points of a star.

If truth be told, half of me too is not old at all. Whatever I may look like, or feel on other days, inside I'm as full of mischief as a twelve-year-old, as strong as I was (well, almost) at forty, as quixotic as an adolescent. When a half-cord of wood is delivered to my driveway, I'll toss it, piece by piece, closer to my kitchen door, stack it, cart some upstairs. I'll stride over hilly trails; I'll make unabashed love. I'll often dance longer than anyone else at the party. And I'm no age at all, or all ages at once, when you and I are talking, eyes flashing, hearts stretched open, minds burrowing for the truth of something together.

But tomorrow, in the bathroom mirror, I'll study my face, trying to really *see* it, see what's been happening, and take it in. Sometimes the face in the mirror is shocking, unacceptable. Where did I go—the younger "I" I still identify with? Did this happen suddenly? Or was I simply not looking? These brown spots on my left cheek: were they so noticeable last week? This lumpiness around my chin: what *is* it? And the sagging under my chin, its absolute *there*ness, its archetypal witchiness, its ancient-spinster-maiden-aunt-hag-ness—these stereotypes appall me, but they grab me even so—can this be me? The grooves around my mouth, the ladder-lines above my upper lip—they're deeper and darker than before, aren't they? My whole face has lost its clarity, its coherence. I take in the losses daily, in tiny increments.

> In the medicine-cabinet mirror I stare at my face. The bathroom door is locked. I am eight years old. The face in the mirror, which I don't really see, is round, with wispy brown hair and large brown eyes. I am searching the face for something I cannot find. "What is it?" I whisper. "What's the matter?" The face in the mirror doesn't answer. It looks scared of being scared.

Toni Packer once said that if a thing is inescapable, we face it. Trying to escape makes everything harder. "Dying doesn't cause suffering," Terry Tempest Williams writes in *Refuge*, "resistance to dying does."

Aging doesn't cause suffering? Resistance to aging does? Let's see. If I were to let go of every idea I have about youth and beauty and strength and suppleness—wait! Impossible! There are layers and layers and layers of ideas, from our culture, literature, media, gestures, vocal inflections, and innuendos—the whole internalized kaleidoscope. This includes even the earliest layer of preverbal experience, the cues that (in my case, as a premature baby) let me know there was something wrong with me: I was too small, too fragile, too hungry, too smelly. My body wasn't strong enough, clean enough, quiet or intact enough. For me, and others like me, physical neediness became associated very early with shame and anxiety.

Last night I took a full-moon walk in the woods with three friends (no flashlights). My eyes were only barely good enough, and I kept them riveted on Kia's white pants right ahead of me. But I couldn't tell what the terrain was like. I thought we were walking through mud when it was just wet grass. In many places it felt as if the trail had narrowed radically, down to a foot-wide ledge that I could fall off easily. I concentrated on my balance while the others ambled ahead, alerting me to rises and falls in the trail—"a steep place here," "a rock coming up," "it dips down now." For me it was like what's sometimes called a "trust walk." I knew the others would keep me alert and prepared for what lay ahead; and I knew that, however unsure I felt, there was really no danger.

But I told no one of the moment in the meadow before we started, as we looked up at the moon, both obscured and dramatized by banks of clouds. Something about the light allowed me to see clearly the fluttering dark spots that sometimes appear in my upper vision, and which I know prefigure macular degeneration, an eye condition that can cause blindness. I felt chilled.

It was natural to say nothing. The activity and the setting made it inappropriate. But there was also an element of hiding.

Aging sharpens acutely our sensitivity to issues of dependence and independence. On the trail through the night woods I depended on my companions. It was a light dependency, inconsequential perhaps. But for me its edge was keen and, for what it portended, a bit ominous.

To ask for help is not an easy matter. On a walk not long ago with a friend, her daughter, and her three-year-old granddaughter, my eyes followed the little girl as she picked her way through a tangle of rocks and tall grasses, examining each new obstacle with care and concentration, finally coming up against a big fallen log that blocked her way. She considered it, then turned toward her mother, who up until then had not involved herself. "I need help, Mommy."

So simple. Just the truth. Lucky child. We are not all taught such things.

There is a drugstore on our corner whose window is painted black up to a few feet from the top, where it is edged by a thin gold border. I'm in third grade, and on my way home from school I walk around this corner, passing in front of the black opaque glass that reflects me perfectly. I'm wearing a white cotton dress with a Peter Pan collar covered with tiny blue flowers, and white lace-up shoes. There is no one else with me. Approaching the window, I slow my pace and pretend to look up at a crack in the yellowing brick wall above the drugstore. Just before I pass the black window I quickly let my gaze fall to my reflection in the glass. I hope that if I wait until the last second and look only for an instant, the mirror will finally betray its secret.

I was certain there was something wrong with me. Something I wasn't supposed to know. To protect me, my parents had magically altered all the mirrors and all the reflecting surfaces in my world, including the drugstore window.

But I knew. I didn't know *what* the secret was, but I knew it was there. I knew something was wrong with me, and I must never let them know I knew.

How long I carried this circuitous plot inside my head I cannot say for sure. It might have been a year or two. What haunts me now is my unsparing aloneness. "I need help, Mommy," was true, but entirely unthinkable.

Even now, with all the work I've done to burn away the false constructions of my mind, echoes of that narrative remain. Aging changes our features, our gait, the acuity of our senses. Anyone can see there is "something wrong" with us. So frailty becomes tinged with shame and fear, and my instinct is to disguise it.

For the past week I've been at Hedgebrook, a writer's retreat on Whidbey Island, off Seattle. This morning, making the fire in the woodstove in this beautiful place, sitting on the floor, splitting kindling on my knee, I felt young. I didn't think that word at the time. I was aware of my body, legs crossed, reaching for newspaper, getting up and down for matches, the energy involved, the unfamiliar movements, the fun and frustration of learning to build a fire a new way.

It was just now, crouching down to check the damper and adding some wood, that I thought that word. Young. I feel young when I tend the fire. Of course, if I weren't thinking about writing this essay, I probably wouldn't have thought it at all, but would have relished my pleasure without commentary. That's how it was when I took a break to go down to the woodshed for more logs and kindling. It was a good-sized load, and I hoisted it up from below and clambered up the bright green hill. I enjoyed the physical effort, my arm and back muscles working, my feet navigating rocks under the load. Back at my desk, I see the fir boughs out my window, swaying their dark green and paler-green-edged fronds in the afternoon breeze. Sun and shadow. A yellow butterfly. Crows cawing. Fire crackling. Our bodies take in the world. As they fail, does the world recede? As the ground did last night when I couldn't see it?

Loss of vision is hard, but loss of hearing is what makes me tremble most. Since an operation twenty years ago, I've been completely deaf in my right ear. Now the left is beginning to fail me. I'm learning how hard it is to ask people to repeat something I didn't quite catch, how easy it is to lose the thread of conversation among a group of people when you miss words and phrases as it goes along. "Wait, stop! I missed the drift just then." That's a possible scenario some of the time, but hardly all. After dinner last night, I sat among a group of lively writers and noticed I was missing the point of swift exchanges, that I had no clue as to why laughter erupted once, twice, three times, more. I began to feel outside the campfire.

Hearing is my preeminent sense. I have told friends over the years that I'd rather be blind than deaf. Often they protest, but the sounds of voices are more important to me than faces. And the sounds of nature! What would a silent ocean mean? A forest without its music of invisible birds? And not to hear Bach, ever again? Strange. It's the last one that makes me cry.

Age is also destroying the cells and synapses of my once-dependable mind. These days, nothing holds. Not names, dates, faces, or the thought I had a moment ago. They slip into the slough of lost objects and dreams. Gone. Not always, though. Sometimes, the next morning, or the next hour, or in five minutes, a lost one may suddenly surface. "Oh yes! It was Karen I was supposed to call." Eureka!

And then there are *words*. I love words, the precision and spiciness of one deftly chosen. Here too, if I wait patiently, sometimes the word I'm looking for appears. Very often, it doesn't. I've lost so many. They hover, maddeningly, just out of reach. But listen to this: my vocabulary has become "exiguous." There's a word I'll never forget. I learned it years ago reading a novel by John Fowles and I don't know why it stuck. It means meager, spare—what my vocabulary has become. Maybe now you'll never forget it either.

So aging does not cause suffering? Resistance to aging does? Aging undeniably causes discomfort and increasing dependencies—on more-able bodies or material contrivances like hearing aids and canes and large-print books. But according to the Dharma, all of this is pain, it isn't suffering. If we don't spin stories of failure and humiliation, what's happening is not a private, personal tragedy, but just what's happening in the great scheme of things. If I can see through my childhood fantasy of a secret flaw, and my infantile shame and fear of helplessness and vulnerability, see them as sad, comprehensible responses to my earliest environment archaic remnants now, no longer true—then my aging, undefended against, becomes fresh and full of surprises.

As I climb a familiar trail, for example, more slowly than before, I notice a perfect spiderweb catching the morning sun between swaying cedar branches. And at my feet, among dark fuzzy leaves that border the path, I see clusters of dewdrops scattered like handfuls of jewels, each a tiny burst of rainbow light. I exclaim out loud, heedless of hidden eavesdroppers, happy that what others might think of me matters so much less than it used to. Such a relief and a lightening. Such an uncluttering of mind!

Still, it confounds me how everything seems to be happening at once—the losses, the continuities; the dissolution, the resilience; the capacities and incapacities; the changed and the unchanged. Sometimes I feel like a Russian doll, the kind that hides a whole series of smaller dolls nesting one inside the other. Who am I? On good days I feel myself pulled by the tides, by the moon, by nature herself. Nature blows through me, and my skin changes, like a windblown leaf. There are changes of color, of texture, and the same wind blows through all of us, all of us growing faded and spotted and frayed over time, over cycles of seasons of sun and rain and wind and drought, sweet years, bitter years. We are soothed, we are buffeted, our hair grows, it falls, we dry, we break. On good days it all seems okay, or it seems like nothing, nothing in particular happening at all.

Our Body and Our Economy

HELENA NORBERG-HODGE

OVER THE PAST TWENTY YEARS, I have spent nearly half of each year living on the Tibetan Plateau in Ladakh in a culture which has been shaped by Buddhism. Ladakhi people seem to have a deep sense of connection to each other and to the natural world, and therefore to themselves and to their bodies. In Ladakh I feel my sense of place, my rootedness on the earth, my feet against the soil, my body embraced by the heavens. When I wake up in the morning I hear the stream outside my window, the yak grunting, and the sheep bleating. Early in the morning I hear Meme-le, the grandfather of the house, chanting in the chapel and Ama-le singing her prayers in the vegetable garden. I hear the sounds of the kitchen: the stoking of the stove, the churning of butter. Throughout the day I greet dozens of people I know—we chat with one another and help each other when help is needed.

An understanding of interdependence permeates all aspects of traditional culture in Ladakh, affecting my body-spirit in many powerful ways. However, with the recent onslaught of "modernization" in Ladakh, the connections between body and spirit, and between humans and nature, are seriously threatened by Western-style development.[1] And when I return to the industrialized West, I am shocked by the society's denial of bodily experience. Life in the West is atomized. Our experiences are separated, and placed in conceptual as well as very real structural hierarchies. The pace of life alone makes it hard for us to listen to our bodily responses to the world. Technologies which supposedly bring us together in fact separate us. Because of the telephone, for instance, it is considered quite unacceptable to just drop in on friends. It has become essential to make an appointment. My friends have much less time for one another than they used to. In order to earn our daily bread we need to work long hours. And when I'm in the West, where we all lead more separate, private lives, I feel the loss of not having children—something which never happens in Ladakh because of my closeness to other people and to their children. Indeed, in the West there are so many forces separating spirit, body, and nature that it takes constant effort to live from a deep experiential knowing of interdependence.

Many Westerners, and particularly Western women, yearn for a more holistic way of life, a way of life that is body-affirming and nature-affirming, harking back to prehistoric days of goddess worship. By observing the process of economic development in Ladakh, I see how our efforts to unify our body-spirits are inhibited by an economic system which perpetuates ignorance and greed. Through my body as well as my intellect I have come to realize that if we want to embrace the body, we must confront such distant structures as the globalization of the economy. The ways that I felt my body-spirit celebrated in traditional Ladakh are threatened under the regime of transnational corporations, and exactly the separations that many of us in the West are trying to overcome are being replicated in Ladakh now.

The dualism that separates body from spirit, and considers spirit as superior to body, has a very long history in the West. In the early days of Christianity there was a splitting of body and spirit, of women and men, of feelings and intellect, of nature and culture. Furthermore, body, women, feelings, and nature were deemed of a lower order, were marginalized and denied. The growth of science and the thinking of Descartes made the separations even more rigid.

All of us in the West have internalized this point of view to some extent. Though we yearn for the understanding of interdependence and believe that such an understanding can heal our suffering, let us not underestimate the profound effects of two thousand years of a vastly different worldview. If we want to embrace Buddhism, the process must be one of refiguring all aspects of ourselves and the structures of our society so as to integrate with the rest of the cosmos.

Emptiness, as far as I can tell, is experiencing yourself as part of an interdependent flow of relationships. I like the word *flow* because it gives the sense of movement; it's the opposite of experiencing yourself as a separate, static entity. Though I think the word *interdependence* closely approximates what is meant by emptiness, the danger is that our Western conceptual mind will create a concept that is bounded. The word *interdependence* can lead us away from understanding the truth of emptiness: at one and the same time we are separate entities and we are also inextricably intertwined with everything that is. We are both our body and not our body.

Tashi Rabgyas, Ladakh's foremost Buddhist scholar, helped me to see emptiness. He said, "Take any object, like a tree. When you think of a tree, you tend to think of it as a distinct, clearly defined object, and on a certain level it is. But on a more important level, the tree has no independent existence; rather, it dissolves into a web of relationships. The rain that falls on its leaves, the wind that causes it to sway, the soil that supports it—all form a part of the tree. Everything in the universe helps make the tree what it is. It cannot be isolated, its nature changes from moment to moment—it is never the same. This is what we mean when we say that things are 'empty,' that they have no independent existence."

Our female bodies, in particular, reveal emptiness to us. To sense interconnections between our bodies and our spirituality is "feminine." The Stone Center in Massachusetts, a center which studies feminine psychology, has found repeatedly that it is through relationship that most women tend to experience life. In the interdependent web of our world we become ourselves, know who we are, and create our lives and our world.

Our bodies bring forth our spirituality precisely because our bodies form a bridge between "inner" and "outer," connecting the personal and the so-called political. Our spiritual practice and our practice in the world are not separate. To experience my body is to experience my nonbody; it is to experience the spiritual fabric of relationships, eco-nomic forces, the media, agricultural realities, issues of age, and ecol-ogy. The way we live in our bodies tends to mirror the way we live in

the natural world. Our environmental crisis is happening in part because of our disdain for our bodies, for our vulnerabilities, for our mor-
tality, for our feelings. And so to speak personally about my body is to
speak politically about my world, and to speak personally about my
world is to speak politically about my body.

My twenty years in Ladakh taught me that spirituality (Buddhism,
in this case) and societal structures are intimately connected. When I
went to Ladakh in 1975 it was the most vital place I had ever been.
The people exuded inner peace and joy. At first, I explained the Ladakhis' laughter and absence of anger or stress in terms of their Buddhist
religion, an important but personal, nonpolitical part of their lives. I
didn't fully grasp that the very structures of their society were Buddhist.
It was only over time, in seeing how new structures, introduced by
economic development, undermined their spiritual well-being, their
deep sense of connection to each other and to the natural world, that
I saw how important their Buddhist societal structures had been to
maintaining their more personal Buddhism. Gradually I realized that
the division I made between personal and societal did not hold in Ladakhi culture.

Having observed the process of economic development not only in
Ladakh, but also in Bhutan, rural France and Spain (for over ten years),
as well as Sweden, the United Kingdom, the United States, and Ger-
many, I see how inextricably linked economic issues are to almost all
areas of life, even spiritual and psychological ones. The global economy
and the "modernization" it brings undermine people's sense of themselves and their cooperative relationships. No longer are harmonious
relations between people and with the natural world seen as vital, for
they cannot be measured as part of the gross national product. To traditional Ladakhis, real development means becoming more compassionate, but the development that is being forced on them today increases
the Three Poisons of greed, hatred, and delusion. The Western model
of development is the complete opposite of a Buddhist vision of development. As free trade and "modernization" continue to affect Ladakh,
Ladakhis will have to strive harder and harder to maintain their Buddhist practices.

Though we tend to think of development as only happening in the
"less developed" world, it is also happening in the North. Here, it goes
by the name of "progress." As the global economy necessitates high

degrees of mobility to remain competitive, a sense of place is undermined. As the pace of life continues to speed up, the rhythms of the body are denied. As we drive at unnaturally high speeds, our relationship to the earth is thrown off kilter. As we are forced to live in concrete structures of straight lines, move on tarmac, and work in cubicles, we come to forget who we are until we no longer even see the unnaturalness of our lives and we cut off responses we might otherwise have to the suicidal direction of the global economy.

But even as these trends continue, our longing for connection with the earth, with one another, and with our bodies increases. This striving for connection is bubbling up in many quarters—in the health movement, where the new direction is toward recognizing the interdependence of earth, body, mind, and spirit; in architecture, where there is a trend toward relating structures to the specifics of climate and place; in agriculture, where there is a shift, even at a government level, toward organic methods; and last, but not least, in the eco-village movement, which seeks to combine all the various strands of this yearning for connection. People are also recognizing that no form of materialism can quench spiritual thirst, that consumerism dampens creativity, and that we must reconnect with the natural world if we are to lead rich and meaningful lives.

As we embody these new ways (new for us, but often very old), we may feel shaky and vulnerable. This process of reconnection can be messy, painful, and difficult, but it brings much joy and peace. It is the acceptance of connection that our body teaches us, and that our society so often denies. We must trust our interconnectedness and reweave the fabric of meaning through relationship. With the earth as our witness and ally, with one another's support, we can find the strength to refrain from capitulating to commercial interests at this critical time on the planet. Calling on the buddhas and bodhisattvas throughout space and time we can transform ourselves and our world.

NOTE

1. I am not making a blanket condemnation of the West. When I write of "the West," I am describing an economic system and a worldview. This exploitative economic system and this worldview of domination have been very destructive, not only for the less industrialized countries of

the South, but also for the West, or North. And since I am speaking of a system, rather than particular individuals, it becomes possible to actively dissociate ourselves from it as individuals while also naming it as a Western phenomenon.

PART THREE

❀

Body as Gender

Piecing Together a Life

FRAN TRIBE

What is required (of you) is not perfection but completeness.

—C. G. JUNG, 1931

No creature ever falls short of its own completeness; wherever it stands, it does not fail to cover the ground.

—DOGEN, 1233

THE SIGHT OF MY SHAVED HEAD shocked my friends and family, yet it felt surprisingly natural and comfortable to me. Some years earlier, a period of intense discomfort with my hair had been the first symptom of my aspiration to ordain. The realization that I wanted to be a priest had shocked me profoundly. I didn't believe in a professional priesthood; I felt it led to an unhealthy separation between practitioners and their teachers and led to corruption and abuses of power. In a lineage which emphasizes the unity of everyday life and practice/realization, there seemed to be no excuse to elevate the priesthood over the laity. In 1970, Suzuki Roshi had told us our practice was to be like a "white bird in the snow," merging completely with our circumstances, meeting each person on his terms, not our own, just as Buddha had. Wearing robes and shaved head in my suburban community, I'd stick out like a black swan in the snow, yet I felt compelled to take this step and to find a way to integrate being a priest with the rest of my life.

The ordination ceremony (for both priests and lay practitioners) is an initiation into the lineage of the ancestors. Until recently they were always referred to as the patriarchs, because they are, of course, all men. One of my sangha friends had expressed concern that in taking this step I could be in danger of deserting the feminine. Long hair has always been a symbol of femininity. My friend cautioned me not to cut off the feminine in myself. I appreciated her warning and took it to heart. In fact, my desire to join the ranks of the patriarchs was part of my own quest to honor and develop all the many aspects of myself. It seemed to be the logical next step in investigating my unconditioned nature. For me this has had a lot to do with understanding and overcoming my personal and cultural conditioning.

Like most women of my generation, I grew up believing that being born in a female body was unfortunate. It was an obstacle to be overcome. My parents and grandparents gave me contradictory messages about how to accomplish this: I should always look and act the perfect lady, be attractive, find and marry the right man, be a good mother, and so on, but never indulge in the frivolous side of femininity. No frilly blouses, sexy undies, or time out for menstrual cramps. We were a family of strong women, serious women, smart women. My mother and grandmother were, in fact, cold women as well. They knew what they wanted and went after it. They didn't know what to do with me. I was too sensitive, too moody, and I got sick too much. I was too dependent in some ways but too independent in others. My grandmother lamented that I'd inherited my father's looks and my mother's brains. My uncle said I was too bright to catch a man and not nearly attractive enough. My father never noticed what people looked like or what they were wearing, but I was not nearly bright enough to keep up with him intellectually.

Shaving my head and mothering my daughter represent two poles of my life as a woman. Both have been central to being fully who I am, as a women, as a human being, as Buddha. The summer after my ordination, Jessica, then nine years old, developed a passion for swimsuits. The timing was probably not a coincidence. Her quest for the perfect swimsuit led us unexpectedly into an investigation of the relationship between appearance and reality and the connections between desire and dissatisfaction. It led us to explore our experience of living in a female body in this particular time and place. This inquiry has been central to our relationship ever since. We are growing together, each of us in her own way, as we try to understand how certain forms of desire push us around, and as we try to figure out what to do about it.

Jessica's passion for swimsuits overwhelmed her easily, and often, especially in summertime. Desire would grab her by the throat, refusing to let go until she had a new swimsuit. But she noticed that soon after she bought a new swimsuit—no matter how lovely—she was dissatisfied, disappointed, and regretful. After a while the suit was not as pretty as she'd thought, or not as comfortable. Some suits didn't swim well; bright colors faded quickly in chlorine. Somebody else had the same suit and looked better in it or had a different suit that looked promising. The search for the perfect swimsuit continued.

She tried passing up promising prospects, letting go of them, even if they fit, even if they didn't cost much, even if Mom was willing to buy them, just to see what would happen. To see if a more perfect suit might come along. Because she had learned by trial and error, by observing the peaks of anticipation and the valleys of disappointment, that no matter how beautiful the suit, no matter how comfortable, sooner or later she would see a nicer one on another girl. She practiced over and over falling in love with a swimsuit and leaving it in the store to tempt someone else. The bathing suits left behind, the "ones that got away" we'd call them, could haunt her for weeks. Perhaps that suit would have been wholly satisfactory. "I bet I wouldn't have regretted buying that one," she would think out loud.

There had been other compelling material desires before this. There was a Cabbage Patch phase, a My Little Pony period, a Strawberry Shortcake obsession. Her pressing need for these items was created by advertising and the conviction that everybody she knew had a complete set of them. And, as with the bathing suits, there was always more of a thrill in the wanting than in the getting. I had a much easier time with the toy obsessions than I did with the bathing suit thing, however. The preoccupation with having the "in" toys was familiar from my first child, Josh, who had been even more intense in his pursuit of popular playthings. I had no difficulty setting limits, leaving toy stores, calmly riding out tantrums. There was something more to the swimsuit pursuit, something deeper than just the desire for more things, something I needed to investigate for myself. Dissatisfaction with how we look and with what we're wearing is such a central fact of life for women, and Jessica's swimsuit fetish epitomized every aspect of this dis-ease. It was especially poignant to watch her at age ten, her moods swinging so quickly from hope to despair and back again as she searched for the wholly satisfactory swimsuit experience. Her lean, supple body was showing just the first small signs of budding womanhood. She was radiantly beautiful, but she didn't know it. (Actually, she didn't believe it.) She didn't hate her body, not yet, but dissatisfaction was dawning—too much here, too little there. "This one makes me look fat," she'd say.

Her difficulty in finding the right swimsuit and the right "look" was just the beginning of her initiation into the world of women. In addition to looking back at suits that "got away" she looked regretfully at those that came only in baby sizes, and she looked longingly at the more glamorous things worn by teenagers. Even as she mourned the end of childhood, she could hardly wait to be full grown. It was the first time I had seen her being at all restless or discontent with the age she was. Most of the time she was still a happy child who lived primarily in the present, but ambivalence about getting older and feelings of loss about time already past were taking root in her mind. How I wanted to save my sweet, beautiful daughter from the pain I saw her in, from the vast bottomless pit of greed, envy, and vanity. How I wanted to be saved myself!

I watched my thoughts and feelings as we struggled with odd-shaped bits of nylon in hot, stuffy dressing rooms. (What was a Zen priest doing spending so much time in department stores?) I observed the tension in my body and massaged her little shoulders (when she'd let me). Directing attention to my (bulging, middle-aged) belly, I'd breathe and remind Jessica to breathe. We got through this difficult time the way we got through so many others. One breath at a time. I remembered Aitken Roshi's ordination gift, a koan: "*Tokudo* means home leaving. How can you leave home without leaving home?" This was it: being at home where I was, helping my daughter feel at home in her own body and mind.

Painful memories from my own childhood flooded my consciousness. My mother's impatience with my pace, my preferences, my looks. She didn't care what I wanted, she just wanted to get the process over with. She didn't want me to be too preoccupied with clothes or looks or what was fashionable, but at the same time she berated me endlessly for not matching the feminine ideal of the time. From the moment I hit puberty (at nine-and-a-half) she hounded me about being too fat. When we shopped she'd often suggest that I might be worth spending money on if I were thinner. Yet, if she liked something, she'd buy it even if it was expensive; but if I liked something and she didn't, she'd make me feel unworthy of it rather than saying no directly or letting me choose for myself. The pain of many long-forgotten shopping trips with my own mother haunted me. I experienced again and again the hatred of my body I had felt as an adolescent, and the hatred I imagined my mother felt.

I vowed to cherish and protect my children as all children should be cherished and protected, whether male or female, beautiful or ugly. It was difficult to do because I didn't know how. It is hard to give what you have never received. I listened and watched carefully all those hours in front of mirrors so that I could see and hear what Jessica needed. My therapist helped me deal with the memories, the tangled web of mixed emotions I had about my own body, and the confusion I had about how to present myself and be myself. I didn't want to contaminate Jessica's experience with mine. I loved her soft little body, and I wanted her to love it too.

But no matter what I did, I couldn't protect her from the messages she was getting from the culture. As puberty hit, the task of helping her grow into a healthy young woman became more difficult and more complex. By the time she was eleven, Jessica already knew one girl who had been hospitalized with anorexia. By her junior year in high school, worry and confusion about the epidemic of eating disorders she observed around her dominated her thoughts. She wanted to save her friends and classmates from themselves, but admitted it was a struggle just to listen to her body: feed it when it was hungry; rest it when it was tired, hurt, or sick; and try not to compare it to the cultural "ideals" she saw everywhere. The monthly ebb and flow of hormones brought sugar cravings, headaches, cramps, moodiness, and self-doubt. Buying a swimsuit became much less fun.

She began to see how her desires had been promoted by the media to satisfy the greed of people who produced magazines, fashions, makeup, and diet products. She wanted and hated all of it. She was righteously indignant that a magazine could print heart-rending stories about girls dying of eating disorders with a cover photo of a probably-anorexic model and pages of ads for diet aids. She wrote letters, canceled subscriptions. I was proud of her awareness, yet heartbroken to see her suffering.

Finally, one day she announced, "I think I understand something . . . the wanting is better than the getting." She had found out for herself how desire leads to suffering and she knew she was weary of this particular form of suffering. She also began to see that looking like the girl on the magazine cover or the prettiest girl in the neighborhood didn't lead to real happiness. The swimsuit fetish dropped away. And although clothing and finding the right "look" remained important to her for many years after that, she retained some ability to observe the rising of desire and dissatisfaction and she has cultivated a kind and caring attitude toward her body and its comfort. Clothing hasn't caught her in the same way since then.

I've always been in awe of my daughter's beauty. I thought it would bring her the kind of happiness my mother promised would come to me if only I were beautiful and slim. But alas, it's not so simple. My daughter has a lovely figure. I think it would have been nearly perfect by the standards of my own youth. The standard now is even thinner. The models in fashion magazines and catalogs look like concentration camp survivors; many of Jessica's classmates look like this, too. She feels trapped between wanting to alert her classmates and their parents to the dangerous behavior she sees and the teenage code of silence. She wrote a paper for school on eating disorders, arguing that teachers should be required to report odd eating behavior and extreme thinness just as they would report suspected child abuse or neglect. We talked about the problem until the wee hours many mornings. I didn't feel bad about not getting up for zazen those days. Practice takes many forms—sleeping can be one of them.

Not long ago, Jessica put herself on a diet. It was moderate and sensible as diets go, but she was miserable and hungry. She felt deprived all the time, and she didn't lose weight. It was easy for her to see how her friends could get caught up in cycles of self-deprivation and overindulgence. We talked about listening to her body and what made her feel good or not so good. The diet was over in less than a week.

Jessica will go to college in a year; Josh is just now graduating from the University of California at Berkeley. They are struggling to find who they really are, to find their niche, to create meaningful and productive lives. I'm looking forward to seeing them launched, to working less, to having grandchildren, and to having more time for retreats, reading, and writing.

My robes hang in the closet, worn infrequently these days. They hang there with my professional outfits, my gardening clothes, and an assortment of shoes, handbags, and accessories. I hope they are not

embarrassed to share space with the silk negligee I save for special week-
ends with my husband. My teacher told me I couldn't wear makeup or
earrings after becoming a priest—"unless you're going somewhere special with your husband," he stipulated. Ironic, I thought, to be warned
not to look too attractive after years of being told I was not attractive
enough!

Regardless of my hairstyle (or lack thereof) or my attire, I will
never fit my teacher's image of a priest any more than I fit my mother's
image of proper daughter. I need all the pieces of myself to make a life
that hangs together.

I sewed my outer robe (*okesa*) by cutting small pieces from a large
bolt of cotton and stitching them together in the traditional pattern
said to resemble a rice field. With each stitch one repeats, "I take refuge
in Buddha." The okesa is the image of my life. My life is like a patch-
work quilt. There are blocks of working as a therapist, squares of
cooking, shopping, and caring for my home and family, patches of
mothering my (almost adult) children, trying to be a decent wife to my
husband. Studying, sitting zazen, writing, and teaching are relatively
small blocks in the quilt. But mindfulness is the warp and woof of each
piece, and Buddhism is the thread that holds it all together. As with my
okesa, each stitch contains the vow: I take refuge in Buddha. Regardless
of my activity, I'm watching, always watching, what comes up in my
own mind and trying to help whoever I'm with to accept the contents
of theirs.

My children will tell you they know nothing about Buddhism. They
have never meditated. They are no longer embarrassed by the fact that
we have an altar in the living room and a sitting group that meets here
on Sundays. But they understand and embody the basic teachings quite
well. They can spot the gaps between appearance and reality, and have
developed an eye for what's genuine. They have learned from their experience how life is characterized by the unsatisfactoriness born of desire. They understand how desire can be transformed through
awareness and that by paying attention to the results of their actions
they can avoid producing more suffering for themselves and others.
We keep learning together, over and over again, noticing our mistakes,
returning to our intentions.

Beings are numberless (filling our minds, moment after moment),
*   I vow to save them.*

Delusions are inexhaustible (and our culture promotes them constantly),
  I vow to end them.
Dharma gates are boundless (opening continuously every day),
  I vow to enter them.
Buddha's way is unsurpassable (there is no other way),
  I vow to become it.

Anger and Meditation

RITA M. GROSS

Human birth is precious in Buddhism because the human body is the basis for the practices that facilitate realization. Without that human body, it is impossible to do such practices. In Vajrayana traditions, we are encouraged to contemplate this premise: "Precious human body, free and well favored, difficult to obtain, easy to lose, now I must do something useful." Such contemplation on the worthiness of the body contrasts significantly with the devaluation and fear of the body found in so many religious systems, including those with which most of us grew up. Such body affirmation is part of the refreshing emphasis on the basic goodness of human beings and the world that is so central to Vajrayana Buddhism.

Nevertheless, traditional Buddhism also contains contradictory teachings that suggest that when the precious human birth occurs in a female body, then that birth is less precious. Female rebirth, resulting from negative karma due to misdeeds in a previous life, was thought to be unfortunate. Women's spiritual and intellectual capabilities were considered to be lower than those of men and their female bodies not disposed to Dharma practice. Women did not deserve to be involved in religious learning and teaching and were given many fewer opportunities to practice the Dharma than were men.

To correct this problematic situation, women were given practices—such as piety, conventional morality, deference, and specific prayers—that would enable them to be reborn as men in the next life. With male bodies, they would then more easily become enlightened. (At the most extreme, some Buddhist texts declare that a buddha would never appear in a female body.) Thus, Buddhism, like many other traditions, declares that men are really the normal human beings, while women are odd, and not full-fledged representatives of the human species.

This stark assessment of the effects of having a female body on precious human birth elicits two observations. First, it is based on circular reasoning. Women have not been trained in Buddhist meditation and philosophy because they have been evaluated as inferior human beings, but then their lack of achievement in philosophy or meditation is used to justify not providing them with opportunities for training. Second, such evaluations of the worth of women's precious human birth have devastating effects on our self-acceptance, our *maitri*, or lovingkindness, in Buddhist terms. Many Buddhist practices encourage us to "start where we are" and to accept who we are as human beings. But this is difficult if we also believe what we've been told about our inferiority and our need to start over with male bodies.

For me, feminism is a powerful antidote to such teachings, whether in Western or in Buddhist guise. Since I define feminism as "the radical practice of the co-humanity of women and men," feminism is about cherishing precious human birth in a female body. When we talk about feminism in the context of spiritual practice, we are talking about taking the buddha-nature of women as seriously as we have always taken the buddha-nature of men, including finding and training young women to be our next generation of teachers, just as we have always been willing to accept young men as teachers.

Unfortunately, the more we know about Buddhist history and some contemporary forms of Buddhism, the more we realize how much we need feminism. Many people do not realize how much negativity toward women is in the Buddhist heritage. This is why it is so important to be aware and critical of the residue of such attitudes still found in current iconographies and liturgies. Feminism is an *upaya*, or skillful means, appropriate to counter such negativity toward women. I cannot imagine taking my bodhisattva vow seriously or working to promote an enlightened society without being a feminist.

When I was a child growing up in the 1950s, before the second wave of feminism, I hated being female, with good reason. I was taught that all the things I wanted to do with my life were not what girls did. I wanted to explore the world, to read, to think, to discover reality. Most decidedly, I did not want to be limited to doing what girls and women did—enabling others, especially men and children, so that their lives can proceed smoothly. Every girl who rebels against the prison of gender roles has her own version of what she will *not* spend her life doing; for me it was dusting lamps. I wanted to spend my life reading, thinking, and writing, not dusting lamps. (I now have many beautiful antique lamps which I dust every now and then, but I dust them because I like them, not because it is my preordained gender role.)

The human activity that I value most is naming reality, especially in religious and spiritual ways. The activity of putting raw, inchoate perceptions into words that others may find helpful has always beckoned me. But every direction in which I tried to go was marked by a sign that read "Stop! No girls allowed." My patriarchal culture insisted that such exploration and spiritual development was not my gender role. The patriarchal prison of gender roles teaches that not only are women not quite real human beings; it also teaches that women should willingly accept having their reality named for them by others.

What do you do in a situation like that? As a child you don't understand that the problem is with the system, not with you—a girl who wants to think about reality. So you accept it as a fact that there's something wrong with you. Either my desire to think about reality was wrong or my female body was wrong. My desire to explore the world was too persistent for me to give that up, so for years as a child I hated my female body because it was the impediment to being the human being I wanted to become.

I don't quite know how it happened but some time in my late teens, I had one of those sudden "aha" experiences that save your life if you can remember them and not fall back into habitual patterns. While dancing between the milk cans in our shoestring dairy operation, I experienced a very strong realization: "It's not me. I'm not what's wrong; there's nothing wrong with my female body. It's the system—the system!" I have a strong body memory of how I felt at that moment. I felt powerful synchronization of body and mind—mental delight meshed with physical alertness—and a sensation of freedom and empowerment.

The insight was very brief, almost instantaneous, but I don't believe I ever again said, "If only I weren't female! Why did I have to be female?"

Years later when I learned Buddhist names for experiences, I realized that this was the first time I had experienced self-acceptance, or maitri. And, years later, when I encountered Buddhist beliefs that my female body needed to be traded in for a male one before I could truly practice, the memory of this experience kept me from taking that doctrine seriously. I knew that in this *female* body I could learn, I could name reality and create culture, I could become a teacher. I knew I did not have to wait around until I had a male body.

That insight was followed by years of what I would now characterize as complaint and aggression, which, though painful in its own way, was a lot healthier than the previous self-rejection. I was a pioneer in my field, the feminist study of religion. I was also angry because I was punished professionally, rather than rewarded for my feminist insights. I responded to the academic establishment with verbal aggression and sarcasm at every opportunity. If on a daily basis you are having your life taken away from you because of your gender, from a conventional point of view it would be logical to be angry about that. If you are going to get angry about anything, that's something worth getting angry about. In terms of Buddhist psychology, I am describing unenlightened *vajra* energy, and I lived with that for many years.

Many people, and particularly those with a meditative practice, dismiss feminism because of the anger they see displayed. While it is true that many feminists often become ideological and aggressive, it's helpful to look at the situation using some basic Buddhist tools instead of glibly writing off feminism as "too aggressive." According to Mahayana teachings, aggression always arises from pain. The angry feminists who are such a turnoff are expressing their pain at having their lives taken away from them by a sex/gender system that doesn't work. Usually, as Buddhists, we try to understand the source of a person's aggression, and also the critical intelligence that is always present within aggression, but feminists are often dismissed—and quite aggressively! What does this dismissal say about women's precious human birth?

For Buddhists to be unwilling, even aggressively unwilling, to examine conventional habitual patterns, such as gender roles, is rather odd. This may be the only realm in which ignorance is not only tolerated but actually encouraged. And this occurs at all levels, from the language of our liturgies all the way to our Buddhist leadership. For example, within my own sangha, Vajradhatu, daily chants still use generic masculine language and the shrine room is often devoid of feminine imagery. In addition, female lineage holders and *tulkus* are quite rare in Tibetan Buddhism. Those who criticize this situation are often subjected to dismissal and isolation themselves. It is very strange and sad that this continues to happen.

I was already well schooled in feminism and the academic study of Buddhism when I began meditation practice. I had no idea how profoundly meditation would affect my self-righteous feminist anger. Observing that effect over more than twenty years has been an interesting journey. At first my feminist friends thought I had lost it. It's one thing to *inherit* a patriarchal religion and try to work with it. Many of my feminist friends were making that choice. But to *convert* to a patriarchal religion was incomprehensible. No wonder they questioned my basic sanity.

My Buddhist friends were not much help either. The generic line was something like, "That's okay, Rita. When you get to be a real Buddhist practitioner, you won't care about feminism anymore because you'll be detached." It was okay from their point of view to care about jobs and families or about Buddhist practice, but not to care about the politics of affirming the preciousness of human birth in a female body. So basically I found myself between two factions, both asking what was the matter with me.

What happened was not what either faction predicted, which is where the magic connecting feminism and the path of practice occurs. After being involved in serious meditation practice for several years, I began to discover that I simply didn't find anger so satisfying any longer. Previously, I always experienced emotional relief through venting verbally, often with extreme sarcasm and cutting intellect, when I was overwhelmed by misogyny and patriarchy. But I no longer found it so appealing to get mad when gender issues arose because the relief was not reliable, and I began to see that in any case my anger was not doing anything to alleviate the general misery brought about by patriarchy and misogyny. I began to realize personally the Buddhist teaching that aggressive speech and action always produce negative counterreactions. I began to see that people tuned out when I ventilated my angry feelings, that my fits of aggressive rhetoric only caused further mutual entrenchment, rather than any significant change in those whom I confronted. I wanted to do something more helpful.

These changes were very scary at first because I feared that I was ceasing to care about concerns that had been central to my life for years. Maybe my Buddhist friends were correct and practitioners are not involved in "causes." But something else was also happening. With practice, the anger that had been so much a part of my feminism had started to transmute. I no longer experienced so much of the time that painful state in which clarity and anger are totally mixed up. The clarity remained but the anger started to settle. My body no longer tensed with hot explosive energy; instead I began to hold a relaxed body state that has nothing to do with giving in and everything to do with furthering communication. Now I test myself on issues. I find that if I explode into emotionalism, felt in the body as cloudy rage, I know that I must work further with the issue by myself before I am fit for public communication about that issue.

As my anger became less urgent, my clarity concerning gender issues and the Dharma increased proportionately and my skill in expressing my convictions without polarizing the situation also increased. I was actually becoming a much more effective spokesperson for feminism. I was not ceasing to care about feminism, as my Buddhist friends had been encouraging me to do, but ceasing to nurse my anger. I did not stop saying the same things that I always had, but when I expressed myself less aggressively, people could hear what I was saying. I discovered a middle path between aggressive expression and passive acquiescence, and at times I have been able to bring about major changes in a meditation program because I simply maintained my position without aggression.

We do not have to choose between confronting someone or getting rolled over, even though that's what the conventional world teaches us. Thereby, some measure of victory over warfare may be achieved, because one cannot be so easily dismissed when one does not respond aggressively to provocation. This middle path is very hard to maintain. It takes a lot of being with each moment, moment by moment, to avoid getting rolled over or becoming confrontational, but that is the magic of the middle way. The point of feminism is not to fight wars but to alleviate the suffering caused by conventional gender roles. Practice can tame the anger and unleash the clarity of feminism so that communication is more possible.

Not only does meditation unlock the power of feminism; it also sustains feminism in the long haul. I don't see any way that, more than thirty years after I began to advocate feminism, I could still be talking about it if I had not begun to practice. If you really want to work with the world on something you care about, practice provides the staying power to avoid burnout, precisely because meditation tames anger and makes it workable. Practice seems to be the foundation for caring about the world without becoming exhausted. It is the foundation of a movement that people are beginning to call engaged Buddhism—and Buddhist feminism will be part of that movement.

However, even after our anger has transmuted into clarity, we women who do not conform to conventional gender roles still often face a long and lonely haul. We are frequently punished by being denied love and companionship. Quite commonly we are told that more conventional women are more desirable companions. Feminist historian Gerda Lerner has commented that forcing women to choose between their intellectual-spiritual concerns and their love lives is patriarchy's oldest and most devastating device for self-maintenance.[1] But few women want to live without companionship just because they will not give over their precious human birth to conventional gender roles. Therefore, for me to maintain some equanimity took considerable effort and watchfulness for a long time. Only in the past few years has that effort transmuted into a steady self-existing cheerfulness, which has been a shocking experience in its own right. The transformation from feeling that my life was so difficult that I didn't know if I could take it anymore to appreciating the richness of my life has been delightful.

But I think you need more than formal practice for that to occur. You need community and you need relationships with people who genuinely care about you. I found it much easier to flip struggle into cheerfulness when I was not only practicing but had an adequate container of relationship and community. This understanding is one of the things that feminists practicing Buddhism have to contribute. We understand that not only is formal practice absolutely necessary, but so is the support of a nurturing community. This is something we will be talking about for a long time to come. That is only one example of the insights that practicing feminist Buddhists bring to Buddhism. The wisdom of women's culture has not been adequately transmitted from generation to generation in the context of formal Buddhist practice and Dharma discourse in the past because of the prison of gender roles. Bringing the wisdom of women's culture into mainstream Dharma discourse is central to the magical interaction between feminism and the path of practice.

NOTE

1. Gerda Lerner, *The Creation of Patriarchy* (Oxford: Oxford University Press, 1987).

Breaking through
the Concrete

LINDA RUTH CUTTS

WHEN I STARTED PRACTICING, about twenty-eight years ago, I was depressed and in a lot of pain, and nothing could get through to me. There was a moment when I was standing in front of Ghiberti's golden doors wrought with many small figures, called *The Gates of Heaven*, in Florence. I knew they must be fabulous because I'd studied them in art history class, and I had been looking forward to seeing them—but there they were and I couldn't feel anything. I remember saying to myself, "You numbskull, this is a masterpiece. Look at it. You numbskull!" Not only was my skull numb, but the rest of me was numb, too.

At a certain point in my life I had chosen to go numb out of self-preservation. I decided that I will not feel any of this pain anymore. I was able to switch off my emotional life, as well as my physical and mental sensations and my sense of relatedness. We can actually do that for self-preservation when we have to. But it's very hard to get back, to get un-numb again. How do we do that? Later, when I was ready to thaw out, it didn't happen just because I wanted it to; I was encased in front of the doors of heaven and I couldn't feel anything.

My shutting down had to do with my family's reaction when, at the beginning of my freshman year in college, I got pregnant. This was in 1966, and it was a major catastrophe for me and for my family. I clicked myself off so that nobody could hurt me anymore. I didn't cry anymore in front of anybody who mattered to me.

It was the change in my body—secret and shameful—that caused me such pain. Not being able to button my miniskirts, the Velcro on my ski pants unfastening if I bent over. And vomiting. Nothing tasted right, or smelled right. The world was no longer safe, no longer felt like home. And my cute little body was disappearing.

This body that had always been loved and admired by those close to me became an object of abandonment and scorn.

My mother took me shopping for maternity clothes in New York, far away from the friendly saleswomen in St. Paul's department stores and the chance that we might run into someone we knew. I bought my meager wardrobe for the mother-to-be: white turtleneck, powder blue shorts with expandable belly, navy and white suit—the skirt of which didn't even have a belly but a horseshoe cutout where fabric should have been. I wore a costume-jewelry wedding ring which seemed to call out its fakeness.

I was sent away, across the country, to a foster home in Philadelphia—to a couple who took in unwed Jewish mothers. My mother left me there after a brief look at the house where I would be living for the next six months. There I was, alone on West School House Lane, Philadelphia, PA.

I was expected to babysit for the couple's two small children. The woman was pregnant, too, but we never formed a bond. Her husband and I watched endless television together while she went to bed early.

I was assigned to an obstetrician by my social worker, and on prenatal visits I was weighed, my blood pressure was taken, and a urine test was done. No discussion, no asking how I was faring, only the repeated warning not to gain too much weight. Natural childbirth was not yet in vogue and I was told nothing about what might happen. I was afraid, because my view of childbirth came from *Gone with the Wind*—Melanie Wilkes writhing and groaning. That's what I thought it was going to be like.

But I felt I had no right to ask for help. "You got yourself into this," I said to myself.

My mother had said little about her own experience giving birth, but I felt her unspoken fear for me. Of her three children, two, including me, had been delivered by cesarean section, lifted out, drugged, delivered by appointment. My older sister's birth had been difficult and traumatic.

In spite of everything, the more pregnant I became, the more I felt a deep connection with the growing baby. When it began to move, the joy I felt was a kernel of life within a numbness like ice.

I tried to prepare myself by reading. There was a small branch library within walking distance, and several times a week I would trundle off to this haven and come back loaded down with whatever I could find on childbirth. One line in one of the books said something like, "Breathing during labor might be helpful." It was the only useful phrase that anybody gave me. Breathing . . . I promised myself I'd remember that.

My mother was visiting me at the foster home when my labor began. The water broke with a rush of warmth. "Oh," I exclaimed, "this must be the water breaking." I had read about that in a book.

At the hospital I was checked in and my mother and I had to part. No one was allowed to go with me into that unknown. The nurse was kind to me as she shaved my pubic hair, and her kindness surprised me. Then I was left to fend for myself on a narrow gurney. Other women were screaming somewhere in the room, but I was partitioned off by screens.

I remembered the library book's advice and did my best to breathe in a relaxed way. At other moments I whistled, "Whenever I feel afraid . . ." from *The King and I*. Keeping myself company, feeling my body do what it had to do, I tried in my own way to take care of myself and the baby that was on its way. At some point I was given an anesthetic.

When I awoke I put my hand on my belly. It's gone. It's over. The nurse said, "It's a boy." I hadn't even thought to ask, I was so groggy. At my request, I saw him a few times and gave him his bottle. I never could have imagined the depth of the love that poured out of me for that baby. The child was given up for adoption five days later.

The baby was gone, just like that, but the milk came in. While I was in the hospital they gave me pills to dry up the milk, but as soon as I left, it all came in anyway. There I was, ready for the next thing, but there was no next thing. I felt a strange discontinuity and sadness, utter sadness.

After my first evening back at home, the whole experience was never mentioned again. I came home from having a baby and giving him up for adoption and my parents said, "What are you going to take in school?"

I lived at home, went back to college as a freshman, for the second time, and pledged a sorority. I felt like an old woman compared to the girls around me. My body had changed; I had stretch marks. The impermanence of the body had come home to me at a young age. Nobody had ever died in my close family and so I hadn't realized it before, but now it came home to me in my own body because my body had changed. Everybody else was young and fit and hopping around, but I was in another realm. I was out of sync. I was numb, a numbskull, and I couldn't relate to anybody. I went through the motions, and I did extremely well in school because all I did was study. But I felt dismembered because I didn't know where the child was—it had been part of me and now it was gone. I couldn't integrate the experience into my life.

In this state of being, I was introduced to zazen practice. I will forever be grateful to the teachers who offered the Dharma to me. The practice was a kind of remembering for me. Another name for mindfulness is *re*-membering. As a dismembered being I was shown some ways of *re*-membering. Very simple things: careful posture, counting the breath, sitting quietly, putting the teapot down on the coaster and not on the table. I remember being told as I was putting the teapot down, "Don't put it on the table, put it on the coaster." In various small ways I was beginning to remember, and it was through the practice.

Mindfulness takes dismemberedness and re-members it. Mindfulness does not judge. Along with my own physical feelings and depression, I had incorporated the expectations and ideals of everybody else. I had been "colonized," as Anne Klein calls it, and I no longer knew where I was. I had ideals—other people's ideals—that I could never live up to, ever, because that's the nature of ideals, and I was constantly being beaten up and beaten down by this kind of thinking. But mindfulness doesn't care about content. Mindfulness says, "I feel anger; anger resides in me." It doesn't add, "and that's a really bad thing to be feeling."

When I first came to the Zen center, I was really nervous. After dinner I was given the job of putting the *gomasio* (sesame salt) away. Someone said, "Here, do this. You'll like this." There were little bowls of gomasio with teeny little spoons, and a special little brush, and there was a big gomasio container. I had to dump the gomasio back into the big container, and then brush all the crumbs out of each little bowl, and stack it, and take another. To be given a job like that was heaven. There was no colonized ideal there, just lift, brush, brush, brush, set down. I got the feeling that we were taking care of things and carefully doing things, and somehow, I was carefully taking care of myself.

For me, just doing that which was before me with sincerity was a new way to be in the world. For years I had been doing things in order to get approval, to get good grades, and to stay very small so as not to be noticed—that was my world. I was living for what everyone else thought I should do; there was nothing else. If you give somebody like that a gomasio dish and a little brush, the relief of just doing that body practice is enormous and unforgettable. It was January 2, 1971. I'll never forget. I was asked to do something fully, with no questions asked—I experienced that as compassion. The person who gave me the job saw my pain and said, "Here—you'd like to do this."

Mindfulness practice holds the possibility of dropping the judgmental, critical mind. Mindfulness focuses on the object and stays steady with it, while everything else is swirling around—billions and billions of universes. You can be steady, and at the same time feel the movement, the impermanence. I was lucky to be introduced to sitting, mindfulness practice, posture, and breath at that point in my life. Over the years the numbness evaporated, the numbskull let go. Life-force began to break through the cement, like little tendrils, until there was a whole bunch of grass.

But coming back to the wisdom of the body was not a smooth process. During the years that I was at Tassajara Zen Mountain Center, I made involuntary movements in zazen. I would crash from one side of the *zabuton* to the other, and I had to hold on tight to the zabuton, because if I didn't, who knew what would happen? It was like riding a magic carpet in the zendo, while everybody else was sitting quietly around me. Then the bell would ring, I would get up, fluff my cushion, walk out, do my work, and everything was fine. But as soon as I went back to the zendo, I was a wild woman. I had impulses to pummel the people on either side of me, to hit the divider. And then, *ding*, bow, and back to normal. What was this? It was a koan for me for ten years. For ten years I sat with involuntary movement. It was extreme at the beginning, and gradually my movements got smaller and smaller until I was finally able to sit still.

I now understand that it took ten years of zazen for me to thaw out. The involuntary movements were a bodily expression of the feelings I had locked up and shut away. These painful feelings demanded to be heard and thrashed me about until I took notice. Gradually I paid attention and admitted the pain that was alive in me; and the feelings worked their way through me at last, cracking the concrete.

I had a different kind of experience of the wisdom of the body some years later. I was living at San Francisco Zen Center, where I was the head of practice, and I was asked to go down to Tassajara to give a Dharma talk during the guest season. I was pleased to be asked. My daughter was a baby then, and she was nursing, so I planned to nurse her and then put her down for the evening. After she was asleep I'd go into the zendo and do the talk; the timing would work out perfectly. So I prepared for the talk during the day, and then it was time to nurse my daughter. She was such a big nurser—she just kept nursing, nursing, nursing. She didn't want to stop, and I could hear the roll down on the *han*—it was time for me to get into the zendo and give my talk, and she was nursing, nursing, nursing.

Finally she was finished and I went into the zendo and tried to speak about Dogen Zenji and Zen. If you're a nursing mother, various hormones get secreted that make you feel completely relaxed, like a big cow, which is just what you're supposed to be. So I had what a friend calls "milk mind." You can't really put two and two together. A cow doesn't give the best Dharma talk. I fumbled, I couldn't remember what I was going to say and it was very embarrassing. I was later chastised: "If you're going to give a talk at Tassajara, and the guests are there, you should prepare. . . ." Many years later I realized that if I had gone into the zendo and said, "I just finished nursing my baby, and now I'd like to tell you about how I love zazen. And aren't we all happy to be here"—if I had spoken the truth—this is who I am, this is what I'm doing, I am a nursing mother—if I had spoken authentically from where I was, without trying to be somebody else, without trying to be a Zen Teacher, it would have been fine. But I was pretending to be something different. I didn't confess who I was. It's not that you have to dig down to your deepest darkest most horrible secrets and express them at every moment, it's just a matter of looking at who you are and what's going on, and speaking from there. And when you do, it's such a relief to everybody around you, and to yourself, too.

We need to take care of ourselves, both women and men, and this is often difficult. I believe it's particularly difficult for women, because in this culture women are socialized to take care of everyone else's needs before their own. We can forget how to take care of ourselves. Our bodies can help us by tipping us off. Our bodies often tell us that there's something we need to pay attention to, that we need to take care of ourselves.

Postscript: A few years ago I received a call at work from a social worker in Philadelphia. I was stunned—this could mean only one thing. For several years I had been trying to find my birth son, and in my search had purposely left a wide trail for him to follow in case he ever wanted to find me. The social worker, once assured of who I was, said, "Your son is here in the office, and he's a very fine person!" Then she gave the phone to him.

"Is it really you? What is your name?" I asked. We talked for an hour and made arrangements for our reunion.

What joy and relief I felt to finally know he was safe and had been brought up in a loving home. He was alive! The deep hole I had carried in my heart was healed. I felt complete once more.

❁❁

What Do Lesbians Do in the Daytime?

JISHO WARNER

I STAND UP IN MY LIFE IN THE Dharma as a lesbian. And I fall down as a lesbian. I have to confront the circumstances of my particular personal life at the very same time that I live as a person no different from anyone else and as a person who is responsible for taking the best care that I can of my meeting with you. This is my whole life of trying to stand up in the buddha way. Dharma practice is all about trying to meet the full reality of life in everything I encounter, and sitting in zazen and standing up in life are not two different things. They are both the one universe of impermanence flowering. They are both the hesitant stammerings and gropings of this particular me.

To be a lesbian is by the nature of the word a body-based identity. This has zero connection to whether I'm sexually active or not. How is this different from life as a heterosexual? Of course it really isn't different in the grand scheme of things. But our minority status pushes lesbians and gays into being identified and judged by our sexuality. Heterosexuals aren't forced into this because their sexuality doesn't appear to be a distinguishing feature.

The all-too-common assumption that heterosexuals are just people but homosexuals are aliens came clear to me many years ago. My partner Joni and I were visiting friends in upstate New York and they were asked to speak on a panel about lesbians sponsored by NOW. Our two friends turned out to be the whole panel, and each spoke about her life as a lesbian. They talked about the ordinary daily issues of raising children, making a home, having a job, and about the special flavor of their lives. Then they invited questions. Silence. Finally one woman raised her hand and nervously asked, "What do lesbians do in the daytime?"

I can't look to my society or my education for models of how to live life as me unless I want to see myself as unworthy and sick. Nor can I assume that I will be accepted or granted normal civil rights. I can't expect validation from outside; I have to define myself, moment by moment. I'm not trying to lay claim to these truths as somehow unique to lesbianhood. Where we turn for acceptance, what sources we take our values from—these are issues for everyone. It's just that I don't have the choice of avoiding them, and that is one of the blessings of being a lesbian.

My life has pushed me to an intensely interesting edge. I get lazy and want to coast along, and I have to be poked and prodded by life to wake up. Difficult circumstances are great opportunities for waking up. Harsh circumstances are something else altogether; they are problems, not opportunities. Great pain, poverty, being cast out—these never did anyone any good. In most times and places lesbians have been stoned, burned to death, outcast, or hidden, like so many other minorities. The United States is often chaotic and violent, but it is also one of very few societies in history with room for me to write these words and for you to read them.

A lot of people don't examine their sexual identity, and so the intricate role eros has in their life can get submerged. As a lesbian I don't have that option. Even if I want to put it aside, the world won't let me. There's no such thing as being finished with people's attitudes and projections, so I have really no choice but to maintain my awareness. I've always felt that we who engage in Dharma practice do so not because we're so wonderful to have understood the importance of Dharma, but because we need it so badly. To live my life with integrity, I need the Dharma.

The blessings of my life as a lesbian go beyond the powerful effect it has had on my awareness. The other side of this gift is personal joy: it is with a woman that I have learned about the deep reaches of loving commitment. That's also not particular to lesbians, of course, but it is in the particular circumstances of my life as a lesbian that I have learned about honest and loving relationship. Once I learned to love one woman, I found I could love all sorts of people, other animals, rocks, sea, and sky. And just as love is not particular to lesbians, so I am not set apart by my loving.

People often get this point confused. When I lived in Minnesota, a member of the sangha who knew me and Joni and a little about our long and loving partnership was in our house one day. She was talking to me about the serious problems in her marriage, and bemoaning that the same was true of most of the other marriages she knew of. And she said she wished there were some role models around the Zen center of successful pairing—how sad there didn't seem to be any. "What about me, what about Joni and me?" I asked. "Oh, that's different," she said. She was confused between what's personal and what's universal. Being a lesbian in a particular relationship is individual, but the heart, commitment, love—these are universal.

The broad view of the heart was offered to me by my first teacher, Dainin Katagiri Roshi. I had been practicing in solitude for some years when I went looking for a teacher and met him. I decided to ask him to accept me as his student and made an appointment to talk with him about what it meant, since I had no idea what I was getting myself into. We talked for some time and I felt good about the arrangement, but there was one last topic I had to discuss.

I took a deep breath and said, "There's one more thing . . . I'm a lesbian." No response. I took another deep breath and went on to explain what a nice, sweet, good lesbian I was, dwelling on all the positives I could drum up. He just sat there looking at me. I took another deep breath and backtracked. "Do you know what a lesbian is, what the word *lesbian* means?" Still no response. I was getting desperate now, and my voice cracked as I plunged ahead. "Do you have *anything* to say about my having a woman partner?" There was another long pause. He pursed his lips and looked thoughtful while I sat there in agony, and then he said, "It isn't bad, it isn't good. What's her name?" Every year after that when I arrived in Minnesota for practice periods at Hokyoji, Katagiri Roshi would greet me warmly and say, "How's Joni?"

Just as I can't take a form from my society for my life as a lesbian, I also can't look to my Dharma lineage, to the sutras and commentaries, or to the Vinaya for models of how to be me as a priest. Most Buddhist lineages would repudiate me first as a woman and again as a lesbian. Institutional prejudice runs deep and has prevented many people from having access to these wonderful teachings. I am grateful for my good fortune in being in a line that has room for me.

I was a lesbian before I was a priest, and many of the lessons I learned as a lesbian stood me in good stead after I was ordained. Anyone who stands out is particularly subject to projections of specialness, and I had had a lot of practice at not identifying myself with what people sometimes projected on me as a lesbian—wolfish sexual predator, pariah, man-hater, and, occasionally, beacon of the future. I do have my share of personal faults, but being a lesbian isn't one of them. Priests tend to draw more positive projections than do lesbians, and so we're more likely to be seduced by them. It's tempting to think I'm as wise and kind as someone wants to think I am, but it's just as important not to identify with positive projections. Besides, being a Buddhist priest is also pretty strange to a lot of people.

I've been mistaken for a man many times over the years, and when I kept my head shaved people yelled "skinhead" at me from cars a couple of times in a tone of voice that made me wonder if it was safe to be walking there. Once a woman approached me at a deserted gas station, hesitantly asking for help. Later she confessed she had been afraid to talk to me because she couldn't make up her mind whether I was a skinhead or a nun. I used to travel alone by train a lot, and I was usually the last person left with an empty seat beside me as the train filled up. After I was ordained I traveled alone shaven and looking even more "different" looking than before—and then I was *always* the last one left with an empty seat beside me.

I decided with some regret to stop shaving my head because people so often assumed that I had cancer or else felt shocked and alienated by my baldness, and I had no wish to promote Buddhism as weird, nor to receive sympathy under false pretenses. It has been painful all these years that my being a lesbian and sometimes my being a priest have led some people to keep away, a distancing that is completely contrary to my aim. So I have had to work at bridge-building, rooting that effort in my aim to practice wholeheartedly.

This deep intention is where we are all alike. In the Dharma it doesn't matter one whit what I call myself. What matters is that I try to live the full reality of my life with all my cells, pores, heart, and sweat, because all Dharma practice is embodied practice. Without embodying our understanding, we have merely an intellectual view. But true practice is with our bodies, not with our ideas about ourselves. Our ideas about ourselves are our impediments, including my ideas of being a particular thing called a lesbian. Or a particular thing called a priest.

At the very same time, truth has no existence apart from me just as I am. I practice embodied as me, nowhere else. Not only do all our actions take place in the body, our actions take place *as* the body. Wholehearted practice is whole-bodied practice.

In my experience of myself—inside my skin and looking out from my eyes—I'm not some thing called a lesbian or a woman or a priest. In my experience I am simply what is. My job is to go ahead as that just-what-is, attempting to love the world no matter what kind of reception I get.

Celibate

I MARRIED AT TWENTY-ONE, WAS A wife for thirty years, and someone else's partner for the next five. The assurance of partnership was built into my agreement with the world. Whatever life events occurred—moves, births, deaths, the long, unaccountable passage of time—all were included in the private, joint account of our "we-ness." What we lived through together, engendered, fought about, and endured was a protected investment in our belonging together.

When the second relationship ended, largely through my choice, I experienced surprising and overwhelming destitution. The loss of the particular man was the drain down which everything else poured.

Breath after breath. It was one of those times when death and new life are in too close an embrace to know which is which; when there is nothing to do but lie low in a patient and vulnerable condition, like a naked crustacean peering out of the deep sea foliage, waiting for the new shell.

I first dared to use the world *celibate* when I wrote to my younger sister in England, a Benedictine abbess. She has lived for more than thirty years in a contemplative, enclosed convent with the vows of poverty, chastity, and obedience. It seemed a little loose to use the word *celibate* about myself, since my condition was by circumstance not pledge, but the dictionary leaves room for ambiguity: "Celibate. An unmarried person; a person bound not to marry." "What does celibacy mean?" I asked my sister. She replied that celibacy had been the most difficult requirement for her. Over the years, as she had chastely wrestled with infatuations, she had come to understand it as "intimacy."

That was invitational. Not a diminishing loss, but an extension of possibility. I recognized the intimacy in my sister's life in the body-to-body embrace of her greeting, the hearty, red-cheeked appetite for whatever came her way, the fullness of her contact with whomever she was with, her vigorous pleasure in the weather, or the cat, or the pure line of chapel plainsong. I knew from her close example how appetite can be enjoyed as connective energy, freed from the restrictions of preference.

Months went by. The sense of depletion lifted and a new appetite stirred—a curious excitement in going places alone, a taste for the adventure of solitude. One evening, in this mood, I decided at the last moment to go to the Berkeley Symphony. I'd read a good review and the theater is a short bicycle ride from home.

Two men stand to let me pass to my seat. The first is familiar, though I can't place him. The second is a stranger. I slither by. Why is it there is some urgency, some anxiety in finding my seat? Is it the background doubt as to whether I belong? (Do I not have my ticket stub?) I used to take my place for granted. Wife, mother, social worker. Now, divorced, retired, friend to my children more than mother, what is my place?

In this case, it is on the back of my chair, F 16. The royal blue plush seat receives my body agreeably. In the zendo, when we find our seat, we bow to it and then to the room and the world at large. Now that I'm located, I feel complete, a member of the body of the evening. As I look about I feel that our orderly rows, balconies, and tiers constitute a request. We have come to sit still and devote ourselves to listening, willing to resolve our many selves into the single event. In this place there is no problem.

The familiar man greets me. "Hello, Maylie." I know him, but memory does not quite catch. We are altering in our sixties, the graying or balding heads, the deepening insistence of wrinkles, as the weight of character overrides innocence. He reminds me, "Gus Franklin." I extend my arm in front of the stranger next to me and he extends his arm across the empty seat next to him marked by a woman's coat and bag. "Hello, Gus." He is a professor, a colleague of my ex-husband's. I have encountered him intermittently for decades. He has become a kindly, sunburnt chipmunk, friendly, but not quite serious. I ponder the empty seat. I remember two attractive consorts who left him. Now, a youngish Asian woman sits in the saved seat, and I wonder if she is another. In addition to his intelligence, his range of interests, his family, and his accomplishments, there is an oblivious streak to Gus's character. He will talk forever.

I am glad to be in F 16 alone and still to have a connection at the end of the row. When I was first single, couples of any age were like magnets drawing out my sense of loss. I searched for the ingredients of their relatedness; the sexual, body connection, or lack thereof; who seeks, who avoids; levels of friction or agreement. A high level of either attraction or anger would be so captivating I would walk out of my way to follow the couple or stare rudely across a room. It was not envy, but a miserly appetite. I wanted to know the experience but not have to go through it, to grab its gist and hoard it in my own empty recesses.

Now the unruly curiosity has largely turned to relief. How pleasant to have unapologetic space; to be no longer subject to the drainage of another's continuing presence, the erosion of another's defining view.

I begin to read my program. When I put it down, the man next to me remarks on the fact that no one in the orchestra is seated. It's unusual, I agree. "Oh dear," he says, imagining a glitch. Since we now have met, we look at one another to take stock. I gaze right down to the bottom of a brown, hazel-flecked eye, and catch a genuinely nice person recognizing me. Contact. Fear. O.K. Leave it at that. There is no need for a star to tumble from its constellation and streak across the sky.

But streak it does, and my susceptible being follows. I am snared, landed on his ground. As his tenant, how shall I be? What do I say? The displacement, while quick, is so familiar, I can pretend nothing has happened. I can make small talk about the program as if innocent of motive. The conductor comes out to explain that the composer of the first piece will open with a brief additional composition on the piano.

The piano strings have been muted, accentuating their percussive quality. The plucked-up notes spill out into little heaps, tumble about into corners, spread flat, heap up again in piles that share the family shape of the whole piece. There is humor and color and structure enough to keep my interest. But the listening is already slightly distracted, tinted with the question of how I might account for it to my neighbor.

Who is the Harris-tweeded vandal whose eye provokes such trouble? Why do I need to be so ready to be courted?

The pianist/composer is a twenty-four-year-old Englishman, already with a credible list of accomplishments. He bows to our applause and then speaks briefly about his works. He hunches around the microphone like an exuberant young bear, delighted with flowers offered, elaborately kissing the bearer of them, innocent, infectiously pleasing. In his young maleness, he is outrageously whole, while I am punctured, my composure hissing out the hapless pinholes.

My neighbor asks me what I think of the music.

Think? Do I really *have* to think before I'm ready? I have tried so much in my life to think quickly, smartly, with no respect for the background confusion. Now because of a curious, friendly look in a hazel eye, I am doing it again.

"I liked it. There was color and just enough of a trace of structure." My voice carries on, disembodied, young, anxious to please.

When I ask him what he thinks, he says, "It didn't move me."

How is it that men take their place so naturally at the center of the world? That I expect them to be there? I do not want to speak any more. Let me be settled as a rock. I do not want ever again to engage in the exhausting labor of forging a relationship. The listenings, the presentations, efforts to match, sly exaggerations and omissions, worries and expectations, false and true rewards, and, finally, like an elephant's footprint over the whole business, the fatal stamp of mating.

What makes a woman? My long-married friend Dorothy says it would be "embarrassing" not to have sex. There is basic status in a sexual relationship with a man. I recall my mother's implicit edge over maiden aunts; they lived on the fringes, diminished by chastity. My friend Eleanor, a professor, tells me that since her divorce, she has been dropped from the "couples" parties.

What makes a woman? My chest is tightening with the panicky grief I thought I'd left behind. The man at my side leafs through his program, while I am at the sheer edge of loss. No living with a man or without a man. To retreat is death by restraint. To move toward is death by surrender. I want to find something stunning to say to him, a way to snatch his attention as he has snatched mine. But I can wait. There is time here to haul in the mind, bind it down. The impossible will pass as it has before.

I read my program as he does, while the orchestra tunes up; cacophony of singular voices—strings, winds, percussion—listening to themselves, practicing their entry—while we, the audience, settle into quietness. Lights dim. The delicate Asian conductor bows, long hair falling over his face, and turns. One lift of his baton awakens the grand, assertive opening chords of the Brahms first piano concerto. Nothing left out. Fearless assumption, by an authority that embraces even as it moves us.

The piano enters, with the impeccable confidence of a single, perfectly pitched voice. The orchestra responds and the unlimited partnership—piano-orchestra—begins, pronouncing, receiving, elaborating, giving way. This is what I have come for. Gratitude rises in my chest and throat.

And yet, as I get used to it, there is a slightly muted quality to the sound, as if a scrim is dropped between the players and my ear. I wonder if I am imagining it, or are our seats poor?

In front of me, a young woman shifts in her seat, crosses calf over knee, leans against the shoulder of her escort. He glances at her, irritated, and leans away. She straightens herself, and, reaching her arm behind her head, separates a strand of strawberry-blond hair. With a practiced twist of two fingers and thumb, she makes a slip knot that is pulled out gently, slowly from her scalp. The skin on the underside of her forearm is white and firm, resilient as a child's. Her quarter profile suggests she is a beauty—well-shaped high cheekbone, gently aquiline nose—but for the bulge of teeth under the upper lip. Something about this protrusion accentuates her boredom. Aware of my own propensity to lose my ground to another, I admire such containment. I imagine her to be an expert in boredom; able to fall into her own pool, sullen, complete, slipping like a lovely stone to her autonomous bottom.

The music receives me, partially or completely as my attention allows. In the flow of notes, I can almost believe in the wholeness of the present, in the condition of being nowhere else. Such generous possibility makes my heart warm. Body itself has opened, listening through its own sensations, as the porcelain-skinned woman in front of me knots and releases her hair and the man in the next seat leans toward me so that our sleeves touch.

We clap hard. Some people stand. I would stand if I were alone, but I don't feel alone. I don't know what he would think. There is a lot of bowing, leaving me time to wonder about intermission. Will we speak or not? Has something happened between us? When the applause stops we do speak, agreeing the music was stunning, and he reflects that the seats are not good. There is a slight blunting of sound. I am glad to have my impression confirmed; we now have a simple, vital bit of companionship.

I walk out in front of him, slowly, through the crowd, keeping my back straight, body supple for him to notice, half hoping he will follow—"Would you like a coffee . . ."—half hoping he won't. I glance back and see him engaged with a couple of his friends. At a distance, he is younger than I had supposed; he's caught up in the point he is making, gesturing with his hands, boyishly excited.

Outside, in the cool night, the air is heavy with cigarette smoke. Not so long ago, people smoked in this lobby. Very long ago, I smoked in lobbies and wore high heels, and could turn a man's head.

There are so many turns in a sixty-year-old life.

The air is chilly with incipient off shore fog. I regret having left my jacket at my seat. I am facing a coffee shop in the basement of the Student Union. Young people are studying at the tables, separately and in groups, talking, fiddling, engrossed. The tangled excitements of mind and body. At Harvard in the early 1950s, all but one of my teachers were men. An instructor asked me to read a paper I'd written on Saint Augustine to the class. I had a crush on him. On my way to the class, I rubbed snow on my cheeks to make them red. Later he became my boyfriend. The next year I met my husband-to-be and the year after took marriage vows.

Over the Student Union roof, the new moon hangs above the horizon; a silver thumbnail in the dark purple sky. She is beginning again. I've always watched the moon, finding refuge in her constancy even as she changes.

I am chilly and turn to walk back in. Gus is coming toward me. My first impulse is to flee, but there is no getting away.

"Maylie. So nice to see you. You look great. What are you up to?" He is a little stout, the belly is new. The positive energy is genuine.

"Well—a lot of things. I retired from County Mental Health ten years ago. I'm a priest at the Berkeley Zen Center. Peter and I split up a few years ago." Where should I start? It used to be easy to explain what I did; now it's harder.

"Oh yes. Betty and I split up, too. I'm with someone else now—you saw her. . . ."

We speak for a while about people we know and used to know, who is retired and who has died. I hear the end-of-intermission buzzer sound from the lobby and motion to Gus. He continues to talk as we head back, placing his hand lightly under my elbow. We have known one another slightly for thirty years and that is something.

"Are you with someone?" he asks.

"No. I'm alone. I'm celibate," I say, although I had not planned it. "It's good for me. Easier to be a priest that way. A different kind of appetite."

Gus blinks. "Yes," he says, "I suppose so. Do priests have to be celibate?"

"Oh no. Some are married and have children. It's just that it's better for me to do one thing at a time."

There's a brief silence—an impasse.

"Oh look," he says, "there's Emma. Let me introduce you."

"Thanks. I need to duck into the ladies' room." It's a lie. I don't want to be drawn again to the academic, Berkeley hills life I left a decade ago. I don't want to try to explain what I can't explain. I want to take one more look at the moon.

I walk in the direction of the ladies' room through the close flow of incoming bodies, feeling their heat, their slight odors, to the far end of the lobby and slip out the door. Venus has risen below the moon, white and shimmering in contrast to the moon's pale yellower evenness. It is steadying to know their partnership will be there, crossing the sky, as I return to the concert, bicycle home, and sleep in my bed.

I am grateful to be a priest, even if I can never explain it well. "A combination of aspiration and commitment," my teacher, Mel Weitsman, says. A place to return to that accepts what is gone.

I will bicycle home to the house I have lived in for more than thirty years. Husband and children replaced by housemates and my ninety-three-year-old-mother. I will sleep across from my altar, in my single bed on the sunporch at the back of the house. The sliding windows look down over the garden and the pink climbing roses that cascade over the roof of the old garage. It is the first time I have had my own room since I was a child.

The lights flicker and I hurry to catch up with the last people going up the stairs to the balcony. The man in the next seat is taking the stairs two at a time just ahead. I keep up, just behind. Glancing back, he notices me.

"Think we'll make it?" he asks, grinning.

"Yes," I say, panting, "we'll be exactly on time."

PART FOUR

∾

Body as Vehicle

Bowing to the Great Mirror

BOBBY RHODES

ONE OF THE UNIQUE ASPECTS OF the Kwan Um School of Zen is our practice of performing 108 prostrations daily. Each prostration begins from a standing position with palms together, moving to a kneeling position, lowering the forehead to the mat with palms upward and returning to a standing position. This "bowing practice," as we call it, was given to us by our teacher, Zen Master Seung Sahn, and is taken from the Chogye School of Zen Buddhism in Korea.

The first time I saw Zen Master Seung Sahn do 108 bows, over twenty-three years ago, my reaction was "he doesn't expect *me* to do this, does he?" Through the years I learned that his expecting me to do daily bows was only the tip of the iceberg. I also learned not to ask what my teacher expects of me, but what I expect of myself.

Some of my students ask me why they should do prostrations. Many people think of Zen practice as being only sitting meditation. In our tradition, we combine bowing, sitting, walking, and chanting as a way of seeking balance. Performing prostrations is a physical manifestation of our Buddhist practice, a symbol of putting our *whole* body into it. Performing 108 prostrations strengthens our muscles and has a wonderful limbering effect on the spine. Keeping the body strong and limber helps keep the consciousness strong and limber. With this practice we gain strength for both body and mind—and we see, perhaps, that body and mind are not different.

Here is a Zen story: One day the teacher asked a student, "Do you see that pile of rocks over there?" "Yes, I do," replied the student. "Are those rocks inside or outside of your mind?" "Why, teacher, they are inside of my mind." "Oh," moaned the teacher, "how are you ever going to be able to raise your head?" Where was the student's mistake? She created inside and outside. We create separations and distinctions between mind and body. Zen has the danger of becoming too cerebral. Bowing helps to remedy this.

In our tradition it is said that there are 108 names for the buddhas and bodhisattvas. Another explanation says that human beings have 108 delusions. We bow to let go of these delusions. In Korea, another name for this practice is 108 repentance bows. By repentance, we mean that we are sorry for our arrogance. Our "I" has gotten in the way and caused suffering. Sometimes the suffering we cause is very subtle, sometimes it is enormous. This doesn't mean we are bowing out of guilt. We bow to open to our wisdom. As I bow I find it helpful to ask, "To what or to whom am I bowing? To what or to whom do I repent?"

When performing prostrations, we place ourselves in a position of humility, a position of receiving. Forehead to the ground, with palms uplifted, the body is saying, "Please teach me." Bowing daily we over-come our arrogance and learn to let it go. In the repentance ritual that accompanies our precepts ceremony we acknowledge our transgres-sions "committed since beginningless time, through our greed, anger, and ignorance. . . ." At the same time we recognize that "our offenses have no self-nature, but arise only from our minds" and ask that these offenses "accumulated during hundreds of kalpas (may) now be totally consumed in an instant, as fire burns dry grass, extinguishing all things until nothing remains."

In the Kwan Um School of Zen, teachers will sometimes prescribe "extra bows" to help a student deal with a difficult situation. Zen Mas-ter Seung Sahn is a strong believer in the benefit of bowing practice, and until very recently he routinely performed 540 bows a day. He often jokes that a human birth can be very difficult, so extra bows are always in order.

Prostrations are extremely engaging, so it becomes possible to only bow and drop ideas about who you are. Just letting go and curling to the floor over and over again. Standing up straight, palms together at the heart over and over again. A balanced movement of surrender and lifting to full height and stance. As a hospice nurse, I am with many people as they approach their death. Sometimes the letting go seems graceful with strong lessons learned until the final breath. Sometimes the process is awkward with fear, doubt, and resentment blocking clarity and peace. I believe that bowing practice strengthens our trust in the process of letting go, knowing that there is a cycle of birth and death—bowing down and standing up. Eventually the dichotomy disappears and there is no gain or loss—being up or being down.

The fully enlightened mind is the mind that has come to completely believe in itself. It no longer separates self and other. It is the great round mirror, the sphere—able to see in all directions at once. This is the state of total grace and compassion that we call our "true self." When we bow, *this* is what we bow to. Ultimately we realize our whole, complete self. With each prostration we fold into this self—this ancient fetal position—just as the caterpillar folds into the cocoon. The fruits of this practice we then dedicate to saving all beings from suffering.

◉

Dance
A Body with a Mind of Its Own

RUTH ZAPORAH

I AM A PHYSICAL PERFORMER OF improvisation theater. As both actor and dancer I weave images through movement, language, and vocalization. I enter the performing arena with no prearranged concepts. I begin with a spontaneous action and then, step by step, build a scenario until the content is realized and the piece feels complete. Within it, I introduce characters, events, and situations that reflect the mingling of imagination, memories, and sensory input. The pieces are often dreamlike landscapes, grounded in humor and pathos. I am endlessly surprised by what happens.

◉ The year was 1976. I was performing in Ann Arbor. I had asked the presenters to create a set within which I would improvise. That evening, the set included a Raggedy-Ann-like doll, which was lying on the floor downstage center. Early on the doll drew my attention. I named her Alice. Within the first fifteen minutes of the improvisation, Alice died. The remainder of the show focused on how others in her life responded to her death.

As I was bowing at the end of the show I noticed three women sitting on the floor near where Alice had been lying. While everyone else clapped, they were completely still. Later, they came to see me backstage. Through their crying, they told me that a year ago, that very night, their mutual and dear friend, Alice, had died. Before my performance, they had gone out to dinner together to honor her passing. A shock went through my body and left me trembling. The territory of embodied improvisation that I had just visited had implications beyond my comprehension. If I were to continue, for my own safety, I would have to observe very closely.

When I refer to the body, I am also referring to the mind, for the two are known through one another and are inseparable. The body knows itself through the mind as the mind knows itself through the body. Sometimes it is convenient to talk about the body and the mind as separate entities. We can talk about taming or disciplining the body, quieting the mind, relaxing the body, focusing attention. But can you imagine doing any of these without both body and mind?

I have been practicing physical improvisation for thirty years. My mind and body, their oneness, is the instrument of my art. Sometimes my body seems to have a mind of its own. It fidgets, slumps, and jerks while my mental attention is elsewhere. And conversely, my mind (as we all experience in meditation practice) fidgets, slumps, and jerks while my body appears to be calm and still. We talk about the mind and body as if they were separate but, in fact, it's our attention that's split. Through improvisational practice, awareness expands to hold the entire self.

෧෧ "Ruthy, dance for us." I'm four years old. At every family event, this invitation is spoken by someone. I never decline. I am shy, but when I dance I have a voice, I am seen. In the family, I am a Dancer.

Simultaneously, another and quite different realization was brewing. At age six in 1942, I began formal dance studies. Three afternoons and Saturday morning of each and every week, I attended ballet class. This regimen continued through high school. Ballet classes in those days were exceedingly impersonal. The student was seen only as a body. A student arrived, silently changed clothes in a gray and metal locker room, careful not to let her gaze turn toward another naked body, entered the glistening white and mirrored ballet room, and, within the vacuum of her isolation, inched along toward mastery. At the end of the session, students clapped their hands, left the room as silently as they had entered, and stuffed their stimulated young bodies into plaid skirts and penny loafers.

As I write this, it's clear that those hours in ballet class were often a place of pure bodily experience. Yes, there were times charged with judgment, moments filled with confusion, self-hatred, or pride. But there were also stretches of nonthought that drew me back and back again. That state of nonthought was restful and calm. I relaxed into the action itself, losing all sense of self, of Ruth, of me.

Dance is silent. The lips are shut tight. The motion can be either serene or violent. Either way, there's no guarantee that because the body is filling every moment with action, the mind can't also be filling every equivalent moment with disembodied thought. For me, the thoughts were often about the action: judging, evaluating, or directing.

Can we stop thoughts so that our body and mind are aligned into a singular happening? I'm not sure we have to stop anything. What I remember is that I came upon a secret place of silence and I was repeatedly drawn to it. Neither my family, friends, nor teachers guided me or prepared me. At the time, I couldn't have talked about it either. It just seemed right. I was continually drawn to this place, more like space, and that space became home.

Dance itself is thoughtless. It is its own event. It doesn't follow anything and it doesn't lead anywhere. It is not about gain or absolution. Dance dances itself and is not at all tied to the conceptual world or even the concept of dance.

Until my thirties, I danced, danced, and danced. I took classes, created dances, and taught both technique and improvisation. Only when dancing did I feel truly peaceful. I knew my body and its capabilities and danced within my limitations. I remained focused on the actions themselves, and they always offered cues for further explorations. I remained relaxed and imagination thrived. I knew that if I was fascinated, so too would be the audience. All of this knowledge integrated into my awareness. Awareness danced.

Then, in the early 1970s, I became restless within the confinement of silence. I felt handicapped. I wanted to talk, to be heard, to explore "real" life, grapple with its issues. I began to experiment with speech, character, and vocalization of feeling. Wrestling with these forms for a very long time, I tripped over myself continually, forcing, analyzing, and constructing. I was determined to create meaningful content. All this led to more separation, myself from myself. Eventually, however, I got a clue. I felt my mouth moving. My mind had relaxed its hold on content. I experienced speech and feeling as their own dance— movements arising and falling away, mouth moving, mind moving, thoughts, feelings, all moving.

I sense the body as no different from the space it is moving in and the sound it is moving to. If I'm improvising with a partner, each of our bodies becomes an extension of the other. I perceive her body as no other than my own; her voice, my voice; her story, mine. If I'm dancing in a public dance hall or a private party, I merge into the larger body of sounds, colors, heat, sweat, motion. I'm not alone in this. Dance has served through time and cultures as a collecting force, a softening of the hard edges that separate one person from another, an activity of communion.

၆၈ Bob and I are improvising together on stage. The performance begins with both of us standing, playing conga drums. We chant. My voice is inside of him and his is inside of mine. We wail. I begin a narrative on top of the clamorous beat. My voice and the sound of the drum rise, swell, and recede together. I tell of a woman sitting before the fire in her living room. She feels the familiar cold wind slipping in under her front door. She's tried to seal the space under the door many times, to no avail. The wind continues to torment her as it slams against her fragile body.

As these words escape from my lips, I sense that I'm following a script that is writing itself. Each word comes on its own. I discover it as I hear and feel it forming itself. The beats of Bob's drum and the timing of my words are riding on the same energy. Even though we're not doing the same thing, our bodies have merged.

Abruptly, as if we were being directed, we stop. Bob crosses the floor. He sees a river between us and is intent on crossing its hazardous waters. I, too, see the river and share his distress. I reach out to him and throw him a line of a song which he repeats. I sing, he sings, again and again, until we are both on the same side of the river.

In the altered state and extraordinary space of performance, Bob is me and I am him. No boundaries exist between us. His river is *the* river, real and tangible; his distress, mine; his safety, also mine.

For many years, I struggled with the awkward moments that follow a performance. Audience members would come backstage to offer their appreciation, to tell me how much they loved the piece or me. If the performance had been a struggle for me, if I had been plagued by judgments, I felt ashamed, as if I'd put one over on them. Or I sometimes felt overly exposed, the soft belly of my psyche hung out on the line of spectacle. Even if I had sailed through the show without a disembodied thought, I was still unable to receive their praise. Here they were talking to Ruth, and yet, ever so vaguely, I suspected that it wasn't Ruth they had witnessed. Ruth wasn't there. Instead the dance had danced itself.

After years of practice in performance, I have learned to no longer identify with content as it arises. I don't know where it comes from, certainly not always from my personal experience. The episode of the Raggedy-Ann doll, Alice, begins to make sense. If the performer is truly riding the energy of the moment, without any ego interference, the audience recognizes this dynamic and relaxes into it. The performance becomes a collective experience, the audience and the performer meeting in a clear space.

> ◐◑ I am leading a training in Freiburg, Germany, July 1995. It is the fourth of what is to be ten days of work. The students are grappling with an improvisation score that focuses on relationship. Whether their partners project an image through movement, vocalization, or speech, they are to respond with a contrasting form. For example, if one speaks, the other must move or make sounds. After several rounds of sluggish practice, I suggest that the students shift their perception and accept their partner's action as their own—to view their partner's body and all its actions as extensions of their own body, with no sense of separation. They are to consider that one body, not two, is expressing itself. They are to experience the improvisation as an ongoing stream of action.
>
> I feel the room lighten and the energy become fluid. Students relax. They are quicker to respond.
>
> Afterward, they say this idea of no ownership has helped them to view all action as having equal value.

"Ruthy, dance for us." The dancing that began with a child's need to be seen became, over the years, a release from the separate self.

Movement, speech, action. It's all dance emanating from the inside out, one moment nourishing the next, uncoiling itself.

꩜

Meeting Vajrayogini

PHYLLIS PAY

I MEDITATE UPON THE FEMALE Tibetan deity Vajrayogini and can feel body as no body. The familiar patterns of my mental identity become fluid and liquid as known structures dissolve into energy. Forms as basic as bones, muscles, and organs transform momentarily into the light essence of red. The female body I have struggled with for what has been my life—more than fifty years in earth time—becomes something formless and nameless as I finally experience scattered moments of peacefulness. I have questioned this existence for so long. The existential questioning itself has led me on my path.

I was born female but never felt that the programming of my Asian lineage with its expectation of the feminine role expressed the fire, the force, the passion, or the aggressiveness that I felt inside of myself. My will felt powerful and strong, although I was trained into passivity. My will was not just the survival will of the body; it was a force inside of me that wanted expression. This force felt knotted, twisted, and locked deep inside of my belly, hidden as a survival mechanism, while consciously my mind created confusion as a diversion from it.

I was confused. I was born into a Chinese body, but not in China; into a female body, but not docile as I was cued to behave. I was born in America, in the heart of a black ghetto, and when I looked around me, I didn't see many Chinese bodies. My first confusion was that if I were embodied at all, I wanted to be black. At least in a black body I could feel as if I belonged there in that neighborhood. In general, I wanted to feel a part of this planet on which my repeated embodied experience had been one of alienation and isolation. This dilemma of race, which still plagues me, was only one sign of the discomfort I felt in body. Ultimately, mine was not a specific problem of race, but only one sign of my general resistance to showing up again here in this physical realm of existence. A part of me, even in my earliest memory, dreamt of other realities. However, here I was, seemingly against my will, immersed again in the wheel of karma.

To understand my existence in this life, I have had to transcend the more obvious levels of identity. The sense that I carried of being on the outside—outside of even a subculture that is the victimized and oppressed shadow of the society into which I was born—forced me to search for a ground that transcended my physical characteristics. As a child, the feeling created by this dilemma was one of simply not wanting to be here. As an adult this feeling often emerges as a form of despair that at times dominates my emotional life and distracts me from the moment. As a result I choose to be stranded between two worlds. In my career as an intuitive counselor, I have developed a perception that moves my awareness beyond the physical plane, believing that what exists physically is only the entry point to multiple levels of energetic reality. I have had to view myself multidimensionally because one identity would not fit. To identify only with the physical characteristics of my body felt limited. Early on, my imagination served as a survival tool and carried me beyond physical realities and identities; it served to buffer both my emotional pain and my isolation.

Yet in the midst of this isolation I would often feel gratitude. I sensed that something much larger than myself was operating in the universe. In some vague space inside of myself, I was nourished by the feeling that even in this experience of pain, there was a form of grace. This faith was an essential part of my being. I had no understanding of faith from a religious point of view, as neither of my parents followed a religion. The only remnant of any religious inclination existed in the home of my grandparents in their ancestral altar, of which I had no understanding. Aside from this small clue, nothing in my environment indicated that there was anything that existed beyond what we physically and visibly agreed upon as reality. Yet there always seemed to be spirits. The spirits were not spoken of, but the superstitions of my Chinese ancestry, referred to obliquely in conversations, confirmed their presence. I knew that I was not to offend some ever-present force more powerful than myself. I felt this most strongly during the lunar new year when my behavior was scrutinized by relatives taking stock of omens that foretold the fortunes or disasters for the year to come. I felt both the isolation of my separateness and the sense that something else was always present. This was not a contradiction. I felt that there was something larger than myself to connect with and to bring into myself, something that I could merge with that was missing from my body. My sense of my own body continued to be painful.

I could not find ground within the identity of my physical body. I could not assume that the external realities that defined other people would satisfy some interior emptiness that plagued me. I longed to have my material surroundings represent my inner experience. It was enigmatic to me that other people seemed to be born into a racial and social class that represented them, and that they could live that reality without questioning it. I didn't have that kind of ground and I couldn't take my existence for granted. At times now, when my heart is able to listen to my soul, I understand myself in deeper ways. I was not able to accept a more superficial identity in this lifetime. As a result of this dilemma my internalized reality became stronger.

I drift back to my Vajrayogini practice. As I recite the refuge prayer in my mind, I feel an expansion of energy at the crown of my head. The mantra begins rotating in my heart center. My body begins dissolving into light. I am no longer aware of the limitations of my present physical identity. I am aware of the skull-cup in my left hand as I visualize myself as Vajrayogini, and I feel the heat and redness of the blood flowing through my mouth into my body. The flow of this energy allows me to be aware of all the spaces inside of my body in which I deny to myself my own warmth, my power, and my passion. My fear of being alive emerges as I feel my pain mingling with my sadness. I remember that Vajrayogini holds the curved knife in her right hand. I know that I must use this to cut through the illusion of fear. I know intellectually that the fear is a product of my ego. It allows me to believe that I have something to lose. I will lose whatever false identity I've created for myself, even the identity of having no identity. When I realize how strongly I am attached even to the idea of no identity, I understand how complex my illusions are.

I feel the potential for beingness, but I am trapped in my own web. I feel the way my body has held resentment, how I have reinforced my own powerlessness. I am a woman of my lineage. I identify with the tears, the sorrows, the pain of my own submission and the submission of elders; the pain of the wars and the lost children. I hold these memories in the cells of my body. I feel the attachment. I am a part of this lineage of women and feel responsible for preserving the memory in my body. This is my only sense of belonging. How can I release these memories without losing the last remnants of my identity? I feel that I must hold this web of suffering until our silence is broken. It is the debt to my lineage. Can I free myself from this web? Even as I contemplate the curved blade of Vajrayogini, I want the comfort of my history and of my illusions. I want what is familiar even if it is painful. I feel the control as a twisted web within my solar plexus, the seat of my ego-self and of past identities. I dread the emptiness that would create the internal space for new stories to flow through me in the purity of my own voice.

As the mantra continues to spin in my heart, I realize that in this fear of release, I, in fact, betray my own heart. I deny to myself the internal space that links that presence that is larger than myself and my known ego. How much of this lineage and memory is part of my ego? How much is it a true expression of my soul? I am the history I hold in this body as woman, as Chinese woman, as Chinese American woman, as mother, as psychic, as victim, and I am also more than this. Vajrayogini dances in the sky. I am earth-bound in the various identities that fill my emptiness and define my existence. I am here to speak. My ego believes in this purpose. It justifies my existence and allows me to occupy space, although deep inside I continue to deny my own sense of value. How can I hold the memory of my earth-bound self and live the wisdom that Vajrayogini represents? Can the histories and memories be transformed into wisdom?

The possibility of this transformation begins to send cleansing waves through my body. I realize that the lineage identity and my history as woman does hold wisdom, but that I have been stuck in the thickness of its pain. Is the pain simply attachment, or is it my real experience? My ego does not want me to forget pain, even if it is past.

If I forget, it can happen again—whatever caused the pain in the first place can be repeated. I must hold this pain to defend against future pain. I feel the tautness and the stubbornness of this belief in my body. In these spaces of holding, there is no movement of energy, there is no wisdom, there is no presence of Vajrayogini's essence.

As I write this I am aware of a physical pain in my right shoulder joint that I have been struggling with now for many months. It extends down through my right arm, often lodging in the elbow joint and causing immobilization. It is perhaps part of the aging process, and at the same time this pain expresses unresolved issues in my sense of self. When I feel this dense holding of tension in my right arm and shoulder, I am moved toward a variety of reactions. The first is fear. It is not simply a fear of pain, but a fear of immobility, a fear that I will not be able to function, that I will not have control, that I will not be able to continue defining myself through my action. When the pain eases in meditation, I visualize this right arm as energy holding the curved blade and realize that I must use this tool to cut through my fear. But I am immobilized. The energy in my arm is frozen. I want to hold on to the past, to identities that have felt safe to me. This fear is a specific sensation in my belly, near the diaphragm, and it causes me to contract my breath. I have to remember to breathe. When I breathe, a wave of grief moves through my consciousness. I feel the sadness of my own denial; how long it has been that I have buried my essence behind a victim identity in order not to be threatening or even noticed. I have allowed myself to defer even when I felt forceful inside. My immobilized arm and the pain remind me of my sacrifices. My position in the world is still dangerous and I must retreat. I am aware of how I have carried others on my shoulders in order to hide my real self. Will I use Vajrayogini's blade to cut through the veils that protect me from contact with my power?

The pain forces me to make an internal decision. I must move toward my own release. I have a moment of anger as red energy flushes through my body. It wants to push out anything that I hold as limitation. I feel a cleansing as this wave moves through me, but I also know that the battle is not over, that the fear will wake me again in the middle of the night, reminding me of past terrors and sending my mind once again into confusion.

I am this female body. I am the lineage and history that has stored itself as fear in my body. I am also energy, passion, will, and strength, beyond which is emptiness. I am in awe of the opportunity I have in this body in this lifetime. When I am centered, focused, and still, I feel myself as an energetic flow beyond roles and preconceptions, beyond my daily drama, confusion, and contradictions. I am able to dance centered in this fluidity, moving graciously through this life, accepting my pain, my sorrows, and my joy as the opportunities that lead me deeper into my knowledge of self.

Vajrayogini is the wisdom *dakini*. She dances through the sky. Her right foot stands on the chest of red Kalinga symbolizing the conquering of attachment, and her left foot stands on the head of black Bhairava representing the conquering of anger. Visualizing myself as Vajrayogini, I become emptiness. My pain becomes wisdom. My personal history and family lineage as woman transforms from fear into knowledge and truth. As I sit in my center, feeling myself as this flow of liquid energy, gratitude arises from the core of my being that I am here, blessed with my body, filled with the history and the experience that will become part of my wisdom self.

Grounding and Opening

Anne C. Klein

Buddhism, like life, teaches
that the things we take for granted are actually changeable and more
significant than we think. Likewise, our sense of how we inhabit our
bodies, something so unremarked upon that it is utterly taken for
granted, is actually an important factor in how we live our lives and,
therefore, how we relate to Buddhist practice. In general, we relate to
our bodies in ways that are largely determined by a variety of historical
and cultural circumstances. More specifically, whenever nature is no
longer viewed as sacred and alive, as in the modern West and the industrialized East, boundaries between our bodies and the external world
seem to harden. This hardening has many causes, and just as many
consequences.

Over the last several centuries in Europe and North America our
relationship to the larger physical environment has changed a great
deal, and this has affected our style of embodiment. In many respects
we have become smaller. Our connection with nature has been so cur-
tailed that, instead of inhabiting an entire landscape and allowing it to
carry some of our feelings—as was the case, for example, in medieval
times and during the Romantic period[1]—all these feelings as well as
our sense of the self that holds them are felt to be contained simply
within the narrow parameters of our own physical form. This makes it

more difficult than before to connect with anything outside of these narrow boundaries—with the external world, with other people—and even with our own minds and bodies. As a result, we are deeply at risk for becoming personally isolated in ways unthinkable among the traditional cultures that produced the texts and rituals many Western Buddhists now seek to practice.

To feel we are located in and even confined to our bodies, yet at the same time alienated from them, is ingrained in modern identity and the individualism that is part and parcel of it. In the pre-Romantic period, medieval descriptions of the humor theory of disease, as well as popular beliefs in magic and in unseen beings that affect or even enter one's own body, suggested a more open boundary between the psychic and the physical, between self and world. Romantic poets saw their own image reflected in the skies and seas. Such porous boundaries characterized every culture to which Buddhism spread, until the twentieth century, when these traditions came west.

To consider our relationship with our bodies is also to investigate how we imagine the boundaries of our own actions, intentions, and physical impact. These boundaries fix our position in physical and mental space. Modern culture does not encourage us to notice how we organize the spaces of body, mind, emotions, and social distance. At the same time, our half-conscious arrangements of these categories color all of our experience, including the ways that we appropriate Buddhist meditation. For example, if at some level I understand my agency as a person to be located in my head, my meditation may affect me differently, on a physiological or energetic level, than if I understand my agency to be located at my heart. The cultivation of compassion, which both metaphorically and energetically is related to the heart, may be quite a different process in the two different cases. I am interested in how traditional forms of practice do and do not match with contemporary women's and men's sense of embodiment, and how we can bring this sensibility into play with our practice.

Modern, urban people often live with a subliminal sense of being caught inside their own silhouettes—that is, of inhabiting a body that is cut off from nature and independent from other human beings. At the same time, modern life presents us with so much information, so many choices, and urges us to attend closely to the multiple feelings associated with these, that we are dealt a great deal to hold in the very small space that is our body. As a result, it is easy to feel overwhelmed, congested by the unwieldy possibilities of our own lives. Indeed, many people practice meditation partly to gain relief from a sense of being overwhelmed by noise, responsibility, agendas, choices—in short, the burdens of individualism that require us to hold a great deal in an increasingly limited personal space. This sense of congestion needs to be addressed if we are to have any hope of creating a practice relevant to our situation, and of easing the sense of congestion, often experienced in physical or energetic terms, associated with our culturally derived sense of boundedness. From this vantage point, much of Buddhist practice can be understood as a way of consciously seeking a more spacious way of experiencing our embodiment.

Moreover, through trial and error I have discovered that the practices I am familiar with, especially those from the Tibetan traditions, work much better if I consciously counter the modern, culturally normative sense of a strictly contained body, mind, and self. Tibetan religious practices were typically enacted, after all, in a radiant open landscape, in vast spaces dominated by bright air over turquoise rivers, with iridescent cobalt skies spanning the distance between darkly colorful rocks or snow peaks. Such grand expanses were vibrant not only with light, but with life as well. To the traditional Tibetan imagination, there is no such thing as dead space. There are no empty forests either. Everywhere there are beings, visible and invisible. Even in solitary pilgrimage across frozen and immobile vastnesses, one is never truly alone, nor, meditating in a cave high above the nearest village, is one confined to just a small space. Even inside caves or darkened temples one's body resonates with the pulsating images of the dynamic arena one has traversed before entering. The imagination becomes steeped in a sense of space it cannot lose, and that space is always alive.

Most of us in the West (and increasingly in modernized Asia as well) live in a personal space much smaller than that of traditional Buddhist practitioners, and far more cluttered. No traditional culture offers its inhabitants the messy assortment of choices, information, or multicultural styles that people in contemporary postindustrial societies are faced with today. This is clear even in a small matter like clothing. A traditional Tibetan woman might have silk *chuba*s and cotton ones, but she does not have shorts for tennis, slacks for shopping, short skirts for work, long ones for formal wear, not to mention heels, flats, and hiking, running, and snorkeling footwear. And these choices are nothing compared with the options regarding lifestyle, careers, places to live, when or whether to have children, and so forth. The proliferation of possibilities and the information that allows us to choose among them, as well as the kinds of education, worries, conversations, and consultations that accompany such choosing, mean that we must contain exponentially greater amounts of data in a far smaller, more enclosed sense of physical space than either earlier generations in the West or in traditional Buddhist cultures. No wonder we often feel swamped, exasperated that things are "too much."[2]

Moreover, we tend to feel ourselves divided into the very different spaces of mind and body. Thus, not only do we now understand mind—as medieval persons did not—to be located entirely within the body, we also feel that mind is in some fundamental way alien to the body and even in conflict with it. In addition, especially since the advent of cinema and television, the mind itself becomes imagined as a kind of small viewer separated from the large screen of the world by our bounded bodies.

This sense of a mind that is localized and limited further contributes to the notion that mind and body form a relatively closed system (breathing, eating, and elimination notwithstanding). These three perceptions are deeply interrelated: A (1) small mind inhabits a (2) closed body to which (3) this inchoate amalgamation of mind and body is only loosely tethered. Such perceptions make it difficult to take real energetic possession of our own bodies.

To inhabit our body fully, and to feel connected through it to the earthy body beneath us is to be physically grounded, able to inhabit our bodies as the mooring and support for all our activities. In this way, we move beyond the sense that we are a small, closed system, not anchored in anything other than ourselves. Such physical grounding facilitates emotional grounding—the strength to hold ground and fill space; in other words, to be present with all our being. With such presence we move past the sense that mind and body function independently of each other. Freed from this bifurcation we can begin to experience the body as the actual locus of enlightenment.

Equally important, such grounding means accepting our body, not trying to escape it. If this sounds sensible, why is it so difficult? For women, certainly there is the difficulty of constant cultural cues that discourage us from accepting our bodies as they are. We are encouraged to care what our bodies look like to others, but not to notice how we occupy and experience them ourselves. We even learn to view our bodies from a distance, adopting a male gaze as we consider our physical imperfections, as if watching ourselves on television (again, the metaphor of mind as disembodied "viewer"). Beyond this, women who have suffered either physical or mental abuse often dissociate physically or emotionally, or even leave the body, especially during meditation. Grounding practices such as physical movement, breathing down to the center of the earth, or rhythmic chanting can help one learn to be in the body and to enjoy the simple experience of being physically present to oneself, others, and the physical elements. Let us consider the difference this makes in specific types of meditation.

In cultivating mindfulness one typically trains attention on an object such as the breath, an imagined image of the Buddha, or an external object that one gazes at with the physical eyes. To the extent that the attentive mind itself is experienced as a small internal gazer, we may have the sensation that we are trying to steady a tiny beam of light that behaves like the jittery hand-held laser pointer sometimes used by lecturers. Such an instrument of attention is volatile and weak; the least movement pulls it from its object, deflecting it from its purpose.

Meditation texts teach us to beware of "distraction" and to bring the mind again and again back to its object. But I want to note that distraction cannot be fully understood if we consider it only a function of mental meandering. It is virtually impossible to accomplish the goals of mindfulness without being well anchored in the body. Similarly, if the laser light, rather than being held by a moving hand, is anchored to a table, it can send a steady beam. For stillness of mind, stillness of body is crucial. Most meditative traditions tell us this, but we are not culturally primed to grasp very well what they are saying.

The focusing of mindfulness is not simply a matter of divesting ourselves of distraction; we must be solidly grounded physically if our mind is to become unwavering. And we cannot gain sufficient groundedness by anchoring in our small physique alone; we must connect through our bodies to a greater source of stability. Observe, if you have the chance, how traditional Native Americans walk on the earth. Caucasian city dwellers walk differently, and I believe this difference, difficult to describe, has much to do with an ancient people's sense that they are participating with the ground they move over, not simply treading on it. To feel such a connection between self and earth is to expand one's own sense of space. One is no longer so small.

To feel that the mind is either a kind of small screen filled with images or a distant gazer at a large external screen is to presume that mind itself is small and limited in scope. Such assumptions make it extremely difficult to be calmly mindful or to remain grounded when strong feelings such as anger, nervousness, guilt, or passion arise. After all, if mind is but a small screen, whatever appears on that screen dominates it wholly. We feel overwhelmed. But when we feel that our mind participates in a limitless arena, even the most fiery explosions cannot wholly encompass or violate it. The atomic bomb, with all its terrible destruction, did not touch the whole of space. Both the destruction and the areas free from it require our attention.

If the mind is only a gazer across distances, wholeness is once again eclipsed. Doris Lessing in *The Golden Notebook* speaks of trying to hold two very different perspectives simultaneously: the vastness of the universe and the smallness of her own immediate being. Both are crucial to a full view of our situation. We are limited and also part of something vast. Too often mindfulness becomes cultivation of a very small internal space, paradoxically making it more difficult to "simply observe" whatever occupies that space for the time being. In the vastness of mindspace, even the most ferocious response cannot fully define us. Understanding this gives us a greater and thus more stable base, making it easier to avoid wholly identifying with what we observe. At the same time, people who are too enamored of this sense of vastness may be tempted to overlook the specifics of what happens within it. The horror of a Hiroshima or a Bosnia demands that energy be directed at its healing; likewise, our anger and other internal bombshells require us to look into their effects and sources. But none of these events owns all of space.[3] Practice means learning to maintain a balanced sense of the finite and the infinite, sustaining an awareness of wholeness, presence, or emptiness through all circumstances, and at the same time dealing with those circumstances on their own terms.

With this in mind, we can understand many Tibetan practices as methods for expanding our sense of the physical and mental space we inhabit. A number of practices involve receiving or sending light, usually emanating from or dissolving into the heart. Though such techniques are often described as visualizations, this term is problematic. In hearing the commonly given meditative instructions that we are to "visualize" rays of light, many of us automatically assume the dynamics of a television viewer. Yet, these practices emerged in cultures where sight always involved real action, not film, and thus a felt presence between the seer and the seen. Likewise, we need to be physically present to these practices in ways not captured by a passive, disembodied vision.

Radiating and dissolving light, or expelling from our bodies whatever negativities the light purifies, need to be understood as energetic practices, not primarily visual ones. We do not work with light in some abstract sense, but from the particularity of our own bodies, our own energetic patterns. Engaging in these practices energetically means experiencing ourselves as part of an open system, a sensibility that contrasts markedly with contemporary styles of embodiment. Most importantly, in order to bring such light into full contact with ourselves, we must *be* there, physically and mentally. Only then can our imagination and meditation really come in contact with our actual situation, including touching whatever pain or alienation might be there.

If, in any of the many Tibetan practices that involve sending or receiving light, we feel we are disconnectedly looking at, rather than feeling, the light we send or receive, then we are not expanding our ordinary sense of personhood and space, nor even remaining grounded in our own body. We may even become more alienated from our bodies, observing ourselves receiving light and so forth, as if watching from the outside. Such dissociation from our own sense of embodiment also makes it difficult to draw light into every part of our body equally— because we cannot draw it into those parts of our being that we ourselves do not inhabit. Such absence can be due to energetic blockages or psychological impasses, which are usually related. When we find such a block, breathing into the area that seems blocked can open that space for us, allowing us to enter and engage our energies there. This is important, because being absent from any part of our body not only makes it difficult to receive light or healing there, but also contributes to our sense of being a closed system. Again, unless we really live in every part of our body, we are absent from much of our own physical basis.

In short, these practices are not at all about seeing, they are about opening our being to a larger dimension and above all opening our heart, from which all light flows. The open-heartedness encouraged by practice is not simply an idea, nor even a feeling, for it also involves a particular way of tapping into the energetic potential at the heart center of the body, and from this point, allowing ourselves playful access to ever-larger patterns of energy and greater dimensions of space. This engages all dimensions of our being—physical, energetic, and mental.

As long as we understand ourselves as a closed system, we feel we must hold all our "stuff" in our own small bodies, for we have denied ourselves access to any other place to put it. We are also less present, less grounded, less available to ourselves, to others, and to the powerful currents of the practices we undertake. We have hardened the internal mind-body boundary as well as the boundary between ourselves and the outside, making it—however much we might visualize—much more difficult to actually contact, much less transform, some of this stuff and send it out, in purified form, to the universe at large. If we can't send it anywhere, we are left holding it. But holding so much soon becomes overwhelming, and in this way paradoxically reinforces our need to distance ourselves from the actual physical, emotional, and mental processes of the self, thereby becoming less and less grounded. We even seek alienation because of the apparent relief it offers from the whirlwind of indigestible feelings and experiences.

Axiomatic to Buddhist, and perhaps all religious, engagement is the ability to experience the expansive area in which we actively participate. In this way it becomes possible to access wider resources than are available in the mind-body as ordinarily conceived. This can be imaged as going inside so deeply that one opens into a vast space that is neither internal or external, or as a kind of holographic expansion in all directions.

If we understand our physical boundaries as selectively porous in ways that allow us to receive what is helpful and release what is not, the space through which we understand ourselves to move is expanded. It becomes easier to sense that groundedness of the earth and openness of the sky are qualities that move through us, not objects to gaze at "out there." This suggests an energetic ability to locate ourselves deep in the seat of our own physical experience, and at the same time be open to the grounding capacity of the earth beneath us. The ability to be grounded is enhanced by the sense that we are part of an open system, able to receive stabilization and support from the larger environment. We are able to experience our energies in intimate interaction with the grounding qualities of the earth and the expansive arena of space. Such a sensibility expands the dimension in which we live. It also brings attention and energy to the complete and present body through which we participate in that dimension.

NOTES

1. Consider Keats, even Wordsworth, and Walt Whitman.
2. I compare Western and traditional Tibetan senses of personhood in Chapter 2 of *Meeting the Great Bliss Queen: Buddhists, Feminists, and the Art of the Self* (Boston: Beacon, 1995). For a superb account of the postmedieval retreat into the body and many related cultural factors, see Charles Taylor, *Sources of the Self: The Making of the Modern Identity* (Cambridge: Harvard University Press, 1989), especially 189ff.
3. This is, however, an extremely delicate point, and only usefully mentioned when a person's or a nation's healing process is quite far along. In almost all cases, trauma must first be respected and dealt with *as trauma,* and as the focus of one's whole attention, before the larger space can be noticed or found meaningful.

❧ ❧

Body on the Line

CASEY HAYDEN

I REMEMBER WHEN I WAS DRAGGED from the courtroom in Albany, Georgia, for sitting in the black section, how calm I was. I was actually completely present there in that body, willing it to stillness, devoted to that practice. I remember being present in the same way when the cops picked me up in Jackson, and questioned me in the jail; simply the embodiment of the practice of nonviolence. And being thrown in the paddy wagon in D.C., after refusing to move from in front of the White House, just a handful of us, demonstrating early on against the Vietnam War, everything in slow motion. There was no effort at all. Everything seemed so still. Sitting-in at the welfare office in Chicago, 1965, I was very still, very quiet, and very formal. Going limp was easy when the cops carried me out. The training, the practice, the devotion was immediately present and that was all that was present.

It was like birthing my daughter Rosie, while looking into Emily's eyes, my friend who had just had her own child, breathing deeply, becoming that breath, so that the birth process just went on around us both . . . no pain, just sensation.

It was the same as typing all those letters to raise money for the nonviolent movement, when I'd work for hours and no time seemed to pass at all, the very same as feeding my infant, as pouring this out now, this secretion of my body-mind. The lunch counter, the zafu, the sink where I washed the dishes as all this was becoming clear to me, the back porch where I sit in a rocking chair writing these words with a pink ballpoint pen as the cat walks by and the train whistles, each place a setting for attention to the activity of this body in it, in interaction with its environment.

Sometimes the body resists. Sometimes the practice is tedious, the insight lacking, the body restless. It is the discipline, what we actually do with our bodies, that matters, that represents our knowledge, embodying the seamless web:

> *my body*
> *you are kind to sit*
> *and wait for me*
> *while I'm away*
>
> *I wander off*
> *but you don't budge*
>
> *when I return to my true home*
> *it is to you*

The practice of nonviolence is the demonstration of that true home; it *is* that true home.

Sometimes the body is afraid. I don't remember fear when I was in a large group of people acting as one nonviolent body. I remember some excitement: beating heart, rushing blood. But I remember two experiences that were not planned, when I was terrified to the point of shaking, trembling, my body wet with sweat having nothing to do with the heat, and dizzy when it was all over. In one instance we were driving from a mass meeting in the Mississippi Delta and a car of whites rammed us from behind repeatedly, trying to run us off the road. Narrowly, we escaped. Another time there were shots fired outside the house where I lived in Tougaloo, Mississippi. All of us were crawling around on our hands and knees telling each other to keep down, sure that the house was about to be bombed, trying to figure out if we were surrounded. Terror. It turned out to be a couple of our friends shooting off their guns.

Perhaps in the formal activities I relied on the civilization of the police? Or on the presence of my many friends? Was it that in the two frightening events I had no time to prepare? I wonder.

Would it be the same now? Would my body remain true to my Buddhist training now? What would save me from terror in a situation without props where nonviolence was demanded? Would my practice save me, my awakening? Is this practice different from my nonviolent training? Do I believe my own training in both instances deeply, in my body? How is this question any different from asking whether I can remain simply present when my children hit rough spots, when my husband is distant when I need him?

When we demonstrated by picketing segregated movie theaters in Austin, Texas, in 1958, we were demonstrating a self-understanding.

> "I know I'm free! Can't nobody—can't no leaders—can't no president tell me this man *here* ain free! . . . if you think you ain free, then you gon try to do things to *get* free, an the more you try, the more set you is in your way a bein not free. . . . Don you see that? but now if you *be* free, then that is how you gon act, cause you ain think a how you act, cause you just *walk on out!* Like the river here—it don ever stop—it stay so still . . ." (Peter de Lissovoy, *feelgood*, Houghton-Mifflin, 1970)

That's what we did. We just walked on out. Anyone could do it. That's how we knew everyone was really free. It is as though we were the remnant, a tattered piece of the original whole garment of humankind, marginal, useless in the culture's terms of profit and blame, acting for all, telling truth for us all, speaking that truth to power. As though I were a cell in the body of us all. I saw us yesterday in the zendo, sitting zazen for everybody, in the same way, doing the same thing.

Using one's body to make the statement of complete freedom by refusing to cooperate with laws that obliterate, blocking actions that destroy, removes doubt. Like making art, like religious ritual, this activity says it like it is with bell-like clarity. The body, doing this thing without the clinging of language, cuts through, reverberates.

The activity of nonviolent action is without goal. It is just a series of means. One tends to think of civil disobedience as tactical, as forcing change. But it's simply a statement, a means of communication. As such, it trains us in renunciation. This commitment to the action, regardless of result, is seeing the oneness of cause and effect. I recall saying at the time of the sit-ins that if I knew not a single lunch counter would change its policy as a result of my action, I would still do it. One is simply being the truth with one's body.

Demonstrating our self-understanding is no different from the dokusan room, really. Sitting in. Just sitting. Sitting on the lunch counter seat, on the green plush train seats on the Freedom Ride to Albany, Georgia. As we engaged together and repeated these activities with our bodies over time, we became community, tribe, family. Our identities were entwined, identity having nothing to do with race, class, gender, age. This shared self-understanding, our solidarity, was what I experienced in my body. It was strong, deep, secure, still, earthy, heavy. It was "I will be with you. I will sit with you."

Being able to say that and know I could be trusted to mean it, even as I trusted my friends to mean it, was empowering, ennobling. It was this nobility, experienced as calm and strength, that kept me going, not anything accruing to me as a personality. It was truth, acted out by our bodies, which strengthened us. In this strength, my experience as a woman is the same as yours as a man. My experience as a white is the same as yours as a black. This body is the same as yours. This was our truth. This is still our truth. The cells know it. The earth.

I've often thought that I have never known anything so clearly right as my time in the movement, so in my cells and body and gut right, except bearing and caring for my children, equally the activity of devotion. But as I write now, the special significance of these experiences is evaporating, and I realize all of life is the moment for this work. Each moment holds the potential for that deep devotion, this moment equal with that one.

When I was in the South, segregation was the law. Every time I went into a black restaurant, church, or school, I was breaking the law, engaging in civil disobedience, nonviolent social change. I was in training for the rest of my life. It was similar to the training of the zafu: practicing what we then try to do in the rest of our lives. A concentration, not a qualitative difference.

Thus in all actions of that time I also recall feeling measured, formal, intentional, the body slow, observational, clear. Or we might say now, attentional. When I sat in the field in the delta of Mississippi in 1963, at the first Greenwood Folk Festival, on planks set on bricks, and whites drove by in their pickups, circling that little field with rifles hanging in the back windows, I was singing and sitting with others. We were all acting out our self-understanding. We were doing it in our whole lives, all of us there, with every move we made with our bodies. It is the same today, the very same life, the same body.

I get it that this conjunction of the movement and the path is huge, some further healing of a conceptual rift I've constructed between then and now, the importance of the movement and the life I've lived since. Some resistance I've been carrying toward mindfulness practice is evaporating. I'm right inside that mindfulness, living in the actual body. And that's it. It's all the same, all just practice.

Just now after dinner, I slack off while washing dishes, that having been my job growing up, never liking having to do it, going somewhere else in my mind, body continuing unattended. But I come back to myself. My body calls me back, breaking through my conditioning, through the illusory fragmentation, attention shattering the conceptual haze I'm in, and I meet the moment devotedly. I'm so relieved, wondering to myself if this means I can really be here and finally get it that buddha-nature is as present in the sink as in the revolution, all the same body. I release myself and seize the time, letting even this wondering go. . . . And, again, my body calls me back to this moment. Oh, and again!

⊚⊚

On the Other Side of Attachment

MICHELE MARTIN

AFTER THE SECOND WEEK OF A long period of intensive Zen meditation, I learned of an unusual experience that has stayed in my mind for almost twenty years. During a morning sitting, one practitioner had experienced a powerful image that came into her mind like a waking dream. She saw her body as a rack of red meat, like something hooked up in a rural Mexican butcher shop. She had a knife and was carving it up, cutting the flesh down to the bone. There was a feeling of great intensity, but no pain; a powerful sense of wanting to remove something, but not to destroy everything. She was afraid and did not know what would happen once the sitting ended and she had left the cushion for walking meditation outside. She wondered if this were a suicidal urge. Before the sitting ended, however, a golden ray of light penetrated her belly near the navel and filled it with a luminosity that radiated warm light throughout her body. She felt a great expansiveness, a connection to all forms of life along with a wish to nourish and protect them. For the rest of the meditation intensive and for many weeks afterward, she kept this sense of being filled with radiant light and a special kind of liveliness. She even developed the signs of early pregnancy along with a certain glow, and friends and strangers would ask her if she was indeed pregnant. Of course, she was not, but her actual ability to be pregnant had changed, for from that time onward, her periods came regularly for the first time in her life.

When I first heard this story, I was amazed that meditation could bring about such profound physical changes. That the mind could change the mind was not so difficult to accept, but that the mind could influence the physical body so obviously and powerfully was close to inconceivable. The striking imagery also lingered in my mind. Zen practice is permeated by the teachings of the Perfection of Wisdom sutras, which emphasize the empty nature of all phenomena from the most subtle mental states to the most coarse and obvious objects, such as a rock or mountain. These are sometimes summarized as the emptiness of a personal self and the emptiness of phenomena. The subject we are so attached to does not ultimately exist, and the objects we so tenaciously cling to do not ultimately exist either. Meditation practice leads to the discovery of this empty nature.

The Zen context had given rise to this spontaneous experience, but within the Zen tradition I could find no reference for the form it took—cutting up the body and a sense of being filled with light that radiated to all beings. It was only many years later when I learned about the Tibetan Buddhist practice of *chod*—cutting through or severing ego-clinging—that the imagery, process, and underlying structure of the experience began to make sense.[1]

The main progenitor of the teachings of chod was the master *siddha* and teacher Machig Labdrön, who lived in Tibet from 1055 to 1153 C.E. She is a highly respected and beloved figure among Tibetans, who have preserved many stories of her miraculous accomplishments and texts of her profound instructions. Machig Labdrön attained realization of emptiness, the true nature of mind, through reading aloud, at the unheard-of speed of once a day, all twelve volumes of the Perfection of Wisdom sutras found in the Tibetan Buddhist canon. For thirty days, she read the whole set every day, and at the end of that month she attained realization.

In the years that followed, Machig developed and taught chod extensively, blending together three strands of thought and practice: the Perfection of Wisdom tradition, with its focus on the empty nature of phenomena; the Vajrayana, with its use of visualization; and Mahamudra, with its realization of mind's ultimate nature as the union of emptiness and radiant clarity or bliss. Machig also composed many vajra songs that spontaneously arose from the depths of her realization and often found their way into the practice of chod itself.

Chod is a radical method for cutting through ego-clinging, the most basic form of ignorance that binds us to samsara and blocks us from enlightenment. Fundamentally, the process of chod works with cutting through attachment to the body. In her instructions on Perfection of Wisdom, Machig gives a definition of chod, which begins:

> You might ask, "What is known as chod, what does it cut through?"
> Since it cuts through attachment to the body, it is chod.
> Since it cuts through the root of mind, it is chod.[2]

The first level of the practice is to sever our attachment to this body, and one way of doing that is to come to see the body as illusion-like. In working with this practice, I saw again how attachment, clinging, and desire all tend to solidify their objects, making them into something that can be possessed or manipulated. But if the object is just illusory, dreamlike, a mirage, how can you grasp on to that? And further, if the perceived object is illusory, it follows that the other side of this basic duality—the perceiving subject, the self that we cling to—is also illusory. In chod, the realization of no-self, or emptiness, begins with cutting through attachment to the physical body as object and then moves to the discriminating mind as subject. In a lineage supplication, Machig prays:

> Grant your blessing that I be free of cherishing
> This illusory body, gathering of four elements.[3]

Earth, water, fire, and air assembled for a while and then dispersed, so should you understand this body that is like a mirror's reflection: though it seems to exist on a level of apparent reality, from the point of view of ultimate reality, it does not. Nevertheless, due to ancient habitual patterns, we take it to be solid and real, and thereby, the body functions as the basis for our notion of an autonomous self, the major cause of all our suffering.

PERFECTION OF WISDOM

Within the Perfection of Wisdom tradition, which belongs to the Second Turning of the Wheel of Dharma, five physical and mental aggregates are taught to constitute a basis for the imputed self. The first of these five aggregates is form, referring mainly to the body, and the remaining four refer to the mind.[4] The practice of meditation on this putative self is to realize all aggregates as being empty of solid, autonomous, or permanent existence. This does not imply, however, a vacuum or void, but simply that these phenomena have a mode of being that is different from what we usually assume.

In the short version of the *Heart Sutra,* Avalokitesvara states the empty nature of each individual aggregate, beginning with the famous: "Form is emptiness. Emptiness is form." Clearly, in this tradition, our body is the first and the most basic phenomenon to be realized as empty or not ultimately existent. This is not an easy task since our greatest attachment is to our own body. Our most intimate confirmation of who we think we are comes from possessing this particular physical form. Any attachment, however, is an obstacle to liberation, and so the Perfection of Wisdom tradition and chod both focus on uprooting this clinging.

Another fundamental teaching within Buddhism focuses on contemplating the interrelation between the idea of a self and the five aggregates. Reflecting on how the idea of a self relates to these five leads to the understanding that none of the aggregates constitutes a self that is a separate, permanent entity. With each aggregate (here using form, or the body, as an example) you ask the following series of illuminating questions: Is the self the body? Does the self possess the body? Does the self rely on the body? Does the body rely on the self? These four possibilities cover the main ways that we could grasp on to a self by taking the body to be solid and real.[5]

The first way we apprehend a self is the most obvious: no distinction is made between what we think of as our self and our body. We say, "I ache," but it is actually our head or our foot that aches. We also treat our body as an object that our self possesses: "my hair," "my face." And further, we also assume that a self exists because it has the body as a support: it feels like some solid basis for who we think we are. So here, the body plays object to the self as subject. Or the reverse could be true. By deeply reflecting and meditating on these four modalities, it becomes clear that none of them is true and that, ultimately, such a self does not exist.

VAJRAYANA

These two teachings on the emptiness of the body and the interdependence of the concept of a self and the body greatly shape the practice of chod. The power of this practice comes in part because chod embodies these two teachings in graphic images, rather than leaving them as abstractions, which might seem too distant and unrelated. This is the gift of Vajrayana practice. Visualized images bring alive the experience of not being attached to the body or the self, and make vivid the transformation this nonattachment produces. Through Vajrayana techniques, our body and mind are transmuted by changing their relationship. One way this is achieved is through the practice of transferring consciousness (phowa), where body and mind are separated. This occurs repeatedly throughout the practice of chod when consciousness is imaged in the form of a seed syllable and projected upward. The mind is then blended with space and returns in the form of the female deity Vajrayogini. This movement reflects a classic Vajrayana pattern, wherein phenomena are realized to be empty, and from this emptiness all the myriad deities arise. A deity can be seen as a purified aspect of our own mind, and it is this aspect of our mind as Vajrayogini that flings our body, now a corpse, into a vast container, visualized in front of us, where it will be transformed into a limitless offering, blessed by the buddhas and bodhisattvas, and given to all sentient beings. Machig summarized this practice of chod when she sang:

> Separate the material [body] and awareness.
> Blend awareness and space.
> Remain within the depths of emptiness.
> The practice is to offer your aggregates as a feast.[6]

In working with these visualizations, I found they had a direct and visceral effect on how I was experiencing my body as solid and weighty or more luminous and light. In particular, the practice of imaging my body as an offering feast had a powerful effect: at first I was afraid to lose the familiar sensation of having bones and muscles to rely on, hesitant to watch my body being carved up and in that vulnerable state, terrified to invite for a feast what are called harmful spirits. Experiencing this vivid theater of my mind was very useful both to reveal what was there and to start the process of detachment along with the deeper seeing that it allows. Over time, it became increasingly clear how chod works directly with fear, eliciting it in order to reach and cut through its source, the clinging to a self, which in turn allows the mind to arise in its luminous forms.

Seeing your body as a corpse is one way of losing your attachment to it. In one of her well-known verses, Machig sings:

> *Leave your body like a corpse;*
> *Leave it without an owner.*
> *Leave your mind like space;*
> *Leave it without any reference point.*[7]

As we have seen, thinking that the self possesses the body is one of the four main ways the self is reified, so you seek to experience your body as having no proprietor, no subject, no agent in control. If a body, taken to be real, is not there to function as a reference point for the self, then the mind can be like space, open, vast, and expansive. In a similar vein, Machig advises:

> *Like space that has no hope or fear,*
> *Don't conjure up these two, but rest at ease.*
> *Like space not fixed on ego,*
> *Don't grasp on to a self, let clinging go.*[8]

Space, like a corpse, is indifferent, neutral, without self-concern: it has no investment in being this or that, no hope of things going well and no fear that they will not. Hopes and fears are all ego's productions, so you practice letting them go and not getting involved. You let the mind relax, which is possible because you understand that just as space has no self to cling to, discriminating mind has no solid, real body to rely on.

Initiations are the lifeblood of the Vajrayana and usually involve the visualization of a deity and the use of ritual implements that touch and bless the body. Machig had her own special way of bestowing them:

> *I do not give deity initiations to the body;*
> *I give Dharma initiations to the mind.*[9]

Moving beyond the relative level of reality, she aims directly at the Dharma, ultimate truth, discovered in each individual's mind.

MAHAMUDRA

When her son Gyalwa Döndrup praises Machig, he sings: "Mother, by separating mind and body, you showed us emptiness."[10] This revealing of mind's true nature is a crucial event in a practitioner's life and central to Mahamudra and Dzogchen practice. Indeed, it is said that your root or main teacher is the one who has introduced you to ultimate reality. In a formal situation or the natural context of everyday life, a realized teacher points out directly the nature of mind to a student who is ready. To help her students prepare for the event, Machig developed the unique skillful means of dividing mind from body and allowing it to settle into its nature. Through this process, she introduced, or pointed out, emptiness, ultimate reality, to her student's mind.

Machig understood Mahamudra, which is both a tradition of meditation and a synonym for the ultimate nature of mind, as the ultimate basis for her teaching:

> *For example, within empty space,*
> *There is no thing that takes another for support.*
> *Like this, the nature of your mind*[11]
> *Does not rely on an object: one thing is not supported by another.*
> *Rest without contrivance in the expanse of the natural state.*[12]

As we have seen, this experience is invoked in the practice of chöd by detaching our mind from our body, blending our ordinary consciousness with the vast extent of open space, and eliminating our basis of attachment by carving up and giving away our body. Machig describes this experience with terms often found in Mahamudra texts:

> You gain mastery of emptiness, which is free of all extremes and is not established through having an inherent nature; [it is] like the depths of space. Great emptiness is [to be] free of a mind that arises, abides, and ceases. You understand and realize that the body is not truly existent, [but] a reflection of emptiness.[13]

This realization of Mahamudra underlies the whole of chöd practice. To understand the body as a reflection of emptiness (a term often found in Mahamudra and Dzogchen) is to know that form is emptiness and emptiness is form, the principle so central to Perfection of Wisdom traditions. The body, experienced as empty form, appears though it is empty and it is empty though it appears. It is emptiness and appearance, inseparable. Since it is empty, it is not solid nor real, and since it appears, it is not a mere nothingness. The reflection of the moon in the water, the reflection in a mirror, or experiencing one's body as a deity made of light have a similar feel—not solid, yet not a void either. This is one of the main experiences evoked through chod practice.

THE FRUITION

In the processes of chod, then, the body is not eradicated, but attachment to it is. Machig states, "Mind is not attached to the body, and the body is not attached to the mind."[14] She adds that you should also not be attached to nonattachment, which is simply shifting attachment from the body to the mind. When attachment to the physical body disappears, what remains is a vivid, clarified consciousness in the form of a deity made of brilliant light, and a body transformed through compassion into a feast offered to all buddhas and bodhisattvas and every sentient being. Thus, in the practice of chod, both mind and body have been freed, allowed to come into a larger, more enlightened world.

By now, correspondences to the experiences I described in opening this discussion may have already come to mind. Cutting up the body, seen as a hunk of meat, parallels the dismembering and offering of the body in chod. In both cases, a practitioner's detachment allows her to enter into another dimension of reality. The experience of being filled with light and linked to all forms of life, which occurred during the Zen sesshin, reflected a transformation of a solid sense of her physical body into a luminous form. This parallels a chod practitioner's self-visualization as a deity, not made of flesh and bones but of brilliant, clear light; further, the essential nature of the deity, which is radiant clarity, or Mahamudra, is not different from that of all sentient beings. In both cases, solidity is transformed into lightness and isolation into relationship. This correlates with the sesshin practitioner's sense of being connected to all beings and also to the latter part of chod practice when our transformed body is offered to all beings.

COMPASSION

In chod, connection and expansiveness of mind are gained through giving. In his praises of her, Machig's son sings: Mother, you give away your body and life force as nourishment.[15]

Thus, a compassionate impulse of giving moves us outward and connects us with all sentient beings. In chod practice, offerings are specifically made to those who are usually forgotten or avoided—our enemies, harmful and negative spirits, those who create obstacles, and those to whom we are indebted. Such a vast compassion is born that we do not abandon or give up on any sentient being, even the most repulsive and harmful.

One of the skills cultivated in chod practice is that in this act of great generosity, we free ourselves from ego-fixation, since as long as we visualize our body as an offering the basis for an ego is not there. Compassion is also developed by reflecting on the sufferings of sentient beings and the way these are alleviated through our generously offering what we cherish most. In fact, compassion is really the heart of chod.

Referents for practices like chod exist both within and without the Buddhist tradition. The *Jataka Tales* tell of the numerous times in previous lives that the Buddha offered his body in order to benefit beings. Of course, the actual offering of our body is not something that we can do right away, probably not for a very long time, maybe lifetimes, but we can make an aspiration to do so and this has its effect. Ritual death and dismemberment are classic experiences of shamans,[16] and calling in all the negative spirits has resonances with the Jungian practice of contacting the figures from the dark side of our psyche. But the practice of chod is special because it works directly, radically, and graphically with our attachment to this dearly beloved self that is ultimately nonexistent. Such practice fosters an opening out into the whole world through a compassionate impulse that has been freed from the confines of a self maintained by misperceiving the body to be solid and all too real.

NOTES

1. Throughout this discussion of chod, I am indebted and ever grateful to Khenpo Tsültrim Gyamtso Rinpoche, who has brilliantly taught the meditation and philosophy of this practice for many years.

For a discussion of the meaning of chod, its practice, and an excellent version of Machig's life story, see: Jerome Edou, *Machig Labdrön and the Foundations of Chod* (Ithaca: Snow Lion Publications, 1996). For a discussion focused on the origins of chod, see: Janet Gyamtso, "The Chod Tradition," in *Soundings in Tibetan Civilization,* ed. Barbara Nimri Aziz and Matthew Kapstein (Manohar, Delhi, 1985). For brief discussions of chod practice in the Nyingma tradition, see: Patrul Rinpoche, *The Words of My Perfect Teacher* (New York: HarperCollins, 1994), 297–307; and Khetsun Sangpo, *Tantric Practice in Nyingma* (Ithaca: Snow Lion Publications, 1982), 161–166.

2. *Shes rab pha rol tu phyin pa's man ngag bdud kyi gcod yul las snying tshom [chen mo]*, in *gDams ngag mdzod*, vol. XIV, 140ff. After a translation by Edou, *Machig Labdrön and the Foundations of Chöd*, 41.

3. From the Lineage Prayer of *rGyun khyer gyi lus spyin bsdus pa, The Daily Practice of Offering One's Body.*

4. These four are sensation, discernment, mental formations, and consciousness. The five aggregates are often referred to by the Sanskrit term *skandhas,* and they are also translated into English as "the psycho-physical constituents," which make up the existence of an individual.

5. For a discussion of how the skandhas and the idea of a self interrelate, see Khenpo Tsültrim Gyamtso's commentary on the views of the transitory collections in his commentary on "Ascertaining Certainty about the View," Chapter VII, Section 3 of *The Treasury of Knowledge,* by Jamgön Kongtrül Lodrö Thaye, trans. Michele Martin (Los Angeles: Rigpe Dorje Foundation, 1995).

6. *Shes bya kun khyab, The Treasury of Knowledge,* by Jamgön Kongtrül Lodrö Thaye (Lhasa: Mi rigs dpe skrun khang, 1995), vol. 3, 427.

7. Ibid., vol. 3, 423.

8. Ibid., vol. 3, 423.

9. Khenpo Tsültrim Gyamtso Rinpoche.

10. *gCod tshogs las rin po che'i phreng ba, A Precious Garland [compiled] from the Collected Chö [Teachings],* by Rangjung Dorje, the Third Karmapa (Delhi, 1981), 31a.2.

11. The Tibetan reads *sems nyid,* "mind itself," which, in the context of Mahamudra, is a synonym for the nature of the mind, ultimate reality.

12. Loc. cit., 446.

13. *Phung po gzan skyur rnam bshad gcod kyi don gsal byed, Illuminating the Meaning of Chö: An Explanation of Casting Away the Five Aggregates as Nourishment,* by Machig Labdrön, ed. Jampa Sönam, in *gChod kyi chos skor* (Delhi: Tibet House, 1974), 177.

    "Reflection of emptiness" is also translated as "empty form."

14. Machig Labdrön, *Illuminating the Meaning of Chö,* 177–178.

15. Rangjung Dorje, *A Precious Garland,* 32a.3.

16. See *Civilized Shamans: Buddhism in Tibetan Societies,* by Geoffrey Samuel. (Washington, D.C.: Smithsonian Institution Press, 1993) 175, 212, 377–378.

Three Methods for Working with Chaos

PEMA CHÖDRÖN

TIMES ARE DIFFICULT GLOBALLY; awakening is no longer a luxury or an ideal. It's becoming critical. We don't need to add more depression, more discouragement, more anger to what's already here. It's becoming essential that we learn how to relate sanely with difficult times. The earth seems to be beseeching us to connect with joy and discover our innermost essence. This is the best way that we can benefit others.

There are three traditional methods for relating directly with difficult circumstances as a path of awakening and joyfulness. The first method we'll call "no more struggle"; the second, "using poison as medicine"; and the third, "seeing whatever arises as enlightened wisdom." These are three techniques for working with chaos, difficulties, and unwanted events in our daily lives.

The first method, "no more struggle," is epitomized by *shamatha-vipashyana* instruction. When we sit down to meditate, whatever arises in our minds we look at directly, call it "thinking," and go back to the simplicity and immediacy of the breath. Again and again, we return to pristine awareness free from concepts. Meditation practice is how we stop fighting with ourselves, how we stop struggling with circumstances, emotions, or moods. This basic instruction is a tool that we can use to train in our practice and in our lives. Whatever arises, we can look at it with a nonjudgmental attitude.

This instruction applies to working with unpleasantness in its myriad guises. Whatever or whoever arises, train again and again in looking at it and seeing it for what it is without calling it names, without hurling rocks, without averting your eyes. Let all those stories go. The innermost essence of mind is without bias. Things arise and things dissolve forever and ever. That's just the way it is.

This is the primary method for working with painful situations—global pain, domestic pain, any pain at all. We can stop struggling with what occurs and see its true face without calling it the enemy. It helps to remember that our practice is not about accomplishing anything—not about winning or losing—but about ceasing to struggle and relaxing as it is. That is what we are doing when we sit down to meditate. That attitude spreads into the rest of our lives.

It's like inviting what scares us to introduce itself and hang around for a while. As Milarepa sang to the monsters he found in his cave, "It is wonderful you demons came today. You must come again tomorrow. From time to time, we should converse." We start by working with the monsters in our mind. Then we develop the wisdom and compassion to communicate sanely with the threats and fears of our daily life.

The Tibetan yogini Machig Labdrön was one who fearlessly trained with this view. She said that in her tradition, they did not exorcise demons. They treated them with compassion. The advice she was given by her teacher and which she passed on to her students was, "Approach what you find repulsive, help the ones you think you cannot help, and go to places that scare you." This begins when we sit down to meditate and practice not struggling with our own mind.

The second method of working with chaos is "using poison as medicine." We can use difficult situations—poison—as fuel for waking up. In general this idea is introduced to us with *tonglen* (sending and taking practice).

When anything difficult arises—any kind of conflict, any notion of unworthiness, anything that feels distasteful, embarrassing, painful—instead of trying to get rid of it, we breathe it in. The three poisons are passion (this includes craving or addiction), aggression, and ignorance (which includes denial or that tendency to shut down and close out). We would usually think of these poisons as something bad, something to be avoided. But that isn't the attitude here; instead they become seeds of compassion and openness. When suffering arises, the tonglen instruction is to let the story line go and breathe it in—not just the anger, resentment, or loneliness that we might be feeling, but the identical pain of others who in this very moment are also feeling rage, bitterness, or isolation.

We breathe it in for everybody. This poison is not just our personal misfortune, our fault, our blemish, our shame—it's part of the human condition. It's our kinship with all living things, the material that we need to understand what it's like to stand in another person's shoes. Instead of pushing it away or running away from it, we breathe in and connect with it fully. We do this with the wish that all of us could be free of suffering. Then we breathe out, sending out a sense of big space, a sense of ventilation or freshness. We do this with the wish that all of us could relax and experience the innermost essence of our mind.

We are told from childhood that there is something wrong with us, with the world, and with everything that comes along: it's not perfect, it has rough edges, it has a bitter taste, it's too loud, too soft, too sharp, too wishy-washy. We cultivate a sense of trying to make things better because something is bad here, something is a mistake here, something is a problem here. The main point of these methods is to dissolve the dualistic struggle, the habitual tendency we have to struggle against what's happening to us or in us. These methods instruct us to move toward difficulties rather than backing away. We don't get this kind of encouragement very often. What's being presented is that everything that occurs is not only usable and workable, but is actually the path itself. We can use everything that happens to us as the means for waking up. We can use everything that occurs—whether it's our conflicting emotions and thoughts or our seemingly outer situation—to show us where we are asleep and how we can wake up completely, utterly, without reservations.

So the second method is to use poison as medicine, to use difficult situations to awaken our genuine caring for other people who, just like us, often find themselves in pain. As one *lojong*[1] slogan says, "When the world is filled with evil, all mishaps, all difficulties should be transformed into the path of enlightenment." That's the notion engendered here.

The third method for working with chaos is to regard whatever arises as the manifestation of awakened energy. We can regard ourselves as already awake; we can regard our world as already sacred. Traditionally, the image used for regarding whatever arises as the very energy of wisdom is the charnel ground. Now, in Tibet the charnel grounds were what we call graveyards, but they weren't quite as pretty as our graveyards. The bodies were not under a nice smooth lawn with little white stones carved with angels and pretty words. In Tibet, the ground was frozen, so the bodies were chopped up after people died and taken to the charnel grounds where the vultures would eat them. I'm sure the charnel grounds didn't smell very good and were alarming to see. There were eyeballs and hair and bones and other body parts all over the place. In a book about Tibet I saw a photograph in which people were bringing a body to the charnel ground. There was a circle of vultures who looked to be about the size of two-year-old children—all just sitting there waiting for this body to arrive.

Perhaps the closest analogy to a charnel ground in our world is not a graveyard but the emergency room of a hospital. That could be the image for our working basis, which is grounded in some honesty about how the human realm functions. It smells, it bleeds, it is full of unpredictability, but at the same time, it is self-radiant wisdom, good food, that which nourishes us, that which is beneficial and pure.

Regarding what arises as awakened energy reverses our fundamental habitual pattern of trying to avoid conflict, trying to make ourselves better than we are, trying to smooth things out, to pretty things up, to prove that pain is a mistake and would not exist in our lives if only we did all of the right things. This view turns that particular pattern completely around, encouraging us to become interested in looking at the charnel ground of our lives as the working basis for attaining enlightenment.

Often in our daily lives we panic. We feel heart palpitations and stomach rumblings because we are arguing with someone or because we had a beautiful plan and it's not working out. How do we walk into those dramas? How do we deal with those demons, which are basically our hopes and our fears? How do we stop struggling against ourselves? Machig Labdrön advises that we go to places that scare us. But how do we do that?

We're trying to learn not to split ourselves between "my good side" and "my bad side," between "my pure side" and "my impure side." The elemental struggle is with our feeling of being wrong, with our guilt and shame at what we are. That's what we have to befriend. The point is that we can dissolve the sense of dualism between us and them, between this and that, between here and there, by moving toward that which we find difficult and wish to push away.

In terms of everyday experience, these methods encourage us to not feel embarrassed about ourselves. There is nothing to be embarrassed about. It's like ethnic cooking. We could be proud to display our Jewish matzo balls, our Indian curry, our African American chitlins, our middle-American hamburger and fries. There's a lot of juicy stuff we could be proud of. Chaos is part of our home ground. Instead of looking for something higher or purer, work with it just as it is.

The world we find ourselves in, the person we think we are, these are our working bases. This charnel ground called life is the manifestation of wisdom. This wisdom is the basis of freedom and also the basis of confusion. In each and every moment of time, we make a choice. Which way do we go? How do we relate to the raw material of our existence?

Couldn't we just relax and lighten up? When we wake up in the morning, we can dedicate our day to learning how to do this. We can cultivate a sense of humor and practice giving ourselves a break. Every time we sit down to meditate, we can think of it as training to lighten up, to have a sense of humor, to relax. As one student said, "Lower your standards and relax as it is."

NOTE

1. Mahayana mind-training slogans developed by Atisha Dipankara Shrijnana, born in India in 982 C.E.

☯

Body as Self

∂∞

Embodiment

EMBODIMENT IS:

emerging into this world of light and sound

joy of skin touching skin, mouth on breast, body sliding into/out of body

separateness of playmates teasing, mommy scolding, dog growling, knife cutting

loneliness of being encased in envelope of skin, thoughts and emotions a mystery to others

confinement to body as a constantly changing piece of luggage, always a surprise to look down and it has sprouted hair or breasts, become fat, wrinkled, thin, peeling, saggy

becoming afraid that this will end.

Embodiment is:

frustration of mind-never-still standing square in the way of Mind wonder of using mind-that-can-grow-quiet to encounter Mind, body-that-can-sit to realize Body

interpenetration of what I call me and what I call paper just now as I read, interpenetration of what I call me and what I call carpet felt, walls seen, air breathed, trees outside, continuously creating each other, mutual verification, no distance at all. Worm bodies, cloud bodies, toothpaste tube bodies, grass leaf bodies, carpet fiber bodies, Sitka spruce bodies, lumber stack bodies, woman's body birthing slippery baby body.

struggling through body of gristle, skin, sinew, synapse, eyelash, sweat, breast, penis; struggling through mind of scheming, dreaming, steaming, jealous, rageful, loving, doubting, antsy; struggling through body of zafu, left-foot-on-right-thigh, thumbs touching, breath counting, seed syllable, moon disk turning; through mind watching Mind watching mind as it opens to no eye ear nose tongue body mind.

Sometimes I think our em-bodies are like clay shaped on a potter's wheel. Each body is different in form and function, just as pitcher is for pouring, pot for holding, lid for closing. There are man bodies, woman bodies, car, butterfly, radiator, and earthworm bodies. No matter how they are coated—pink slimy, shiny metal, skin, fur, feathers, bark, stone—all are of the same substance. In this universal potter's studio everything is made of clay: the floor, walls, potter's wheel. Nothing enters and nothing leaves. Being born, clay is formed. Living clay bodies chip and gradually or suddenly! break down. Dying, they disintegrate into clay particles again, are gathered, kneaded, and made into new bodies. In the potter's studio are millions of vessel-bodies, continuously being formed, functioning according to their purpose, breaking down, being remade as something new. Nothing enters and nothing leaves.

After hundreds of thousands of millions of years, every particle of clay has passed through every kind of vessel. Every body has particles that have "belonged" to every other body. The vessel-bodies are so tightly packed that there is no distance between them, one shape curving into the next, a valley in one is a hill in another. So close that molecules interpenetrate. What is the clay? Who is the potter?

Of Mud and Broken Windows

MICHELE McDONALD-SMITH

Once I was on a retreat in British Columbia when it poured for five days. There was mud everywhere. Afterward, a woman told me that she decided halfway through the retreat that she had to leave because the paths were getting so thick with mud. She had become obsessed with the mud. In the Vipassana tradition we call that yogi mind: she couldn't let go of the thought that there would soon be nowhere to walk because of the mud. And she felt the need to let somebody know about it. So she went to the cook and said, "What are you going to do about all this mud?"

The cook looked at her strangely, so she thought, "Well, maybe I'm just a little off." She went back to her practice, but she couldn't stop thinking about the mud—how it was getting deeper and deeper. She again decided to leave, but again felt a need to make sure the problem was being dealt with. So she went back to the cook and said, "Really. What are you going to do about the mud?"

This time the cook said, "Don't worry. We'll have maintenance take care of the mud." This was really all she needed to hear—somebody reassuring her that the mud would be taken care of. She decided to stay.

In Buddhist practice we don't always get the reassurance that the mud is okay. I see a split between the clear, unattached mind, the nondual perspective of the Absolute, versus the body, the emotions; the Tao versus the Te. The mud is like the Te. For years in my practice they were very separate.

When I first came to practice, I was desperate to understand and to be free. I was willing to die meditating. I'd been running away from pain all my life. I had no idea what was going on, or why, but by the time I managed to get myself to the end of the first three-month retreat in Maine, I knew that I needed help.

As I continued my practice I touched so many places of freedom that it seemed there was nowhere to go from the pain but up; the model was linear and direct. I didn't have any idea that I would hit many hell realms after that.

When I practiced longer retreats, I began to have an ever-deepening experience of freedom, a very positive sense of the loss of self. It was healthy, awakening, bright, everything that you read about. But soon after that I would experience the opposite. It was like falling into a black hole. The self was disappearing, but it was agony; it was annihilation, everything that you don't read about. Over and over again in my practice I would experience incredible freedom, followed by the black hole, and I didn't understand what was going on. At the time I couldn't even describe it—the sense of going back and forth between such clarity and such darkness. The more I had access to the deep places in meditation, the more I was accessing the darkness.

Eventually I started having preverbal memories of profound trauma from when I was two or three years old, and from birth, and also memories of deprivation and neglect. These were all memories I'd never had before. It was as if Pandora's box opened up. Having access to deeper levels of meditation has consistently given me the strength to face and work with what opened up then.

I'd like to try to describe the initial years of working with that sense of annihilation. It was as if I was a beautiful glass window and someone took a giant rock and threw it through the window. It was like being totally annihilated. In the beginning I rarely had enough power of awareness to go through that experience. Gradually I learned to do it somewhat mindfully, but I would have to look at the experience from a distance. (I learned very young to leave my body and look at myself from a distance.) I'd look at this broken, damaged being and think, "Well, should I try to replace the window? Or should I try to glue all these pieces together?" I had no idea what to do. And I wasn't getting any clues from those around me; no one else seemed to know what to do, either.

Now, after years of working with this in and out of retreat and getting some skilled therapy, I feel I finally have a language for it. Gradually—and it's important to emphasize the gradualness—I started to have the strength to go through the experience mindfully, from inside the body, not from a distance. But it's taken much more strength and equanimity than I could imagine.

I had to learn about regression. The word wasn't in my language. When my practice got concentrated, there would be a certain point where I would regress to very young ages and just be going through the trauma. I had never learned to bring my adult presence to that child part of me. That hurt part of myself was totally alone, and I wouldn't know what to do. So what accompanied the annihilation were layers of terror, rage, grief, hopelessness, and deprivation. When I started going through these layers I felt betrayed. I had supposed that because I had had very deep experiences in practice, I wouldn't ever have to go through anything like that. It wasn't in the model. How could I experience such intense hopelessness after such bright insights? It took me a long time to understand that this was a regression. I was just right back there at three years old, not having healed it. There was a tremendous split between the wise part of me and the damaged child.

I can say now, of course, it's by re-experiencing those emotions with mindfulness and compassion that the pieces of the window get glued back together. Then there is no need to split off from the body or the emotion, because one is no longer afraid of them. The child is safe. But twelve years ago, I had no idea. I think it really helps to have a language. Most people on this planet have a split between their emotional world and their spiritual clarity, unless they've learned to work with the mud.

Several years ago, I started noticing that some people sounded so clear when they taught the Dharma, but the message felt disembodied. I became distrustful of anybody—including myself—who could spout such clear Dharma while their life was a mess. Or while they behaved in damaging ways. How could that be, unless there is an emotional component that's not getting acknowledged? What about need? What about longing? We don't talk about these things much in meditation, and often, the more people practice, the more they hide them, because people who are advanced in their practice are not supposed to have unresolved difficulties. But when they don't acknowledge the emotional side, people get further and further away from healing the split.

We hold difficult areas chronically in our bodies, emotions, and minds. Our bodies particularly are sacrificial areas. Actually, I think of these areas as sacred sites. Parts of our bodies hold our difficulties, until we have the strength to experience them with mindfulness. Without mindfulness, the cycles only continue, because there's still identification.

A change I see now is that our spiritual attention is coming into the body and emotions. I've seen a lot of the lack of such attention in spiritual circles, and often there is considerable "acting out" all over the place, because there's a denial of the body and emotions. I call it "disembodied clarity." But we can learn to integrate the body and emotions with the clarity we develop. I don't even see the Tao and the Te as separate. Wherever we are is where we work, with ourselves and with each other. It doesn't matter. Why isn't that what we're learning? That we're supposed to be with our life and just be aware of what's happening.

As I found more and more compassion to go through the layers of hopelessness and rage in myself, and as I started to glue the pieces of myself back together, I became less and less afraid of the process.

In 1989 I did a three-month retreat, and when I came out I felt that the integration had started; I began to taste the benefit of working with this Te, this body. I felt a balance of the light and the dark. When I came out a friend asked me, "Well, how was your retreat?"

I said, "It was wonderful to taste that freedom again and the deep places in practice, and there was a lot of hard stuff, the traumatic stuff."

She said, "Still?" As if to say, "What's wrong with you? I thought you worked with that five years ago. Isn't that all over with by now?" I felt immediately vulnerable. What *was* wrong with me? I also felt angry. What was wrong with *her?*

I tell this story because the process of gluing the pieces back together through compassion and mindfulness is much slower than I ever dreamed. It takes so much patience. Much depends on the extent of the trauma, the age of the person at the time of the trauma, and if anyone was really there for that person, then or later. Also, each person is unique. Everyone has a story, everyone has a lot of suffering. We must be willing to listen to ourselves and each other without knowing what to do, or trying to fix it. You can't fix the pain. You can only help a person along on the journey of learning how to experience the body and the emotions with mindfulness.

Sometimes people become very identified with their story, or with their pain. That's a protection. It's a defense against experiencing the annihilation. I can assure you that identifying with the pain is much easier than re-experiencing the annihilation. It takes extraordinary strength to be able to go through that annihilation. It took me many hard years. Everyone has to unfold at their own rate. That doesn't mean that a person can't at the same time go very deep in the practice and experience deep levels of freedom. It's important not to be judgmental about how long certain layers of reality take to heal.

For all of us, no matter what our path, the spiritual journey takes patience, compassion, and wisdom. Wisdom is learning to let go into emptiness, to let life flow just as it is; this requires the container of compassion and patience. If there is no container of lovingkindness, the insights into emptiness can become unbalanced, hollow, dry, difficult or impossible to realize, and even more difficult to integrate into our lives.

I have been practicing Buddhist meditation for twenty-one years, and this journey reminds me of how long it takes a tree to grow, bear fruit, and reach maturity. My family and I planted a mango tree together twelve years ago in Honolulu. It grew slowly the first five or six years. Then it started growing very quickly. It grew quite tall, but it didn't flower. Two years ago it flowered but we had no fruit. Last year we had baby mangoes and we were so excited, but they didn't mature. It takes time for the tree to grow strong enough to bear fruit, and to hold the fruit to maturity. This year we had twelve delicious golden mangoes. The tree is like the container for the wisdom I am talking about. The tree is the lovingkindness, the compassion, the patience. The fruit is the maturing wisdom and freedom.

Tracking the Two Bodies

A Conversation between Toni Packer and Lenore Friedman

Toni and Lenore are sitting in front of the fire in Lenore's living room, two days before Toni's annual nine-day retreat in California. It is the end of a rainy afternoon in late December. People will be arriving for dinner in a couple of hours, but right now there is time to continue a conversation started a year before, in which Toni had mentioned "two bodies—the conditioned and the unconditioned." This year Toni is not so sure about these terms and suggests we look at them freshly, to see if they are a good description or not.

LENORE: What I understood last year was that the conditioned body is the one that corresponds to all our ideas and thoughts about ourselves, our expectations, our resistance, all the repetitive stuff that goes on because of past conditioning and present conditioning. Which we keep repeating and re-creating.

TONI: It keeps repeating and re-creating itself. Yes.

L: In this conditioned body there is rigidity, holding, contraction . . .

T: Patterning. Yes.

L: As contrasted to the unconditioned state, which would be fluid, open—open to change, to the present moment.

T: Open in awareness.

L: Where does awareness reside?

T: I don't know. I don't know where it resides, but it isn't separate from the body either. It permeates and contains everything and yet it is beyond everything. Language is problematic, the thing itself is very clear. It is the clarity, the wholeness of it all. And the sharpness of the senses, functioning as one whole perception.

L: Let's go back to two bodies . . .

T: Two bodies, a conditioned and an unconditioned, or a new and an old body I've sometimes called it.

L: A new body . . . a place you arrive, as opposed to a place you've been?

T: No. It's not something you have achieved. It is the real home, one's true being. The other is distorted, with blocked functioning, self-enclosing thoughts and emotions.

L: So these days do you prefer the terms the new and old body?

T: No . . . these days I don't hang on to words. None of them are as good as seeing, experiencing directly what is actually happening.

L: We should just quit talking now! (laughs) Still, I want to ask if we're talking about actual structures—organs, muscles, bone—or are we merely talking about processes? I mean, is there a difference in the way that the structures function in the two bodies?

T: I'm quite sure that there is.

L: How would you describe that?

T: You mean is there a difference in how the physical structures are functioning when there is presence right now? When there is clear awareness? If I stay completely with what is observed at this very moment, habitual tensions become transparent and smooth out.

L: Yes, in fact that just happened to me! I first noticed a thought, and it had to do with the time. There's something I have to do in about twenty minutes, to prepare for dinner, and in my belly I could feel this tightening. When I noticed it, it relented.

T: If it hadn't been detected it would have continued. But let's look further. Does a physical tension of stress, hurriedness, "I have no time"—the kind of physical tension that goes with those thoughts—does it keep on going without supporting thoughts?

L: Perhaps habitual tensions *create* thoughts.

T: Yes, because a physical tension creates the thought, there must be something to worry about.

L: And we're up in our heads again—with tension in our shoulders and our necks, we're thinking, figuring things out, problem solving. It's self-defensive and self-preservatory and it has a kind of "up-there-ness" to it. Which I guess would correspond to the conditioned body. Whereas residing in the lower body seems to allow things to slow down.

T: There's a danger here, though, that I went through in Zen training, where we were deliberately trying, forcing, to put our energy into our lower belly. I called it the "elevator effect": first the intention from the head to let the energy go down, then some sensation in the belly, then wondering up in the head how I'm doing. Up and down, down and up. And yet there is definitely something to this energy gathering low in the body that allows the head to be light, free, open, unencumbered. And therefore naturally intelligent.

L: Could you amplify this?

T: Entering into silence, sitting quietly, allowing whatever is happening "inside" and "out" to reveal itself freely, meditatively, brings about a natural shift of energy from head, neck, and shoulders, to the foundation of this body-mind—an enlivening of the entire organism.

L: Would you say that the new body or the unconditioned body would be one where there isn't this kind of split (top from bottom) in the body? Is that what's intelligent? That there's a feedback loop, a conversation or collaboration going on?

T: Yes.

L: I know that awareness is not just inside our skins. The organism is fully awake and perceiving reality and responding to it. Resting in it, part of a vaster awareness.

T: It *is* reality. One wholeness of functioning.

L: Toni, would you articulate the two-bodies idea in a way that really feels accurate to you?

T: Can we say that the new body is no separate body? No-body? It is the best I can come up with. You said you know it is not just within our skin, but is there even a skin?

L: Not without holes.

T: The more powerful the microscope or telescope, the more empty space reveals itself. That is not just an item of physics that we can know, but something very palpable.

L: When the energy is high up, in the head, then there is absolute conviction that the skin is not only solid and separating us, but that it also requires defense.

T: Yes. And when the energy knots up high in the head, entangled in thoughts and images and proclamations imagined to be real, the whole body becomes mobilized or immobilized with emotionality. It cannot perceive that it is an integral part of everything else that's going on around it. It feels encapsulated, enclosed, isolated. Thought has an uncanny ability to trigger physical processes that originally were not meant to react to thought. They evolved to react to real dangers or needs.

L: Can you say some more about this?

T: When a deer in the meadow notices you approaching, it instantly stops grazing and looks at you motionlessly. The white tail, used to signal danger to other deer, twitches slightly now and then, ready to flash at any time. If you come too close or move too abruptly, up goes the tail like a torch and the animal bounds gracefully into the woods for cover. For us humans no presence of genuine physical danger is needed for the whole body to be flooded by waves of anxiety. All it takes is one scary thought, one fearful memory, one threatening image to trigger physical flight or fight or freeze reactions. Imagining we are alone and isolated, abandoned, causes immediate pain and sorrow. Deer most likely don't ruminate about being separate creatures—it spares them a lifetime of mental grief!

It is clear that the body itself learns something about this amazing being-in-awareness. At Springwater, I usually go to our beautiful sitting hall in the morning, and in the freedom of sitting quietly, the seamless depth of it—the body is learning the organismic way of open being. It becomes natural. Awareness is here on its own. When any effort is made—the intention to be aware—there isn't this ease of just being here. That is the beauty of it: when there is the ease of simple being, which means no blockages, no enclosures, no separation, there is not even the possibility to make an effort. In the state that we've been calling the "new body," there is no need for effort because the barking dog "outside" is right here, it is not separate. There is no effort "to be one with it" as we used to say in Zen. We're already one whole movement in sound and silence.

L: There's no need to get from here to there.

T: No need to get from here to there because there is already here! This just needs to dawn fully! The aware body does not feel that anything is outside of it. Nothing is separate.

L: As we've been talking, at moments that's felt quite palpable.

T: Yes, just sitting here and talking together, feeling the inwardness, intensity, and depth, there is immense energy—not so much a physical body feeling, but palpitating, vibrating energy.

L: A very alive energy . . . with no sense of where I begin or end particularly, just that alive moment.

T: The intelligence of awareness leaves that whole network of self-reference, I-centeredness alone—it needn't be entered. All the energy gathers here right now. Body is energy. In the presence of this aware listening—voices, breathing, noises—there is no need for energy to travel into the "me" network. (Once the me-network is mobilized through inattention, the body contracts into its old habitual patterns.)

About twenty years ago, sitting in a zendo, trying to be a good meditator way into the night, I noticed clearly for the first time how every once in a while in the midst of quiet, unconcerned sitting, the brain would click in with the question: "Am I doing all right?" "Am I getting somewhere?" When the "am I doing it right?" tape became transparent, it was also clear that I don't have to know how I am doing. Sitting quietly is not knowing. But first you have to recognize the tremendous desire to know. This is how we're built, how we've evolved. It's wonderful to see this powerful urge to know, to question it, and to realize that maybe I don't have to know everything. Not knowing, the body is at ease. Not knowing doesn't mean not hearing the words. The words arise but the brain isn't concerned.

L: In that state, it almost feels pointless to talk.

T: Yes!

L: As I sit here and settle, following your words, letting go of self-preoccupation, the impulse, the fuel behind my questions seems to subside. The charge has gone out of them.

T: What is the charge behind the question?

L: A couple of paradoxical things sort of gnaw at me and also excite me. But if I'm just being, the energy drains away.

T: Let's articulate the paradoxes, because the brain wants to make order, wants to finish its business and does not want to carry a lot of things around. It wants to resolve conflict. What are the paradoxes?

L: Well, there are times, usually when I'm sitting, that I experience a kind of quietness in which there isn't any edge to me. The body exists and doesn't exist. It's filled with open spaces and holes, breath and energy moving in and out, or back and forth. The idea of inside and outside seems arbitrary. So one paradox I guess is the body and the no-body, both present in a sort of embodiedness that rests in a larger, undiscriminated whole.

T: Does it rest in it or *is* it that large, undiscriminated whole? Where does the arm end and the fingers begin?

L: There—I started thinking again and I moved right back to self-concern!

T: So thinking creates the conditioned body. We know how certain ways of thinking either twist our faces and bodies or relax them. Our faces express our past thoughts and feelings, fears and desires. Our bodies grow and relax or contort according to how we think about ourselves and how others think about us. We embody what our parents thought about us. I see so many subtle changes in children growing up, the way they walk, the way the eyes look, the way the mouth and shoulders are held. Yet it is simple to let openness permeate this physical structure and let it dissolve.

L: The physical structure dissolves?

T: The idea about it does. Without the idea about my body, it all feels quite different, more natural.

L: Is there time for one more paradox? We've been talking about the openness of the body, but there is also the defensive structure of the body. This body that seems so obviously to be us—there's me and you and them, all in our separate bodies, and then all the defensive operations come into play from perceiving "them" as separate.

T: The body hardens, stiffens, mobilizes for defense or aggression.

L: Yes. Because the separate you can threaten the separate me.

T: Instinctive protective impulses stay alive because the organism loves to live—life loves to stay alive and propagate itself.

L: Love? Can we talk about love, and how it is of the body and *not* of the body?

T: Love is intrinsic to the openness of being. The enclosed, imprisoned, is not loving, it can't love, it is choking.

L: But when you say the body loves to live . . . is that another kind of love?

T: Love is to live, love is to continue. Life loves to live, loves to continue and propagate itself, to create ever new forms. Are you asking, how does that relate to the love that naturally lights up the human heart when self-concern is quiet? Do we need to first differentiate, and then relate again what the mind has separated, or can we behold it all in silent wonderment?

◎◎

The Formless Form
BUDDHISM AND THE COMMUNITY
OF RECOVERY

CHINA GALLAND

I WAS A BUDDHIST BEFORE I GOT sober. I entered Buddhist practice at San Francisco Zen Center's Green Gulch Farm in 1977 in an effort to get control of my life, which was rapidly fragmenting as I plummeted through the last phases of my struggle with alcohol. If I got up earlier, if I did more meditations, if I studied harder, if I went to more retreats, if I lived inside the Green Gulch monastery instead of outside in the community, if, if, if . . . then everything would be all right.

I went through four years of "controlled" drinking after I started sitting. Sometimes I could drink my self-set limit of two beverages and sometimes I could not stop, no matter how conscious my intentions were when I started. At other times during this period, I would abstain for months to prove to myself that I didn't need alcohol. It didn't occur to me that social drinkers don't need to prove to themselves that they aren't dependent upon alcohol.

I had gone through a divorce the year before I started sitting zazen. I knew something was terribly wrong. Buddhism was my last resort, a last attempt to get control of my life. When I was still married and living in another part of the country, I would down stiff screwdrivers of nearly straight vodka after the rounds of domestic violence that sometimes accompanied arguments with my spouse. I stayed in the relationship, deteriorating right along with it in a commitment to make that marriage work, at all costs. I had three children. Alcohol let me tolerate the intolerable and stay the course to disaster. I remember putting my fist through panes of glass, punching out one pane after another in sheer frustration after a terrible fight, then walking into the kitchen to collect myself by pouring a stiff drink, washing the blood off, and fixing dinner for the children. It took a lot of alcohol to get dinner on the table that night.

After moving and getting divorced I realized that although outer circumstances had changed, my feelings of being out of control had not. I continued to fall apart. It finally occurred to me that alcohol might have something to do with my problems. This is when I turned to Buddhism and the discipline involved.

During the following four years that it took to realize that alcohol was my primary problem, I tried a variety of methods to control my drinking. I struggled to not drink every day. It was an accomplishment not to touch alcohol for twenty-four hours. I spent a lot of time in my head not drinking, being acutely aware of what I was not doing. Few people saw me perceptibly drunk at that point in my life. I tried a variety of ways to keep myself in line: no drinking before five in the afternoon, no hard liquor in the house, only beer or wine. When that didn't work, I stopped keeping beer or wine at home so that I would have to leave the house to drink. With three school-aged children, that made having a drink increasingly complicated. I was constantly making deals, with my children, with myself. "I'm just going to the neighbor's for a minute," was my refrain to them, knowing that I could always count on being offered at least a beer or a glass of wine. "When I come home, I'll . . . ."

I told myself if I sat two periods of zazen at Green Gulch Farm in the morning and ran three miles round-trip to Muir Woods and back, then I had not only proved that I was not an alcoholic but that I deserved those two beers or two glasses of wine that I stopped in for at the local pub, after five o'clock. Though I now know that the exposure to the Dharma, the instruction in meditation, and the daily sittings were helping lay the groundwork for the new life I would one day step into, no amount of practice could stop the inexorability of the process of bottoming out on alcohol for me. Sitting zazen became one more activity that I was engaged in—like running, like wilderness trips—in order to prove to myself that I didn't have a problem. It was an elaborate, rarefied form of denial.

Nonetheless, like many active alcoholics, I still functioned in the world of work, despite increasing difficulties. I had gone from a successful career in public administration as assistant to the city manager in one of the largest cities in the country, to helping organize and run nonprofit organizations, working as a wilderness guide, and beginning my career as a writer.

Yet, inside the despair was growing exponentially and the bottom was coming up hard and fast. After a rough trip to Nepal on which I broke my leg trekking and came down with severe amebic dysentery, I slipped back into a favorite old routine, cognac before bed. I broke agreements with myself more and more often. I could no longer rely upon myself. One night I would stop at the pub for my two glasses of beer and walk out in time to get home, prepare dinner, and help my children with homework. The next evening I would be calling my children at nine o'clock, well over my two-drink limit, to say I would be home shortly. They had given up on me hours before and had made cereal for themselves for dinner. They couldn't rely on me either.

The unpredictability, repeated again and again, against reason, against everything I knew about being a good mother, against the way I was mothered, against the way I wanted to mother my children, beat me into the ground. It fueled a self-hatred that burned like a summer wildfire in the Sierras.

"Sit, just sit," I kept telling myself when I entered the meditation hall each morning. That's exactly what I was doing with my life—sitting on it, suffocating it. I kept quiet about the pain. Wounded, enraged, and frightened by the dissolution of my marriage and the increasing speed with which my life was unraveling, I sensed that events were backing me up against a brick wall. Meditation allowed me to see and feel that more clearly. Sitting two periods with a hangover was miserable. I remember facing the blank white wall in the zendo at Green Gulch at five o'clock one morning, the temperature near freezing, trying desperately to remember to count my breath and to let go of my thoughts of shooting either myself or my former husband. I knew that would only destroy my children, and they were my only reason to live at that point. Time in the zendo helped me become aware of the descent. Still, I couldn't tell my teacher or the practice leader what was happening because I didn't know myself. The problem was alcoholism, not my former husband, no matter how bad the marriage had gotten. The practice leader and the teacher were very kind and tried to be helpful, but it would have taken someone experienced or knowledgeable about alcoholism and addiction and that wasn't part of their training. No one could see through to a problem that I would have denied anyway, had I been asked point blank. I went on blindly, rigidly, dying a little more each day in my long black robes and my ever-present smile. But rather than dying from the "ego-killing" meant to occur in Zen practice, I was succumbing to the living death that alcoholism and addiction bring.

On February 25, 1981, after drinking myself into a blackout in the middle of the day following lunch with an out-of-town friend, I drove home, buying more beer to drink in the car on the way, walked into the house, lost my temper with my daughter, Madelon, and passed out on the couch. I woke up at six o'clock at night thinking it was the next morning. I didn't remember being upset with my daughter, then fourteen, or what I had said, until she confronted me.

I asked her to pour me a glass of wine while I pulled myself together to make dinner, but she refused. She was crying and she was furious with me and rightly so. Her brothers had disappeared into another part of the house. She would not hear the apologies that I tried to make, and her willingness to stand up to me, to cross me, saved my life. She called my bluff. She refused to play her role in the alcoholic family. Her "no" woke me up. In a moment of clarity, I could see that my primary problem was alcohol. I picked up the phone and called a childhood friend who had gotten sober, three thousand miles away.

"Can you control your bowels when you have diarrhea?" he asked bluntly. "Of course not," he went on, cheerfully answering his own question. "Well, that's what trying to control your drinking is like if you have a problem with alcohol. Stopping drinking isn't a moral issue and it doesn't have anything to do with willpower. This is a disease, sweetheart, and you've got it."

I held the phone in my lap for what seemed like hours. The desk light shone overhead. My children were off in their rooms, still upset with me. This wasn't the kind of mother I wanted to be, or the kind that I'd had in my family. I couldn't imagine anyone at the Zen center behaving like this. Everyone seemed so calm. Not only was I failing as a mother, but clearly I was not a good Zen student. I was missing something; all the practice hadn't changed me. It was time to try something else.

How could my friend say that being an alcoholic wasn't a moral issue? I was convinced that I was a terrible person. Yet his insistence that I was not in an insoluble moral dilemma, but suffering from an illness from which I could recover, cast new light on my situation. It gave me enough hope to pick up the phone as he suggested and call the one person nearby whom I knew to be sober. On the phone that night she told me that I could find help, as she had, in the community of recovery. I gave up trying to stop drinking by myself or controlling it through prayer and meditation alone. That was too passive. Mindfulness practice was helpful but I needed a program of action, steps I could take to recover. My experience forced me to admit, to myself first of all, that no matter how much I wanted it to be otherwise, Buddhist practice wasn't going to cure my addiction. I would have to go to a different hall for that, and I would have to learn to speak up, not to be silent.

Sunday mornings were emblematic of the painful transition that followed. During my first year in recovery, in addition to daily attendance at zazen, I continued to go to the abbot's Sunday lecture. I would stand in my meditation robes, talking and sipping tea after his talk, when suddenly my heart would start pounding, my palms would begin to dampen, and my anxiety would skyrocket. It was time for me to leave for a noon meeting. I was too ashamed to tell anyone why I was leaving and too polite and self-centered to just walk out and realize that no one cared and that if they knew, they would probably be supportive. My heart sank every time I turned my back on the community and walked up the road beneath the pungent eucalyptus trees to the parking lot. Standing there in the doorway of my car, I would quickly pull on long pants underneath my robes. Then, when no one was looking, I would unknot my corded belt, whip off the three layers of robe, under-robe, and blouse, until I was wearing only a t-shirt, pull a sweatshirt on over my head, roll up my robes, and drive away to the meeting on the verge of tears.

By the end of that first year of sobriety, I discovered that it's not only the alcoholic or addict who is busy destroying herself. Often there are many people who unconsciously encourage the addiction, despite their intentions to do the opposite—from the wife who finds that she can get what she wants after her husband has had his requisite cold beers, to the children who discover that mom doesn't mind that they take money from her purse after they bring her another bourbon. This realization helped alleviate the guilt and shame that made me think I was different from everyone else—especially from my own family. Just because I had identified myself as the alcoholic didn't mean that I was the only one with a problem.

Still, as I sat in meditation every morning, shame would bubble up in the silence to taunt me. The spiritual program of recovery that I found had taught me that there are moments when it's essential to reach out to another person. During a difficult visit to Minnesota, when it seemed impossible to keep moving between the world of recovery and zazen, I called Katagiri Roshi at the Minneapolis Zen Center, whom I'd never met, and was invited to visit for a private talk.

After listening over tea, Katagiri Roshi put down his cup and smiled broadly. "Other Zen students have problems with alcohol too," he assured me. He said I was only seeing people from the back in the zendo. "If you could see them from the front like I do, you would know that everyone struggles with life, and some of them struggle with alcohol." He encouraged me, "Don't judge, don't compare—just keep going!"

Katagiri's description of a Zen meditation hall where people often sit facing a wall, their backs to the interior of the room, illuminated part of what was lacking for me in Zen practice at the time. His comment was a metaphor for the traditional hierarchical structure where only the teacher "sees" everyone's face. With our backs turned to each other, we saw each other only partially. There was no mechanism in the community for the level of self-disclosure necessary to confront alcoholism.

When I began to study Buddhism in the late seventies, the honeymoon of Buddhism coming to America wasn't yet over. Many of us idealized it and saw it as a way to transcend the world and get out of it, not into it. Buddhism was just heading into the period of scandal and crisis that would mark the eighties. In 1983, San Francisco Zen Center became one of the first communities to experience the trauma of confronting an abbot for abuse of power. The request for the abbot's resignation was preceded by charges of sexual misconduct.

When I started sitting at Green Gulch Farm, the setting was idyllic, still peaceful, calm, and quiet. The denial of my private dilemma was a perfect fit with the community's denial of the abbot's behavior. After I got sober and the crisis broke, I found myself angry, sad, and relieved—relieved to now understand that the strange tension I experienced in the community wasn't only my private difficulty. What happened at Zen Center had not only taken years to develop but had required the unwitting participation of many fine, well-intentioned, intelligent people, not only the abbot.

The dam had broken; the abbot resigned. Some senior members left, others stayed. The difficult, perilous work of restructuring began. San Francisco Zen Center had broken through the denial, brought in professional help, organized itself into small groups, and people started talking, really talking to one another, telling the truth about how they felt. The transformation of San Francisco Zen Center and Green Gulch Farm is the hard-won result of walking through that crisis, and it took years.

I now understand that the abyss I had to cross when I left Green Gulch for my Sunday meetings was in my mind. It was imaginary. I feel quite differently after a few more years as a student now of both Buddhism and sobriety. It wasn't that Buddhism "wasn't enough," rather, it was my own practice that was limited by rigid, narrow, monastic concepts. Maybe some alcoholics and addicts can get sober and clean by sitting in meditation. I couldn't. Alcoholism is a chronic disease with physical manifestations, not just a state of mind. Detoxifying one's body can be a dangerous matter, depending on the stage of the disease. While it certainly isn't always the case and it wasn't in mine, some people go into delirium tremens. Some people die detoxing.

I got off easy. I only had to sleep a lot and go on crying jags for a year. I was exhausted. Sober people were almost the only ones I could talk to at the time. Those rooms were full of people who had been through the shocking experience of re-entry—life without an anesthetic for the first time. My skin didn't begin to cover me. I had a life, three children, and a career—all in full motion.

This is when friends in recovery would say, "Come with us for coffee," even though it might be ten o'clock at night and I didn't drink coffee at that hour, I went, just to be with sober people. There was always an activity to join in: a dance for sober people, a picnic, a party without alcohol, and gatherings of sober people to be with, to call, to come over, to go visit—if I needed it.

I'll never forget the first time I went grocery shopping after I got sober. I marveled at the large number of people who were coming and going and not buying alcohol. I zipped around the store, examining the contents of everyone's shopping cart in disbelief. What strength, what character "normal" people had. I was astonished. When I walked past the liquor section, I read a wallet card that I'd been handed at a meeting: "God grant me the serenity to accept the things I cannot change, the courage to change the things I can, and the wisdom to know the difference," reciting it over and over like a mantra and walked on until I was out of the store and safely in my car.

Finally the day came when I had to choose between what I call my sangha of sobriety and my morning meditation practice at Green Gulch. I was getting up at four-thirty in the morning and going to bed at eleven P.M. I couldn't keep up the schedule, it was too demanding for me in early sobriety. One of the irritating acronyms in recovery is H.A.L.T., meaning, don't get too hungry, angry, lonely, or tired. Those states, and especially combinations thereof, are considered set-ups for what's called a "slip," taking a drink or using a drug. It's also called "going out." People do it—a lot—and a lot of people never make it back to sobriety. Sobriety, like the Buddha's teachings, is an infinite storehouse of wisdom, to be guarded, deeply valued, and treasured. I would have to expand my concept of practice, enlarge it, cultivate it to include the steps of the recovery process I was involved in. It was with great reluctance that I let Green Gulch go, but without sobriety there was no point in my Buddhist practice. I began to sit at home alone.

Because I already had a meditation practice established, it was easy for me to follow the steps that were suggested for what I call the practice of sobriety. One of the most important means for staying sober and one of the primary ways in which Buddhism is compatible with the commitment to recovery is the counsel to seek through prayer and meditation to improve our conscious contact with God as we understood God, seeking only the knowledge of God's will for us and the power to carry it out."

But this suggestion and earlier ones also introduced me to one of the major barriers I would encounter: the language of recovery—the jargon that accompanies it set my teeth on edge. As a newcomer and a student of Buddhism with years of Catholic upbringing behind me, the all-male God talk I initially found in meetings was almost unbearable. I had to force myself to go. I complained, embarrassing myself often, but I wanted desperately to stay sober, and what I had been afraid to say in the past was what I drank over. I knew that I had to speak up if I wanted to to keep up this newfound practice of sobriety. I wanted to drink again, but beyond these meetings, I had nowhere else to go, and I knew that. My choices were to stick with the community of recovery, keep complaining, or die.

At every gathering people are encouraged to "take what you need and leave the rest." It was simple. I did my meditations at home and ignored the God talk. I also created my own gender-neutral text with white-out fluid and a fine-line pen so that I didn't have to keep up the constant translation in my mind of the one sacred text of recovery, written over fifty years ago when it was assumed that women did not have problems with alcohol. In my messy, marked-up copy of this book, women, too, are alcoholics, and God is both a "Him" and a "Her" or the Buddha, the Great Spirit, or whatever I need it to be.

The commitment to prayer and meditation has been a key to my recovery and has provided the bridge between Buddhism and the community of recovery. This suggestion includes a clear-cut directive to develop a spiritual practice but—blessedly—no particular kind of prayer or meditation is prescribed. Since few Western traditions include meditation or instruction on how to do it, increasing numbers of people in recovery seek out Buddhist centers and teachers to learn how to meditate.

For myself, Tibetan Buddhist practice, with its emphasis on visualization, has been particularly helpful. By practicing at home alone, I was forced to a new level of study and questioning, which caused me to seek out teachers. I found Buddhist vows to not use intoxicants support the practice of sobriety. But it was the Tibetan deity Tara, one of the female buddhas, who deserves as much credit as the recovery community for saving my life. Tara, the Great Bodhisattva of Compassion, the Goddess of the Khadiravani Forest, called also Liberator and Savioress. Most important—Tara was a fully enlightened buddha whose vow was to become enlightened only in a woman's body.

Before Tara became enlightened she was Princess Yeshe Dawa— Wisdom Moon—so renowned for her wisdom that all the monks and holy men in the kingdom gathered around her and urged her to pray that her body be transformed into a man's. Enlightenment, it was believed, was impossible to achieve in a female body. Nonetheless, she was so close to it that she only needed the male form, that was all that was lacking, they said.

Yeshe Dawa thanked them but refused to pray either to be transformed into a man or to be reborn as one. The monks and holy men were surprised to hear her say that she had given a great deal of thought to this subject of "what is male" and "what is female" and had decided that worldly beings were sadly deluded in this matter.

"Nowhere can I find what is male, nowhere can I find what is female," she explained. "These are forms of being, no more separate than a wave is from water. But since most buddhas have chosen to come in a man's body, I think it would be most helpful if I came in a woman's body. Therefore, I vow to only become enlightened in a woman's body, for all time, in all worlds, until all suffering is ended for all beings."

The Buddha Tara proved the antidote to the self-loathing I experienced at finding myself in a woman's body. Underneath the need to anesthetize myself (biochemical components and physiological predispositions aside) was self-hatred. "The disease is in the thinking and the feeling," it is often said, and I felt bad, especially bad about being a woman. I was a feminist before I got sober, but nothing really changed for me until I could see women as spiritually empowered—all kinds of women, all colors of women. Tara was known to have at least twenty-one manifestations in different moods and different colors: white, green, red, yellow, blue-black, orange, gold, and black; peaceful, pacifying, magnetizing, and fierce.

Having had no image of the divine as female (Mary's powers were only derivative of her son's and his father's), having been raised with the belief that women couldn't become priests because "they weren't made in the image of Christ," having grown up in a racist culture where, in the not-too-distant past, black women couldn't enter convents because it was believed they couldn't remain celibate, to have found the Buddha Tara with all her many different forms—fierce, compassionate, red, white, yellow, and black—was a discovery that made me ecstatic. Tara seemed a marvelous antidote.

It was commitment to the practice of recovery and, paradoxically, my Buddhist practice that allowed my Christian roots to resurface. Over the years of sitting, Christ began to emerge, as did Mary. At first

I wanted nothing to do with my Christian heritage. I wanted these presences to go away; I had done with them, they were part of a useless past I no longer claimed. But the Buddhist saying, "The Way is easy, no picking or choosing," changed my mind. I began to allow their presences in meditation. With them came the first twenty-five years of my life that I had thought needed to be cast out. It was tremendously healing to allow them into my meditation. Yet by now I was deeply engaged in Tibetan practice. How did they fit? Would I have to choose between Tara and Mary, Buddha and Christ? Was I really a Christian after all, and on top of that, a Catholic?

The late Tara Tulku Rinpoche gave me the answer and supported my faith in the particular form of practice that was evolving for me. I didn't need to imagine all these presences as separate. Because of her great compassion, Tara is famous for taking whatever form is most helpful to us. So I came to see that Mary could be a manifestation of Tara in the West. Yes, Christ could be a buddha, too. They were not to be reduced or denied their identities in the Christian tradition by this possibility. No one could say that Mary was Tara or that Jesus was a buddha, but conversely, no one could say that they weren't. This turn of events had a profound impact on both my recovery and my practice, and cut through the illusion that Western tradition held nothing for me.

Tibetan Buddhists have a term, *rangjung,* which means the self-arising of a teacher or a deity. Sometimes I think of the sangha of sobriety in a similar way, as the self-arising of the Buddhadharma, a wisdom called forth for our time. I have found more of what I understand the Buddha to have taught actually practiced in the community of recovery than I've found in any Buddhist center or monastery. The recovery community, with its focus on anonymity, its lack of money, property, titles, and prestige, leave little for one to cling to, unlike Buddhist organizations that end up struggling like any other institutionalized tradition.

Brother David Steindl-Rast was lecturing at San Francisco Zen Center one day not long after I got sober. He said that when he first entered his monastery thirty years prior, the abbot surprised everyone by announcing that the model they should uphold and strive to emulate was that of the recovery community. Recovery was to be their model because there was more of the spirit of early Christianity to be found in the companionship of recovering alcoholics and addicts than in any other situation. The monks were to remember that they were entering the monastery not because they were particularly holy, but because they had problems. They needed help. They could not work alone, they needed the community and one another. His comments were enormously helpful to me because of the shame I was struggling to get over. He made his remarks as a matter of course, not because he knew that anyone listening was newly sober. Nonetheless, his words felt like a special gift.

I now think of the process of recovery as the formless form—one of the most demanding forms of spiritual practice in Tibetan Buddhism—a practice so thoroughly integrated into one's daily actions as to be indistinguishable from everyday life. Meetings have become Dharma talks for me, teachings given by the whole sangha for the ongoing practice of sobriety. There are no senior students, no abbots, no hierarchy; we have only each other's experience to draw from. It is here in the sangha of sobriety, in the community of recovery, that I am brought back to life again and again, through being witnessed. Here I am nourished and made ready to be of use to others and to the larger community. The very structure of meetings creates an atmosphere in which I catch a glimpse of that nameless wisdom, buddha-nature, arising here one moment, there the next, belonging to no one and to everyone all at once, like a wave out of the blue ocean breaking then falling back into itself and disappearing, leaving only the vast, glistening expanse of living waters washing over me, fully and freely.

Craving

LINDA HESS

BETWEEN 1975 AND 1980, I KEPT a detailed journal on my experience of compulsive overeating, a problem that started in the mid 1960s and increasingly dominated my life. I had begun Zen practice in 1974. The "eating notebooks" turned out to be a very long, cumbersome (since everything had to be recorded in words on paper), and powerful exercise in mindfulness. Combining Zen with this writing practice, I began to see addiction as the whole problem of human life, the cause of suffering that the Buddha tried to help people understand.

Doing the notebooks was an act of despair. Having always been a writer, I felt I might as well write while dying. There seemed no way to change my disastrous habits. I had tried everything, and failed. What I learned in the writing—impossible to anticipate—was that the "eating problem" was connected to many other things, to everything, really. It was connected to sex, rage, fear, and bodily encodings of childhood experiences. For a long time, as these matters came to consciousness, I could experience only the ways in which I was imprisoned and suffering. But eventually, I began to experience ways of release: fear and rage melting to sadness and even love. I also learned about the patterns of my behavior, previously unknown to me. For example, I learned that the "payoff" to a fully successful binge was a short period of utterly

unconscious sleep. The binge would be structured to produce unconsciousness; there would be cravings not only to eat, but to eat lying
down, while reading, under blankets, until I fell asleep. Sometimes I
compared this perfectly blank sleep to the sleep one falls into after lovemaking.

Acting out my addictive inclinations in a very gross way on my
body, I had to learn through the body, not just the mind, how to get
free. I knew, of course, that body and mind were not separate. But if I
hadn't been regularly destroying my body through my eating habits, I
might have been inclined to focus excessively on the mind. The following excerpts highlight bodily experience, body-mind connections, and
the continuing thread of Buddhist practice. During these years, I was
moving back and forth between California and India; the settings are
part of the story.

Since the point here is more process than plot, I'll tell one version
of the ending. By 1980, compulsive eating was gone from my life.
There has never been another binge. This leads me to doubt the Twelve
Step gospel that the particular form of one's addiction is an incurable
disease that one must expect to bear until death. Addiction in general,
I believe, is definitive of the human condition. I equate it with the word
often translated as "craving" in the Second Noble Truth.[1] The forms of
addiction are legion and transformable. They are a major part of what
we study when we study the self.

ⓒⓞ

STOPPING IN ISRAEL ON THE WAY TO A PERIOD
OF DOCTORAL RESEARCH IN INDIA

I can't let go of addiction and obsession, can't feel good for too long.
If I am free of binges for a few days, eating lightly, beginning to feel
open and alive, then I must have a big binge, quickly wipe myself out.
Nightmares, ruined morning, hangover, dead surfaces, hiding from
people, making mistakes, canceling plans, sucked into the vortex, not
available for contact with the world.

Yesterday at 1:30 I bought food in the street, ate walking, stopped
short of a binge but craved figs, bought them, craved to get them home,
lie down in bed with a newspaper and eat till I slept. I felt the relief of
a baby getting its sucker and blanket as I finally lay down with my figs
and newspaper.

VISITING A ZEN GROUP IN JERUSALEM

Friday, after not eating too much during the day, I came home with Hannah. She is dieting, and we had a healthy dinner. Then came the usual cravings and nervousness, my evening withdrawal. Intending to get up early for an all-day sitting, we went to bed at 9:30. At 9:45 I got up and started to hunt everywhere, quietly, as is normal for me in such situations. I found two pieces of candy in a bowl and ate them. There was practically nothing in the kitchen—just her tomatoes and cucumbers. But I kept searching and found a box of sweet cocoa that belonged to her housemate. Mixed one full cup with a little milk to make a thick sauce and ate it in bed while reading. Made a second cup, even fuller, and took it to bed. Then fell into a drugged sleep.

Sat through four hours of meditation this morning. Body feeling terrible as it feels only when I've overdosed, this time on chocolate and sugar. Kept falling asleep while sitting, no power to resist. Then the violence and anger. First: want to die, want to kill myself. Then: want to break the windows in front of me. To smash, smash. I imagine smashing people, beating their bodies against pavement until they are dead. My body shakes tensely because I have to sit still.

I think of the space I would have to get through in order to resist the urges to eat—an empty space, a no-man's-land of yellow flat rock—and I know I can't do it, can't do it, can't do it. A scream starts up in my head: *I hate you, I hate you, I hate you.* Immediately I remember the time when, as a small child, I screamed this at my mother. I imagine taking Hannah into a room in her house tonight and asking her to listen to me. I'll sit cross-legged on the couch with my back to her and shout, "Hatred and destruction, hatred and destruction, hatred and destruction!"

Once my mind starts yelling "I hate you," there is enormous crying, tears and snot running down my face, but silently because I'm sitting in meditation. After that I am wiped out and start falling asleep again.

If I hadn't eaten the chocolate I would have felt happy and energetic. I would have made good efforts and come out of this day's experience with depth, openness, serenity—experiences I can't now imagine, they're lost. I spend two-thirds of my life this way.

The craving takes over my body and mind, the tension is filling my shoulders with pain, my head is hurting, there seem to be lines on the surface of my eyes, pulling them apart, the exterior world becomes strange, it is a great effort to stay in contact with it, and within this difficulty the urge to eat comes every five minutes, then every minute (like labor pains). There is no escape, no relief, no end to it. Eating is the escape, the false relief. If I try to resist even for a minute while food is calling to me from every side of the street—I am writing this now on the street in downtown Jerusalem, leaning on a car—if I try for even a minute, I want to break down crying, deprived of my relief, feeling the pain and craving will go on forever.

No use resisting, it will happen again and again and again. If I resist at 10:00, it will get me at 10:30.

Yesterday's *Jerusalem Post* quoted a woman from the United Nations, saying how intolerable it is that in poor countries millions are starving or undernourished, while in rich countries people are making themselves sick by overeating.

The old woman at Kare Deshe on the Galilee saying to me, "Eat, eat," and I making a joke about it, and she saying seriously, "I have been hungry. It is better to be killed in war than to be hungry."

Staying with Friends in New Delhi, India

Last night I broke apart, stuffing myself with a big extra meal at midnight after everyone had gone to bed. The ten-day resolution was forgotten. I made no attempt to stop, to be conscious of the conflict for even one minute, but waited impatiently until the coast was clear, went down and got two successive bowls of heavy leftovers from dinner, ate while reading Jack Kerouac's description of a horrible alcohol hangover and despair. I fell asleep in a stupor.

This morning, my familiar hangover. Body puffed up, especially face and stomach. Surfaces deadened, especially eyes, which feel like cold gels. I'm trapped inside this puffed-up, dead-surfaced body. I want to avoid contacts with people. Imagining everyone is angry with me. When the cook says, "Good morning," he speaks angrily because he's noticed how I've eaten the leftovers. Karen and Michel are annoyed with my presence at the table. I've made my chest worse and interrupted my recovery from bronchitis.

Feeling sick, hands trembling, brain unusable, made of caked clay.

Very shaky, could easily fall into eating again at any moment. I forget, when enduring the anxieties of withdrawal, how bad this is. I think *those* feelings are unendurable, but forget how much worse *these* feelings are.

Proceeding with difficulty to ordinary activities, late in the morning found myself starting to eat again—in the worst way, like a drunk who starts to drink again when he's not even out of the last drunk. Out of control, I managed to go to Karen and talk and cry. But there's no escape, I'm locked even now in these horrible feelings, physical pain, mental torpor, while outside the wind blows the eucalyptus leaves, everything is green and yellow and blue, birds are singing and children shouting, horses' hooves clopping, but my ears hear the tap of a typewriter, tick of a clock, all noises detached and ominous, and a dead heavy body.

The symptoms of malnutrition seem to be the same as those of overeating: "A malnourished child is listless, lacking in curiosity, and unresponsive to maternal and other stimulation . . . the mother herself is often a victim of nutritionally induced lethargy."[2]

A TRIP TO BODHGAYA

I'll only describe the end of that afternoon. After giving in to the binge, I started to wander around eating. From stall to stall, eating cookies and sesame cakes, with each bite closing myself off to the life around me. Finally I bought a large bag of roasted shelled peanuts, intending to eat them while lying in bed in my room. As I walked across a field toward the guest house, two little girls came running at me, dressed in dirty cotton. They were laughing, about nine years old. Thoughts flickered as legs kept moving. "Beggars. I'm not giving them anything this time. Often I give. Not this time." But as they approached they saw the bag of peanuts, smelled the roasted nut smell. Their eyes glittered with desire. They reached for it. I couldn't keep it. The planned completion of my binge receded as I started giving peanuts to them and two others who had come up. Soon there were ten ragged children, clamoring, pushing, and grabbing while I tried to distribute the peanuts fairly, tried to make them keep quiet and not attack each other.

One tiny girl started crying, hit by a bigger boy. I gave her more. Another girl, the most aggressive, kept trying to rip away my bag like the monkeys at the red temple. After I had distributed nearly all the nuts as equally as I could, the bag was torn from my hands and ripped to shreds, with children scrambling for fallen bits. I went away appalled, wanting to kill myself for my hopeless inability to come to grips with my crude craving, even in the midst of such raw hunger, even in the very place of the Buddha's enlightenment.

AT SAN FRANCISCO ZEN CENTER

Came home with inner peace and quiet from sitting, and immediately overate badly. Unless I refrain from overeating, I will never penetrate anything. Only by refraining can I see the life I have been missing.

What gets liberated when I don't eat is love. There is an experience of love and freedom that is so wonderful—why am I afraid of it? Only by experiencing it can I find out the answer to that question.

Paralysis during and following dinner. Talking to someone at the table, I find myself blanking out on about every third word he says. At moments I feel truly insane but it doesn't frighten me too much, because parallel to it is a state that is rational and in control of behavior and speech. It has taken me an hour and a quarter to write these lines. I'm like a person in a hypnotic trance. The world before my eyes is two-dimensional and portions of it keep getting blotted out. Extremely difficult to write—my head fills with some indescribable substance. The only thought allowed to enter my mind during this time is "Eat. Eat." It is very difficult. This notebook will not be complete until it has many instances of writing at such times, and not eating.

From 7:00 to 8:30, moving from dining room to kitchen to living room and back again. Finished dinner at 7:00 but can't leave. I eat about five more helpings of salad. Heavy. Can't leave. I stand in the hallway browsing through cookbooks and eating salad. People walk by. I am withdrawn and ashamed. I go to the bread room but someone is there, and I'm ashamed to take bread right after dinner, where people can see me. Back to reading room. I read a whole magazine just to fill my mind the way I fill my stomach. I stand in the hall. I pace. I stand still with hands dug into pockets. I am not free to move my limbs or break the spell that is on my head.

I am trying to get to the stairway. I get close to the bottom of the stairway but don't go up. I walk to the front door, pretending to look at messages. Back to the bread room. Still someone there. Don't go in. Survey dinner leftovers and fruit bowl. Don't take any. Stare at people in a class. Somehow I push myself upstairs. It has taken one and a half hours. Even then I don't go to my room but stand in the hall, pretending to look at notices. Someone passes and says, "What's up?" I say, "My usual evening . . ." and then make a gesture of tension and difficulty. He smiles and says, "Me too." This brief moment of normalcy breaks the spell long enough for me to get to my room. I go in, go out again to the bathroom. Then I realize I've done it, broken through it, got through that bewitched period without eating, and *moved away* from it. Realizing this, I start shaking all over and crying, an almost dry, teeth-chattering crying. It was so difficult! Just that much! And not in the clear yet. While writing I am still crying, teeth still chattering. Desires to eat still come, threatening to take me over. But I know I have got through something. The shaking and crying tell me.

Following lunch I was caught in the iron grip of compulsion. With all my will I held back from eating more, then returned to my room and went through the most infantile crying. It was down at the bottom of the breath where you keep sobbing like hiccups, like a tiny baby who is out of control and cries like that until it is exhausted and falls asleep. I imagined someone coming and trying to comfort me, holding me while I cried, and in my fantasy I told them, "I'll kill you, I'll kill you," though I actually wanted them to hold me and care for me.

A life's worth of love is locked up, blocked up against the dam of my stomach. That is the greatest thing that has to be got out, that is the whole secret of life, but before that all this pain, murder, fear has to be got out, again and again. Just this crying, this total, shaking, guts-emptying crying, not worrying about what it means.

Yesterday felt, as many have said, that it's laughable to moan about loneliness or the lack of love. Love is there, contact and relationship are there, infinite supplies of it, if we just let down the elaborate apparatus of barriers that keep it from touching the one pulsing vulnerable center that is actually in the heart but sometimes seems to be in the clitoris.

Was eating an apple when I thought of my mother's death, and how I wrote in the notebook last month that I didn't care, it didn't touch me. Fleetingly I pictured her alive, then started to cry. The same crying again. I started to cry more, dropped the apple, shook my hands wildly, jumped from foot to foot like a child in a rage-grief tantrum, got down on knees and elbows with head down, cried with voice and breath unencumbered, like an infant. It would subside, then start up again strong as ever (like orgasms when masturbating), wailing, sobbing, hiccuping, gurgling, always coming up from the guts, shaking the guts.

Again the bottomless crying, for my wasted life, how I have destroyed the beautiful mind and body which were given to me. Can anyone possibly still think I'm worth saving?

Experiences Remembered from a Seven-Day Sesshin

A woman sits next to me, overweight, with a pile of extra cushions to make it possible for her to sit. She is in pain. I know just what kind of pain she is experiencing. I imagine putting my arm around her and encouraging her. The thought that I could help someone brings tears to my eyes.

I am looking at breakfast, served carefully in three bowls in front of me. The first bowl holds steaming oatmeal; the second, a mixture of cantaloupe, bananas, and peaches; the third, a heap of fragrant, herbed eggs. My legs are crossed, my hands held formally at the center of my body. I wait while everyone is served; after a signal and chant we all begin to eat together.

It looks like so much food, each bowl piled with something different. I think of the children who lived around my house in India. Most of them hardly ever tasted fruit—it was too expensive. I think of children in railroad stations chewing on leathery bits of bread. I remember holding babies with snotty faces, scabby scalps, dirty hair, who looked at me with dull eyes. The glistening pile of fruit in front of me—how can I *want* to eat all this when they exist? Not just that I shouldn't eat it; I shouldn't *want* to.

In a line of slow-moving black-robed Zen students, I think of something I wrote about my mother—"hard, snarling, merciless, ferociously selfish, constantly afraid . . . arteriosclerosis of the heart." Now I want to say to the teacher: "My mother died last September while I was in India. Actually I didn't much care. I hated her and many times wished for her to die." Imagining these words I begin to cry deeply, hiding it so as not to disturb the slow-moving Zen students. How sad, how bitterly sad to feel that way about anyone. Especially your mother.

"I am happy. I am happy." For the first time these words keep coming up, and I don't know why. Then: I am beginning to feel. Beginning to feel. Beginning to feel. From the bottom of my gut to the top of my heart, melting.

The teacher is saying, "In Buddhism we have no revealed teaching. So you just have to reveal yourself. Is there a way to end suffering? Is there a way of living that puts an end to suffering?"

And inside I am shouting, "Yes! Yes!" like someone at a football game, "Yes, there is a way to end suffering!"

൭൭

Months ago I asked about the "mystery of responsibility." Why does one person stand up and another lie down? How does a person who has been lying down all her life find it in herself to stand up?

I know the answer now. It is simple effort. Effort is an inner movement that has nothing to do, or only incidentally to do, with results. You make a big effort, a small effort, an infinitesimal effort. When you're up against something enormous, you make a tiny, a pitifully tiny effort. Never mind. It is a movement. It can be "merely symbolic." You may hold your food up to the sun before you have a binge, as a gesture to light and life. Or you may just consciously stop for one second to hold the thought, "sunlight." For me the effort was often writing in the notebook. Countless times I thought it was useless, disgusting, that I went on writing and writing without results, without abandoning the behavior. But it isn't useless. All the efforts are valuable, although you may not be able to see the value.

After a binge don't collapse. Try not to go to sleep. Try to have one conscious moment at the end of a day that you feel you have otherwise obliterated. It doesn't matter that this effort will not bring you success in your larger goals. Just make the effort. Again and again. Each effort is like a grain of sand. Your enemy is like a mountain. But after a long time you will find that the balance has shifted. It has shifted by one grain of sand. There is something under your feet. The grains of sand have become something under your feet, you can see what you are doing, and you stand up inside. That's how it happens.

NOTES

1. First Noble Truth: Suffering pervades life. Second Noble Truth: The cause of suffering is craving. Third Noble Truth: There is a way to end suffering. Fourth Noble Truth: That way is the Eightfold Path.
2. Alan Berg, *The Nutrition Factor,* (Brookings, 1973) 10–11.

A Conduit for Love:
Adopting a Positive Daughter
An Interview with Furyu Nancy Schroeder and Grace Dammann

Lenore Friedman and Susan Moon

Furyu Nancy Schroeder and Grace Dammann live at Green Gulch Zen Center in Muir Beach, California. Fu is a priest and one of the teachers and practice leaders in the community. Grace is a Zen student and a doctor who works at Laguna Honda Hospital in San Francisco. Grace has reduced her medical practice to part-time work in order to be able to work with the residents of the Green Gulch community.

In June of 1993, the two women became the foster parents of Sabrina, an immuno-compromised baby girl born to a European American mother with AIDS, and an African American father. Sabrina was a month old when Grace and Fu took her home. Eighteen months later they became her legal guardians.

Lenore and Sue interviewed Grace and Fu in their house at Green Gulch while Sabrina played around and among them.

GRACE: Sabrina is like a meditation on impermanence. The day we brought her home I said to myself: I just hope she lives long enough to enjoy the sunshine. She has already done that, and everything else is a gift. I live with total impermanence, and I think about it every day.

We got the call about Sabrina on a Saturday. We were sitting with a group of women having breakfast at the Dixie Cafe, and I got a call on our cellular phone. I said, "Let me ask Fu. Call back in ten minutes."

SUE: You mean somebody called in the middle of your breakfast and said, "Here's a baby. Do you want it?"

G: You got it. She was a month old and was just getting ready to be discharged. They were looking for somebody to take her. Fu said, "Let's go see the baby." I just kind of rolled my eyes because Fu hadn't seen many newborns.

FU: I knew nothing from babies. I knew puppies. That's how I got my puppy. I went to the kennel and looked and said, "That one." So the next day, Sunday, we went to see her. As soon as they handed her to me, she opened her eyes and looked at me. "That's it," I said, "I must be your mommy."

G: We knew she was at risk because her mother was infected with HIV. It was kind of a catch-22, because they can't release information on HIV status to disinterested parties. They wouldn't tell us her HIV status unless we agreed to be her foster parents first.

On Monday I talked to the chairman of the pediatrics department at San Francisco General, a doctor who had been my mentor, and he said, "The odds are only 20 percent that she is going to be HIV infected." Our friends were saying, "Don't do it. It would be crazy, given the work you do and the fact that your mother just died." I thought I was crazy myself.

F: In that first week, before we decided, I went to the Green Gulch staff meeting about it. I was the director at the time, and I felt very vulnerable asking such a personal question. But I knew I had to get permission from the community. The way children usually come into the community isn't exactly by permission from the staff. Usually people get pregnant and then the community gets used to it after a while. So I was kind of scared. I didn't know what would happen. At the meeting it turned out my fears were unfounded. Everyone said, "What do you need? Do you need an Uncle? Do you need a fence? Let us know what you need." There was not just support but 100 percent encouragement.

It reminds me of a conversation I just had with Brother David, down at Esalen. He has a little picture of Sabrina on his altar and he has always been sweet about remembering her and praying for her. I took her to see him, and he opened his door and she just reached out and went into his arms. And he was so honored. I asked him, "Brother David, do you think every monk should have a child to raise?" And he said "Absolutely!" It used to be traditional for a monastery to raise children. They took care of the sick and they took in orphans. It still happens among the Tibetans.

G: Green Gulch has totally embraced Sabrina, and totally embraced us in getting Sabrina. They love this child to pieces.

So when our friend Pauline, who was the contact person for Sabrina, called up to see what we had decided, we looked at each other and we knew it was a go. We realized this was something we could do. We have the resources, because of this community and because of our practice.

There was just a week between the first phone call and the day she came home with us. And in that time we had to get certified as foster care people and get all set up for her. We were both working full-time.

F: Her grandmother showed up and said, "Don't worry, I know everything." She bought all the clothes for her and she arrived with a whole layette, a baby bassinet, car seats, two beds. We put our own things in storage to make a baby's room, and after a while every room in the house became the baby's room.

S: Hadn't you already been making attempts to adopt a baby?

F: We had considered both adoption and insemination, and then given up these ideas a couple of years before. I was planning to study in Japan, and Grace was going to do some work in Latin America. And then Sabrina came along, and we both said, "This is it."

G: The day we were wrapping her up in the nursery, putting her new clothes on to bring her home, the test results came in a sealed envelope, that she was HIV positive. It was the day we were bringing her home.

We all had a good cry right there. We were holding Sabrina when we opened the envelope, and it was not what we had been praying for. So we cried; but we haven't cried about it since. That's just what we're working with here.

S: Grace, you have a doctor self and a mother self. Are they separate? Or do you think about medical information all the time when you wish you wouldn't?

G: Yes, I do. I learned about this when my mother died. I learned that I didn't have to be the doctor with my mother, but there was no way out of the fact that I also have this other knowledge. I can't choose to just ignore certain knowledge. In fact it probably helps that I am a doctor, because there are certain things we have been able to do for Sabrina because of it.

S: What kinds of things?

F: The reason they let us bring her home when she was so tiny, and still drug addicted, was because Grace was a doctor. We actually detoxed her ourselves. And at first, I thought, "Grace is a doctor so she'll know everything about how to take care of a baby." But it turns out that being a doctor doesn't give you magic knowledge that's going to fix all the problems. We still had to figure out how to do it.

G: She received paregoric, which is opium, every couple of hours for the first three months of her life. We decreased the dose and increased the time interval, based on how jittery she got.

F: She had all kinds of drugs in her system at birth, but her mother had been on a really high dose of methadone right before she was born, and that's probably the hardest drug for a baby to withdraw from.

G: I talked to all my doctor friends and nobody had ever detoxed a baby as an outpatient.

F: We called a foster mom who had taken care of a lot of kids with drug addictions. She was great; she had the most information of anyone. She said, hold her, give her a bath, don't worry; the baby is stronger than you think and she'll come through okay.

Lenore: How long did it take?

F: Four months. It was pretty pain-free for her. She would go into withdrawal, and that's when we would give her medication. At the end, it was a very smooth transition for her, getting off the drugs.

L: It must have been an incredible bonding for all of you.

F: Well, I think the bonding happened the minute we saw her.

S: How is your practice a resource for you in relation to Sabrina?

F: I got practice at sitting still in the middle of something frightening when I worked at Zen Center Hospice. I learned to sit still with what's happening. When someone's dying, they don't want you to entertain them, but they want you to be there. And if they need water they will tell you "water." So I felt some confidence that I would know what to do with Sabrina. And people said, babies will tell you what they want. I think it would help any mom to have done some sitting, in order to be patient with the constant needs of the child.

L: But you're grappling with something that most moms don't grapple with. As the attachment grows, you have to be preparing to let go.

F: Yes, that's what I thought at first. I thought I was in a unique position. But I've also understood from talking to other moms that something could happen to any child, any day—something terrible. You never know. Terrible things happen. Everyone who loves someone is always in that position because we're all mortal. My practice doesn't make me more ready for Sabrina to die or get sick; I get scared to death when Grace says her virus is particularly active. My whole body just goes, "Oh, please! No, no!" But I do know grief and I do know that my sitting is where I'm going to take it. I can sit still and just let it keep going through me, and I'm grateful for that.

G: When we thought she was deaf, we were so upset. And then we found out she could hear.

S: What are her difficulties right now, physically?

G: Her gross motor development is not normal. She doesn't walk very steadily yet. When we got her they thought she would never be able to walk or move the lower part of her body. We thought maybe she had cerebral palsy, but probably she had a really bad initial HIV infection. Most kids in her category die. They didn't think she'd make it.

F: She's already gone way past anybody's expectations, as far as life expectancy goes. Every birthday is amazing! She's three!

S: Three years is a pretty long time. It's a big piece of your lives already.

G: It's a lot more than just having experienced the sunshine.

F: I never thought that she would call me mommy. I'm getting so much from being her mommy that I can't even begin to say it. It's embarrassing how lucky we are. And because we are in a community, that gift is being shared by all the people here. We pass her around. It's great for us—we just say, "Do you want to play with Sabrina?"

G: She channels love. She has a way of recognizing everybody—she'll sit in the dining room and she'll say "hi" to everybody. Her way of relating to people is so immediate and so focused that *we* have to ask *her* what people's names are sometimes. Before she was speaking in sentences, she already knew everybody's name in this whole community.

L: Do you try and divide the responsibilities?

F: Yes, we have a little schedule on the fridge. We take turns getting up in the night.

G: Initially, we were both getting up every night with her, because we were sleeping together. We both had full time jobs and we would crab at each other—something had to give. We broke up about a month after we got her, and moved into separate rooms. And that has given us each a little space away from her. We both felt like we were dying. And it wasn't because Sabrina is not a terrific kid, but it was true.

S: Do you think Sabrina experienced any difference when you broke up?

G: I think we are both happier. And we both still live here, so she didn't really lose anything.

S: Is being a mom a basic part of your identity now?

F: I felt a mysterious transformation when she arrived. It happened through my dreams and in my physical body. I felt like my cells were being reordered to be responsive as a mother. I hadn't gone through pregnancy, which I think quite organically adjusts you, but I would wake up at night in a panic, thinking, "Where's the baby? Where's the baby? I can't find the baby!" One night I dreamt she was in a toothpaste tube and I was trying to squeeze her out of the tube.

S: It sounds like a birth.

F: The feeling of my body was that I was being changed so that I could do this thing, so I would have the right instincts. And at a certain point I knew the process was done. I was tuned in; I had the equipment.

L: So in some ways you did become a biological mother.

F: I did, I swear it happened. We provide for the survival of our children in our body. They need a mom; they have to have someone who responds to them immediately with her body.

S: Are you more responsive to the world in general now? Do you relate differently to other people?

F: She was like a crowbar that opened my heart, and I haven't been able to close it since. I'm not protected the way I used to be. Especially with kids, I'm just a total sap. I never looked at babies before, but now I just want to follow every baby that goes by.

I'm not the same person. Years ago I asked one of the moms here, "Does one need to experience being a mother?" and she said "No." After I got Sabrina I went back to her and I said, "Why did you say that?" Of course it's not a matter of literally being a mother as much as being open in the way that a mother gets open. It's having that unconditional relationship with another human being. I think it's necessary for our own evolution, and Sabrina came along and did that for me, although I wasn't headed in that direction at all. I was studying the tea ceremony.

L: Does your body feel softer?

F: A lot softer. I'm more at ease, more "at ease" than "at attention," in the military sense of those words.

S: How about you, Grace? Did you feel a change in your body when Sabrina came?

G: It was different for me. My mother had died nine months earlier, and my father was very sick at the time we got the call about Sabrina. I was shell-shocked and Sabrina was a lifeboat; she brought me back into life. My heart had already been cracked open by my mother's dying, so it was different. But I feel Sabrina in every cell of my body. I took her to work with me at the hospital last week, and she took off down the hallway, and everybody was watching out for her. Somebody looked at her and said, "God, she looks so much like you!" Yeah, really!

F: That's so funny.

G: Her hair is almost the same color, and that's about it. But she's always felt like the right child. She felt like my child from the minute she came to life, which was when she was about six months old.

S: What do you mean, "came to life?"

F: Until she was detoxed from the drugs, she was very introverted.

G: She didn't really claim her body and her life until then.

S: When she was detoxing, was it just agonizing to think of what she was going through? Or were you able to stay separate?

G: Sometimes she would start screaming nonstop. The first three months she had a very high-pitched scream: it would empty rooms.

F: When we went to get her, the nurses told us, "This is a power baby." I think that Grace, because she's a doctor, is more tolerant of other people's pain.

G: Yes, that's true.

F: But I don't feel like I have any tolerance. I didn't know what the limits were. I couldn't tell when her pain was excruciating and when it was tolerable. I was always more interested in giving her the paregoric. And we didn't argue about that, but I just feel that our reaction times were different, and Grace was able to push the detox program along, to wait a little longer each time.

G: Until she was detoxed, she didn't have any stable internal environment. In two- or three-hour cycles she was either drugged out or she was uncomfortable. There was no way to smooth out the peaks and valleys until she was totally off the drugs. I knew with every cell of my being that as uncomfortable as it was going to be, we had to go through with it, because her body was a roller coaster. It wouldn't do any good for us to be a container for her until her own body could be a container. As a physician, I had seen kids go through withdrawals much worse than anything we were letting her experience. She was always responsive, she let us hold her, she was consolable.

F: When we first got her I was still keeping my hair very very short, almost shaved, and one of Sabrina's main comforts was to hold on to hair, which I didn't have, so that was the main reason I grew my hair. At night, she still reaches up and grabs hold and then you just sit there and she hangs on to your hair until she's drowsy.

G: When we brought her home, we looked at each other and we said, "They let us take this baby?!" Then when she had to go back to the hospital when she was two months old, that was so awful.

F: She was such a sick little thing, and she was so tiny. I brought her a teddy bear that was just about her size. That was when I felt the most helpless.

G: I promised myself I wasn't going to let her be tortured by Western medicine. When my mother was dying and there was nothing more they could do for her in the hospital, I decided to take her home. I just wanted to keep her with me. I can imagine having that same feeling about Sabrina. I would do anything in my power just to see her little smile.

F: I'm always worrying about Sabrina. I'm always looking around and seeing which fence she's going to crawl through. I have such anxiety about not wanting her to come to harm. I'm a worrywart and it's uncomfortable. Grace is more realistic.

G: But I worry about a different part. I worry about the HIV status. I carry that, and I don't talk to you much about that.

F: Yes, and I have the same worries for her that I have for myself, that some terrible accident will happen. It's physical; it's in my body, I can feel it in my throat. I'm willing to throw myself in front of a train to keep her from being hurt.

L: What about the role that Sabrina has played in bringing together many different people? Her family, and her extended family?

F: On her first birthday, we invited all the main characters in her life. Everyone introduced themselves, and everyone was connected to each other through Sabrina. The connections are always there, but Sabrina's coming has made them visible. She shows us how we are connected; she shows us our community and our family.

G: And love, she shows us our love. That's a biggie. She's a conduit for love. She's like a spider weaving a web. I really believe she wanted to be here. She's a gift, just a point-blank gift.

F: If I didn't have Sabrina I wouldn't know what I was missing, but now that I do know, I am so grateful that I'm not missing this part of my life.

Tulku

JULIE HENDERSON

STUDENT: For me, Rinpoche, the body is just very slow mind.
KUNDUN GYALWANG DRUKPA (*a little testily*): Of course.

I HOPE THERE IS SOME POINT TO this. I have to act on the assumption that remarks by a person this side of realization will be of some help to others on this side. I can know without hope that whatever I say will be wrong from the other side of that radical shift in perception that is usually these days referred to as enlightenment.

On the other hand, many different levels of understanding and teaching are held and supported within the tradition, so, apologia in hand, I leap over the cliff.

Enlightenment refers to a real state. Enlightened beings do not perceive what we do—or as we do. They can, but they are not bound to. Most Westerners, whether practitioners or not, do not behave as if that were true. In fact, in the West we have most often been called upon to practice without the presence of one-who-is-awake to entrain our attention.

Tulku is the word in Tibetan that refers to the embodied presence of Buddha.

My training over the last twenty years has been in bodywork, body-oriented psychotherapy, and, more recently, the study of the embodiment of consciousness at all levels of tissue. Over the same period of time, I have been held and guided by tulku, though for the first half of that time without my noticing.

I don't know if I am a Buddhist or not. Probably it doesn't matter. I study tulku. I expect that all the living spiritual traditions would reveal the presence of tulku if anyone went looking.

So what is it about tulku that is so important? Tulku is the evidence. Tulku is the demonstration that enlightenment is a real state. If we were able to perceive this directly, there would be no need for tulku, but we aren't able. Most of our consciousness is tied up in making body. That body shapes perception to a great degree, so that to open consciousness beyond the usual options of a human being is nearly impossible. After all, if we were capable of waking up—given the constant, persistent attention of all the buddhas—we would have already awakened. Or so they say.

Tulku shows us enlightenment in a form we can, if lucky, perceive directly. It carries conviction. It's persuasive. Why? Because tulku is the flesh of boundless love inseparably luminous as wisdom. To be touched by it opens the mind, staggers the heart. If *this* is possible, anything is possible. Even enlightenment, however improbable.

> VAIROCANA TULKU RINPOCHE: Any kind of being can be tulku. There are human tulkus, dog tulkus, insect tulkus. The form is the same, but the mind is different.
> STUDENT: How is the [tulku's] mind different, Rinpoche?
> VAIROCANA TULKU RINPOCHE: It's *clean*.

On some four or five occasions, because of my vocation as a body-worker, I have had the opportunity to touch the body of a Tibetan high lama in the category of tulku. (Actually, it is because I trust information received through touch more than that of seeing or hearing that my teachers have used my work to reach me.) In the context of twenty years and more of conscious observation of tissue in literally thousands of human beings (and other beings), I feel confident in saying that the tissue embodied by tulku is different from ours. The tissues are happy. Open, spacious, formed without being bound. Presence without pattern. Even when there is pain or dysfunction in the tissue, the tissue is happy—and conscious. The tissues themselves at every level—from muscle groups to cells—*know;* they share in the realization of the tulku.

This is not true of ordinary tissue. Ordinary tissue can be invited to be conscious—and, indeed, it will function more fully and happily conscious than unconscious—but our ordinary tissues are full of pattern, story, attitude, preference, expectation, hope, and fear. Just as we are.

It is not a matter of knowing a lot or having practiced for twenty or thirty years. Not a matter of being a great scholar or of having learned very advanced exercises of mind, energy, and attention. I have also had opportunity to work with the tissues of the most fully trained lamas within the Tibetan tradition (called *khenpo*s)—very fine human beings they are, too, and they know all the exercises and have usually done at least two three-year retreats—but they are not tulku. The tissues of their bodies are just as patterned, unconscious, bound as those of us with less practice experience. In fact, because of the tendency at most levels of teaching and practice to ignore the body—and therefore all the mind that makes the body—their tissues are often holding quite dreadful stories of abandonment and annihilation.

So, better to say I am not a Buddhist. But I do study tulku. And to the best of my capacity, I devise ways to move directly to the *embodiment* of those qualities of love, joy, compassion, and freedom from bias that characterize enlightened mind.

It scares me to say that publicly. The siren call of "who the hell do you think you are?" arises. Better to say nothing. After all, one of the overriding characteristics of tulku is the willingness and capacity to be in disguise pretty nearly indefinitely, waiting for the right moment with the right student. To let almost all advanced instruction be situational and nonverbal. To go a whole lifetime without saying anything "important." We can suppose they have reason for their disguise.

At least one person out there is saying, "What a neurotic, this is nothing but hysterical projection." To a certain extent that has to be true. The currency of the study of tulku is what we think we are, and all that we think we are has to be released—or, more reasonably, torn away like a succession of grossly adhered Band-Aids. In this process, projections onto the tulku are spotlights showing where to rip.

Studying tulku could be conceptual, I suppose, as long as the student never encountered actual tulku. But as soon as tulku is directly felt, the heart is seized, and the slow, gentle, quick, brutal process of divesting self of itself begins.

The action of tulku is direct, indirect, immediate, pervasive, sneaky, shocking, and seductive. Also bloody accurate. How tulku moves with one student will never be remotely similar to what he or she does with any other.

There are two things to be considered. One is the demands of the relationship between "us" and "them"—all the issues of balancing self-responsibility and surrender, the means by which they drive us sane. The other is to look at the means my colleagues and I have developed, through a marriage of somatics, psychotherapy, and Tibetan practices, to support the embodiment of the four great catalysts, the four primary states: love, joy, compassion, balance.

For myself, I am enjoying speaking the unspeakable.

> You are hiring someone to destroy your ego.
> —*Dzongsar Khyentse Rinpoche on* guru yoga, *1995*

Practically and technically, whatever we are experiencing as "how we are" arises as the complex outcome of how we are moving, how we are breathing, and what sounds we are making. Or, as is more common for us who are practiced in repression and suppression, how we reduce breath, how we reduce movement, how we refuse sound. More simply, there is a particular combination of movement, breath, and sound that is "being angry." Unless we move, breathe, and make sound in one of these ways, we will not be angry. Further, if we are angry and we have the capacity by practice to change even one of these factors—to breathe differently even if we make the same sound, or to move differently even if we breathe in the same way, and so on—then we will change what we are feeling. If we are willing. If we are open to being less driven by conditions.

What this makes possible is the discovery and practice of those combinations of movement, breath, and sound that "make" joy, compassion, love, equanimity. Needless to say, the movements, breaths, and sounds that make bodhicitta are more subtle than those that make anger or sadness or fear, but they can be learned and practiced in a very ordinary and effective way.

One other technical piece of information is helpful. Recently it has been discovered that there is a protein—cyclic AMP response element binding protein, or CREB—in the brain that facilitates the creation of long-term memory. There is a particular way of learning that directly stimulates the secretion of CREB, which is to work a little at something (say, an exercise) and then to rest, to do the same exercise again for a little while and then rest, to repeat again for a short time and then rest. We have observed over many years that this procedure—doing a bit, resting, doing a bit more, resting, and so on—facilitates the movement of information from cortical functioning to midbrain and hindbrain functioning. That is to say, this way of learning leads to the incorporation or *embodiment* of the information. It is no longer only a matter of something you know about conceptually; it has become a part of what you do and how you are.

These two technical bits are the basis for the practice of embodiment of well-being and, for the courageous, bodhicitta.

We are extraordinarily influenced by primate and tribal needs. What this means practically is that we want very much to fit in with those around us. We are far more likely to take on the states of being of the folks around us than we are to create "cleaner" states on our own. Even when the states of the people around us are miserable and unpleasant, it is simply easier to participate in them as they are than to make our own, separate from theirs. Noticing this has led to an understanding of sangha as that group of people who actively and consciously pursue embodiment of the four primary states and, in so doing, make it easier for all to do so.

My colleagues and I have developed a form of practice that supports the embodiment of well-being and bodhicitta as directly and fully as possible, but we still need a map, we need a model to follow, a pattern to match. That is what tulku provides. Tulku shows us and shows us and shows us, in every moment. By embodying the unlikely, tulkus startle us—a little or a lot—into noticing new options of perception and being.

Noticing the new options and embodying them means giving up the old options, and that feels like loss of self. It is loss of self in a psychological sense. Without tulku as guide, as reminder, as catalyst, as mother hen, as frightener, we would never even contemplate radical change because we think we already know what's true.

To engage in the "enlightening" relationship with tulku is, from a purely human perspective, madness. To give permission from heart's ground for the annihilation of who you think you are, not only once but over and over until attention is no longer drawn to "I" as a concern, is certainly not sane if enlightenment is not real and not really possible for us. So the surrender to this possibility is far more likely to take place piecemeal than to happen all at once. Perhaps we can tolerate only so much being "somebody else," let alone "nobody in particular."

In any case, we surrender a bit, have our panics and our blisses, and integrate. We surrender to the degree that we trust our perception of tulku. We integrate as we recognize pragmatically that we create what we feel (even more radically, that we make what we perceive) and that we have the choice to change the feelings we are making. Our link to tulku is both catalyst and provocation; the willingness to remain aware of tulku and to bring all experience into that relationship provokes every possible projection in order to dissolve it. We are stretched between those two poles—of trust and surrender, on the one hand, and self-responsibility and self-regulation, on the other. All the finely laminated layers of habituated perception and location and warping of consciousness begin to move and dissolve. Enlightenment begins to show through. The four primary states of love, joy, compassion, and equanimity reveal themselves as the ground of being.

> Guru is very important for all of us, and especially for me; I mean, I'm just surviving on guru, nothing else than that.
> —*Jigme Pema Wangchen, 1995.*

I see I have made the whole process seem rather horrible. It is regularly ghastly, but only for ego, only for our identification with any pattern, only for what we think we are. In any moment that we accept the constant and continuing invitation to settle down simply into what we are, prior to all pattern, then for that moment at least, nothing could be easier or more luscious than this resting without separation as presence in presence. Like a cat basking in the sun, completely surrendered to warmth. Easy, easy, easy.

All that is necessary is this relaxed shift of attention, repeated over and over, until no shock or distraction can startle us back into identification with pattern. In contrast to traditional teachings, I find that the body can be our friendly ally in this. When this shift of attention becomes embodied, when all consciousness and the whole body, every muscle, organ, and cell, knows tulku and agrees to rest there, what could be easier?

> *This* is the body of Buddha.
>   —*Lama Wangdor (indicating the entire phenomenal world)*

The Lonely Body

SUSAN MOON

Here's the thing about my body that gives me grief, and it's not what you might guess. It's not some piece of me that doesn't match the magazines, like my thighs. No, it's this: I'm stuck inside my body, all alone.

Buddhism teaches us that our suffering comes from a belief in the separate self. We suffer because we forget that we are all interconnected. And our bodies, these lovely, mortal bodies in which we live, make a convincing argument that we are separate.

Before we're born, we're not separate in our bodies—we actually share the same bloodstream with at least one other person. But birth is the big separation. It's such a big change we don't even realize it right away; fresh from the realm of the Absolute, we think everything is part of our body. But when the breast we drink from moves beyond our reach, we finally understand that it's not part of our body after all. Everyone goes through this cruel separation one way or another. Thus the sense of self is built on the experience of loss and separation. From then on, our life is defined by a longing for reconnection. At least that's how it feels to me.

When I was a child, I couldn't understand why each person was trapped in their separateness. It was a terrible mystery. "I" was something inside my body peering out at the world through two holes in my head, like an animal in a cage, like a kid in a stifling rubber Hallow-een mask that I couldn't tear off. Why was there just this one spot from which my point of view originated? Why weren't we all in this together, in one giant point of view?

I sensed that we were all made of the same stuff, and that our bodies were just the packaging. Or that we were all part of the same landscape, but we were divided by fences into separate fields. I always wanted to jump the fence.

In my childhood summers, our family went to the seashore. I had no one to play with, my little sisters were too young. I had a secret place, a clearing in the high bayberry bushes where no one could see me, and there I practiced handstands and backbends, lay on the sweet grass, watched faraway white sails on blue water, and tried to figure out who I was, alone in my body, alone in the bayberry bushes. That's not what I would have said I was doing at the time, but that's what I think now. I would have said I was planning a Robin Hood club, or collect-ing butterflies. But even then, something compelled me to study my loneliness. I knew I felt sad in the secret place, but I had to go there. Watching the sun go down across the pond, behind Lobsterville, I was trying to jump the fence. I was wondering: Can the self inside the body get out sometimes and join the rest of the universe?

The body is a physical thing, and so we look for physical solutions, mechanical reunions. One of the best ways to blur the edges is to get really close to another body—a kind of skin-to-skin transmission. When I was a child, wrestling with other neighborhood kids was good, and playing doctor in the bushes—those times I didn't feel lonely. And get-ting into bed in the morning with my grandmother, loving the cool floppy skin on her arms.

I used to play a game with my best friend—not skin to skin but eye to eye. We took turns leading each other around the neighborhood blindfolded, and after a while the guide stopped and the blindfolded one had to guess where we were. "On Brewster Street in front of Tra-cy's house?" Then we'd take the blindfold off and be surprised. But what I loved about the game, more than the guessing, was being the blindfolded one and giving myself up to my friend's eyes. She had one point of view for both of us, and so I wasn't separate. I might as well have been inside her head.

Maybe the best example of the physical experience of reconnection is pregnancy. When I was pregnant, feeling a baby kicking inside me, I was not alone in my body. I liked having company there—it made me feel a sense of purpose at a primitive level. "What are you doing with your life?", a question that has often plagued me, was easily answered. "I'm sharing my body with an unborn person. Just by breathing, I'm keeping somebody else alive."

And the first few months after giving birth, when my children were infants, they were not yet completely separate from me. Feeding a newborn baby in the rocking chair in the middle of the night, the two of us staring into each other's eyes, I didn't feel alone in my body. What other time can two people look so unblinkingly at each other, so free from self-consciousness? And that was exactly it: free from consciousness of the self. I was still sharing my body with somebody else, and I had to be careful about what I ate and drank, because the baby would get it, too.

Speaking of skin-to-skin transmission, there is of course that most democratic way, available to mothers and nonmothers alike: sex. What else but the longing to jump the fence of our separate selves makes us perplex our edges like this, arms and legs all tangled? Peninsulas and headlands of one floating island push into the bays and inlets of another. Close enough to say, in happy confusion, "Is that your stomach or mine growling?"

And what a wonderful thing, to want something really badly *and* be able to get it. To whip up your desire to a fever pitch, to groan and cry out with wanting, and then to feel fulfilled. Is there something wrong with this? As a Buddhist I'm used to thinking of desire as something that can't ever quite be satisfied. But sexual desire *can* be satisfied. I guess what Buddhism knows is that we don't *stay* satisfied. All too soon we drift apart again.

Anyway, Buddhists or not, we need to touch each other. Children need to sit in the laps of grown-ups. The older we get, the fewer opportunities our culture allows us for physical contact. I know a man who teaches neck and shoulder massage at a senior center. He says that older people who don't have a spouse are hardly ever touched by anybody.

A few years ago I went to the dentist to have a cavity filled. I had no lover at the time, and had not had any cavities for a long time. I like my dentist—he's kind, and I've been going to him for twenty-five years. So when he squeezed my shoulder, told me I was looking well, put my chair back, rested his forearm on my chest and began poking around in my mouth, it felt great. I realized it was the first time in a long time that I had been touched. It seemed a sad state of affairs, but still, the dentist's hands in my mouth kept me from feeling lonely.

But the connection doesn't have to be skin to skin. Past experiences of transcending the body's loneliness have included, for me, rock climbing with another person at the other end of the rope—our lives in each other's hands, playing chamber music, folk dancing. Can you imagine feeling lonely while doing the Virginia reel? Now, most often, it's just having a heart-to-heart talk with a friend. There are lots of ways to connect.

But let's face it. Most of the time I'm not having sex, or wrestling with the next-door neighbor, or pregnant, or at the dentist, or even having a heart-to-heart talk with a friend. In fact some of these things I'll never find myself doing again. So how can I practice with loneliness all the rest of the time?

I have experienced an agony of aloneness and fear in my body, not only before I began my Buddhist practice, but after. There is nobody here but me. How could this be? This pain of loneliness is obscured—even erased—by lovers, friends, family. But when they are gone the pain can come back. Particularly at times of separation it comes—at the end of a relationship, or when children grow up, when friends or family move away, when somebody dies. In the middle of a stormy night it can come back. Even in the middle of a meditation retreat it can come back. This is the feeling: that I am sentenced to solitary confinement for life, and the prison cell in which I serve this sentence is my body. A couple of times the pain of separation has been so intense that I have wanted to die, because dying seemed like the only way out of the prison cell. To be alive is to experience separation.

But here is where Buddhism comes in. I am encouraged by the teaching that there is no such thing as the separate self. This must mean that I am one with all beings. John Daido Loori, a Zen teacher, says, "When we believe that our 'self' is whatever is inside this bag of skin, we feel incomplete, cut off from everything else in the universe. Our desire is to heal the split, to become one with what we think is 'out there.' Without the illusion of separate self, there is no gain and no loss."

So I bring my lonely body to meditation practice, hoping to transcend the separate self. Dogen says, "To study the way is to study the self. To study the self is to forget the self. To forget the self is to be enlightened by the ten thousand things."

But for a person afraid of being alone, it's a scary thing to sit down on a zafu, with nobody to talk to, and face the nothingness of a wall. Could be the hardest thing I've done. The very same teaching of no fixed self that comforts me also frightens me. Emptiness is frightening. No fixed self is frightening. If I'm by myself and I don't even *have* a self, then I figure I must be really alone.

A few years ago I attended a three-month meditation retreat at a Zen monastery deep in the mountains. I wanted to study myself and my loneliness. The question I took with me was: Do I have a self or not? Is there anybody home inside this body? When I'm alone, am I alone with one person (me) or am I alone with nobody at all?

In a mirror I can't really *see* myself. How strange that I go through life able to see other people's bodies, even the bodies of complete strangers, in the sauna at the gym for example, and yet the body that lives my life I can't really see. I look for myself in the mirror: "Who *are* you? Are you the same person I was looking at just a few seconds ago?" But the image I see is backwards, the mole on the wrong side of my face. Or looking at myself in a photograph, it's not myself I see, but an image. I can't reach my hand out to the self I see and touch warm flesh.

While I was on retreat, pondering these things, I had a dream that I was at the bathhouse. I'd just gotten out of the tub and I was standing with my profile to a long mirror, looking at myself sideways. Then I turned to face the mirror, but to my surprise the reflection in the mirror didn't turn. The reflected body just stood there, still in profile. I reached through the frame of the mirror and touched the reflection, and it was a solid body. I felt the warm skin that had just come out of the bathtub. It was a really good feeling. It was as if the "I" in the dream, the dreamer, became the witness, and what had been mere reflection became a solid body. I think I was dreaming that I do have a self. Not a fixed self, but a warm body, a place to begin. There's somebody home when I look into the mirror of myself.

Some years ago I heard a Dharma talk that made a great impression on me, given by Blanche Hartman, now an abbess of San Francisco Zen Center. It was at the end of a long sesshin, and I was in a wide-open frame of mind. Blanche said that in the early days of her Zen practice, in her forties, she greatly admired a young male monk. When a friend pointed out to her that she was unconsciously imitating him, she realized it was not her job to be him, it was her job to be herself, a middle-aged woman, and that nobody could do that job as well as she could. Hearing her say so, after days of sitting, I suddenly knew the same about myself—that nobody else but me could do the job of being me. And no matter what happened I couldn't abandon myself, because I couldn't get away. Even major surgery could not separate me from myself. I saw that I could take good care of myself by being me, and I was elated to have myself for a friend. It lasted a couple of weeks.

These feelings come and go, but some part of me remembers that I am whole, that I am Buddha in my body. It is not *in spite* of my moles and fear of earthquakes that I am Buddha, but *because* of them— because I am here, being me.

If we're going to transcend separateness, we've only got our separate bodies to do it in. But this is increasingly difficult in our Western culture, because we are so alienated from our bodies. We think our bodies are objects we make. We think we are the authors of our bodies. Body becomes expensive product, molded by aerobics classes and hairstylists, the worn-out parts replaced by surgery. Body is a capital asset. Still, no matter how much money we spend on it, few of us own the body-object we'd like to own.

Or, we think of our bodies as big pieces of luggage we have to drag around with us. Carry-on luggage: no matter how heavy they are, we can't check them. No wonder we all want to lose weight.

But I don't want to *have* a body anymore. I want to be it. I don't want to carry it around. I don't want to look out through it as if through chinks in a wall. I don't want it to be my pimp, to send it out looking for people to bring home to love me. I don't want to dress it up like a doll to show to my friends. I don't want to treat it like an enemy soldier when it causes me pain, and fight back with chemical warfare. I don't want to lie in bed, trembling and alone *beside* it, as if beside a sullen lover who refuses to be cheered. I'm tired of having a body. I just want to be my body. Not be in it. Not be over here, relating to my body over there. Let me remember that my buddha-nature is drenched in flesh.

I need my individual body to get to the big body of the universe. And I need this small self to get to Big Self. This is my Buddhist practice: to pay such close attention to this body, this life, that it bursts apart.

So I practice with my loneliness. I look the demon of loneliness in the face every time it returns. And it does come back. I have to assume it will keep on coming back, and that it will still be scary. But it's not going to kill me. I'm going to die, but it won't be of loneliness. I stare into the darkness at three o'clock in the morning, after a bad dream, alone in my bed, the sheets damp with my sweat, the windows rattling in the dark wind. And somewhere inside the insomnia, I remember I'm Buddha. I remind myself that the universe is taking care of me. My body is not a prison. It is not a product. It is me now. I offer love, in this quivering body, in this very moment, to myself. In the morning I can offer it to others. That's all there is for me to do.

One of the old sutras we chant says, "Take care of this life, which is the fruit of many lives." The sutra means we've been born and reborn countless times in many forms, before we got to this precious life in a human body. My body is fruit. This is what it means to be incarnate. Whether or not you believe in reincarnation, you can't argue with incarnation. After all, here you are, and that's pretty remarkable in itself, isn't it? *In-carnate* means in flesh, in meat. I live in my own meat. I *am* meat. This body is not just my house, not just where I live, it's me. The meat of me. I dive into my lonely body; it holds me tight. Starting from here, with this old pair of used lungs, I exchange myself with the universe with every breath.

∾

Our Substitute Life

CHARLOTTE JOKO BECK (WITH EZRA BAYDA)

As WE LIVE TOGETHER, IT BECOMES painfully clear how important a life of practice really is. The mayhem and pain we cause when we don't know what our life is, the punishment we inflict on ourselves and on others—it's almost inconceivable. And there is no medal given for practicing, no trophy. But if we don't practice, and understand *what* practice is, we will continue to suffer.

Many of us still have the strange belief that having an enlightenment experience will dispel all of this pain, that it will completely cancel our unhappiness. But the ambition to "become" enlightened can be a serious distortion of practice. Our very nature is enlightenment. What practice is about is seeing how we block our natural state of being, and what it means to work through this blockage.

So let us consider our basic illusion—the blockage—that is the source of our unsatisfactory, substitute life. And make no mistake: all of us, to some degree, are living a fake or substitute life.

How does this misfortune come about? Our substitute life is born out of a core of conditioning, which is formed from the inevitable and innumerable disappointments of our early years. Our struggles with them result in more and more fixed beliefs about ourselves and the world.

In time, our core belief—always negative and always painful—

becomes more fixed and rigid. It becomes a truth we hold so deeply that it is not even open to question: "I am unlovable," "I am hopeless, worthless," "I am alone, abandoned," "I am unable to succeed," "I am unable to do it right," "I am separate from the rest of humanity." The devastating and painful character of our core belief drives each one of us to find ways to hide its existence from ourselves and others.

To do this, we develop many strategies for covering the aching, quivering hole of pain. If my core belief is "I am unlovable," I may try to please and placate others in ways neither appropriate nor wise. Another strategy might be just the opposite: to withdraw and deny any contact whatsoever. We may remain confused all our life about our puzzling behavior.

Our strategy may often look like the opposite of our hidden core belief. The hard-driving businessperson (or artist, or mother, or athlete) may look as if he or she is doing great things in the world—and such may be the case. But if in these efforts there is a feeling of dissatisfaction, or of something missing, then the action or work is being pushed by the poisonous and hidden core belief. "I am unable to succeed . . . I am an impostor . . . I never was any good . . . If they really knew the truth about me . . . I don't deserve to live." Sounds strange, doesn't it? But it is true of all of us, at least some of the time.

As we sit, we become increasingly sensitive to our patterns and strategies. Therapy can also help uncover them. But sitting—day after day, year after year—also builds the power or courage to move beyond seeing the mental "stuff" to the even more crucial step of returning to the bodily experience.

Why return to the body? Why is it crucial to our practice and therefore our life? We return so we can experience directly—not in words—the quivering pain out of which our core belief was formed.

When, in sitting or in life, we become aware of any disappointment, any emotional reaction—any sense of dis-ease in our body—we know that we are picking up a trace of our core belief. So we need to ask ourselves, "What is the core of this dis-ease?" It's not a simple question that can be answered by a simple thought.

In fact, thought of any sort, simple or complex, rational or irrational, cannot lead us to freedom from our core belief. (Thinking is, of course, a valuable and indispensable tool in living. It just isn't the best tool in understanding what our life is.) Only one endeavor helps. We must abandon our mistaken trust in *thinking* as a path to freedom and turn in one direction only: to experience in our body the pain of the core belief itself. We have to face the pain we have been running from. In fact, we need to learn to rest in it and let its searing power transform us. When we truly rest in this bodily sensation, there's a knowing, an exact resonating in the body. And finally there is a spaciousness and peace in which we see ourselves and our actions in a new light.

It should be emphasized that experiential practice and investigation of our core belief is not analysis. Nor can it be reduced to some formula. Teachers can help keep us on track. It's not that they have completed their own work, but still they can help us to clarify what we're seeing and doing.

Until this return to bodily experience is the base of our sitting (and our daily practice), our lives will not transform. Why? Until our core belief is experienced directly in the body, even if mentally we "understand" it, it will continue to run our lives. Its poisonous footprints will be all over our living—our relationships, our work, everything—with accompanying discomfort and dissatisfaction. For instance, if we have the core belief, "I'll never make it," we'll make sure this belief is realized in our life: we will fail. Our core belief may be almost unconscious, but we believe it, we fear it, and we obey it. In fact, we believe in our core belief as the deepest truth about ourselves.

Often, questions arise: "What does this have to do with Zen? Isn't this just psychology?" What these questions reveal is that the basic human problem has not yet been grasped. The fact is that we are definitely psychological beings—many of the barriers to leading a more open, more free, more giving life come directly from our psychologically rooted core beliefs. These beliefs are like boundaries; they cut us off from awareness of our true nature, our naturally open heart. And Zen practice has always been about exactly this: seeing through our boundaries, our self-images, our artificial separations of mind.

This is not to say that psychology is all there is to practice—nor that we are following most standard psychological models, which are often (not always) primarily concerned with changing our self, fixing our self up. What we are talking about is not fixing ourselves up—it's about *seeing*. It's not about judging, or changing, or improving, or analyzing. It's about seeing the truth about who we really are, seeing from a much bigger container of awareness.

To do this, we have to see the extent of our belief-based substitute life. And further (and this is where this practice departs from most traditional psychologies), we have to willingly experience the pain or the "hole" that this substitute life was originally meant to cover over and protect us from. We begin to look at our disappointment, our anger, and then perhaps to go down layer after layer to the hurt, to the grief, to the fear which usually lie underneath.

If we really stay with this experience, it will eventually take us back to the original hole—whether we experience it as being separate, feeling abandoned, feeling utterly hopeless, full of fear and dread—whatever its flavor. Only by uncovering and entering this most dreaded part of ourselves can we see through this artificial construct of our substitute life—and ultimately connect with awareness of our basic wholeness.

So the "secret" of life that we are all looking for is just this: to develop through sitting and daily life practice the power and courage to return to that which we have spent a lifetime hiding from, to rest in the bodily experience of the present moment—even if it is a feeling of being humiliated, of failing, of abandonment, of unfairness. We learn to rest in our experience *without thought,* to sink into a nondual state. Even if we can stay only a few seconds at first, with time and development we can learn to rest there for long periods of time.

As we rest in this nonduality, we leave behind the phenomenal world of problems and dualistic solutions. We start with including and clarifying our psychological world, but we end in a transformation that cannot be really described in words. We can only suggest a way of living that is free, compassionate, functional. And in this way our so-called problems can be dealt with in a more open and compassionate manner.

Call this enlightenment if you wish. But please remember: we do not do this bodily experiencing just once, or in one sitting. We are describing a lifetime process with many ups and downs, probably one that is never complete. It doesn't matter! What does matter is the slow, slow shift in the way we see and live our lives. This is Zen practice and an end to our substitute life.

ABOUT THE CONTRIBUTORS

Connie Batten is a mother and grandmother. She is also a woman in midlife, for whom the passage of menopause has been profound. Her work in the world is with children and adults, helping them to build relationships and respond creatively to conflict. Her work and play at home are about living as simply as possible in close connection with the earth, sky, and changing seasons.

Jan Chozen Bays is the resident teacher of the Zen Community of Oregon and Larch Mountain Zen Center. A Zen practitioner for twenty-two years, she was ordained as a priest in 1978 and received Dharma transmission (authority to teach) from Maezumi Roshi in 1983. She is a wife, mother, and pediatrician working in the field of child abuse. In her teaching, she frequently works with problems of balancing practice with work, family, and community involvement. In recent years, her focus has broadened to include residential Zen training as an opportunity for deeper practice.

Charlotte Joko Beck lives and teaches an approach to practice that many have regarded as radical—however, it simply represents awakened practice in the midst of daily life circumstances—which, in the case of most practitioners at Zen Center San Diego, involves practicing with family and primary relationships, the marketplace, and other societal institutions. Her experience raising four children and working in both education and industry until retirement age have provided her the experiential base for illumining classical practice of the Awakened Way as it applies in everyday life.

Barbara Brodsky has been practicing meditation since 1970, with dual roots in the Buddhist and Quaker traditions. She teaches Vipassana meditation and Dzogchen (nondual awareness) practices all over the world, and she is the guiding teacher of Deep Spring Center, which offers meditation classes and retreats. Barbara has been profoundly deaf for twenty-five years. Living with silence has greatly influenced her life and teaching, as have years of active involvement in nonviolent social change. She is married and the mother of three children. She is also a sculptor and writer.

Pema Chödrön, the resident teacher at Gampo Abbey in Cape Breton, Nova Scotia, is one of the foremost students of Chögyam Trungpa Rinpoche. She is the author of *The Wisdom of No Escape* (Shambhala Publications, 1991), *Start Where You Are* (Shambhala Publications, 1994), and *When Things Fall Apart* (Shambhala Publications, 1997).

Linda Chrisman is a Somatics educator and practitioner who uses touch, movement, sound, and breath as a means of facilitating awareness. She has a B.A. in psychology from Stanford University and an M.A. in philosophy and religion from the California Institute of Integral Studies. Linda has studied and practiced Buddhism for over fifteen years, and has led wilderness journeys in India, Nepal, and the United States.

Darlene Cohen earned her graduate degree in physiological psychology in 1966 and began sitting at the San Francisco Zen Center in 1970. She was lay-ordained in 1974. After developing rheumatoid arthritis in 1977, she was led to explore the potential of meditation training for addressing chronic pain and catastrophic situations. In 1980, after receiving her certificate as a massage and movement teacher from Meir Schneider, she began instructing people with chronic illness in meditation practices and self-awareness exercises. Currently, she sees private clients and leads arthritis workshops, classes, lectures, and pain seminars in California, Washington, and Illinois. She is the author of *Arthritis: Stop Suffering, Start Moving/Everyday Exercises for Body and Mind,* (Wacker and Co., 1995) and is completing a second book, *Suffering and Delight.*

Linda Ruth Cutts is a Zen priest, teacher, and head of practice at Green Gulch Farm, in Muir Beach, California, where she lives with her husband and their two children. In December 1996, she received Dharma transmission in the lineage of Shunryu Suzuki Roshi, from Tenshin Reb Anderson.

Grace Dammann started practicing Zen in 1983. She is a physician who works primarily with late-stage AIDS patients, and she lives at Green Gulch Farm, in Muir Beach, California.

Lenore Friedman is a writer and psychotherapist in Berkeley, California, and the author of *Meetings with Remarkable Women: Buddhist Teachers in America* (Shambhala Publications, 1987). She has worked intensively with Toni Packer since 1983.

China Galland is a writer whose work includes *Women in the Wilderness* (Harper and Row, 1985); *Family Secrets* (Harper and Row, 1987); *Longing for Darkness: Tara and the Black Madonna* (Viking/Penguin, 1990/1991); and the forthcoming book *The Bond Between Women: The Journey to Fierce Compassion* for Riverhead Books/Putnam, 1998. She is also the founder and director of the Images of Divinity Research Project at the Center for Women and Religion at the Graduate Theological Union, Berkeley, California.

Barbara Gates is a writer living in Berkeley, with her husband Patrick and their eight-year-old daughter Caitlin. She has been practicing Vipassana meditation since 1975. As co-editor of the journal *Inquiring Mind,* she explores Buddhism through writing about daily life. She is currently working on a book based on this theme.

Rita M. Gross, a longtime student of Chögyam Trungpa Rinpoche, is an author and lecturer who teaches both in academic and in dharmic contexts. Her book *Buddhism after Patriarchy: A Feminist History, Analysis, and Reconstruction of Buddhism* was published by State University of New York Press in 1993.

Casey Hayden makes a home with her husband, Paul Buckwalter, in Tucson, Arizona, Sonoran Desert Bioregion, where she practices with the Zen Desert Sangha, writes, and gardens.

Julie Henderson is the author of *The Lover Within* (Station Hill Press, 1986), a practical handbook on opening to energy exchange in relationship, as well as the forthcoming *The Jiggle Book: How to Feel as Good as You Can in Spite of Everything.* She has combined Somatics, body-oriented psychotherapy, Ericksonian hypnotherapy, and twenty years of study with Tibetan lamas into a form of personal work and training that emphasizes direct movement to pleasure and well-being. She calls this work *Zapchen,* after a Tibetan word that describes a salubrious, mind-changing naughtiness. She is also known for her unrehearsed once-upon-a-time stories.

Linda Hess has been a Zen practitioner on and off since 1974. She's a scholar of the religions of India, and has taught at several universities including the University of California at Berkeley and Stanford. Her translations of the poetry of Kabir were published by North Point Press. She lives with her husband and two children in Berkeley.

Anne C. Klein has been a student of Buddhism since 1969. She is currently Professor and Chair of the Department of Religious Studies at Rice University, where she teaches courses in Buddhist thought and Tibetan language. She is the translator or author of several books, including, most recently, *Meeting the Great Bliss Queen: Buddhists, Feminists and the Art of the Self* (Beacon Press, 1995). She is a founding director of Dawn Mountain, a Tibetan temple, community center, and research institute in Houston, Texas.

Michele Martin founded Bodhi Mandala Zen Center in New Mexico with Sasaki Roshi, and was acquisitions editor at SUNY Press. She now lives in Kathmandu, Nepal, is fluent in the Tibetan language, has translated numerous Tibetan Buddhist texts, and has traveled widely as interpreter for Khenpo Tsultrim Gyamtso Rinpoche. She has done intensive training in the esoteric meditational practices of the Kagyu lineage, and currently teaches at the Marpa Institute in Kathmandu.

Michele McDonald-Smith has practiced Vipassana meditation since 1975. She is a senior teacher of the Insight Meditation Society in Barre, Massachusetts, and a cofounder of Vipassana Hawaii, and she also teaches worldwide. She has a deep interest in preserving the ancient teachings and in finding ways of expression that make them more accessible and inspiring. She lives in Honolulu, where she has a sand-play therapy practice.

Kuya Minogue is an adult education instructor in an isolated First Nations village in northern British Columbia. Her introduction to Buddhism was in 1981 in Ojai, California, at the first meeting of Wallace Black Elk and Chagdud Tulku. She has been training in Soto Zen since 1986. She invites the feminine divine into her Buddhist practice.

Susan Moon has practiced Zen since 1976, at Berkeley Zen Center, Tassajara Zen Mountain Monastery, and Green Gulch Farm with Sojun Mel Weitsman and Tenshin Reb Anderson. She is the author of *The Life and Letters of Tofu Roshi* (Shambhala Publications, 1988) and the editor of *Turning Wheel,* the journal of the Buddhist Peace Fellowship.

Naomi Newman is currently a writer, director, and performer with A Traveling Jewish Theater, which she helped found in 1979. She has an MFCC and in the 1970s worked with people who had life-threatening illnesses at the Center for the Healing Arts in Los Angeles, focusing on the psychospiritual aspects of illness. She has been practicing Vipassana for seventeen years.

Helena Norberg-Hodge has worked for the last two decades with the people of Ladakh, in the Himalayas, to demonstrate ecologically sustainable alternatives to Western-style development. She is the author of *Ancient Futures—Learning from Ladakh* (Sierra Club Books, 1991). She is founder and director of the International Society for Ecology and Culture and the Ladakh Project, and cofounder of the International Forum on Globalization.

In 1981, **Toni Packer** founded the Springwater Center for Meditative Inquiry and Retreats in Springwater, New York. She had been a student of Roshi Philip Kapleau since 1967 and later served as teacher and then director of the Rochester Zen Center. In addition to her own doubts, contact with the teachings of J. Krishnamurti led her to abandon the rituals and formalities of Zen and its inherent hierarchical structure. She spends about half the year at Springwater Center and several weeks of the year leading retreats in California and Europe. She is the author of *The Light of Discovery* and *The Work of This Moment* (both published by Charles Tuttle), and *Seeing without Knowing* and *What Is Meditative Inquiry?* (published by Springwater Center).

Phyllis Pay is a psychic and intuitive counselor, minister, and group facilitator who maintains a private practice in Berkeley, California, and teaches in many parts of the United States, Europe, and South America. She is the founder of the Intuitive Energy Center and is the originator of the Intuitive Energy Process, which integrates clairvoyant training with somatic awareness and emotional release work. She has practiced meditation for more than twenty-five years, and in the past few years she has studied Tibetan teachings within the Sakya lineage. Her current work integrates Western mysticism and Tibetan Tantric practice.

Bobby Rhodes received Dharma transmission from Zen Master Seung Sahn in October 1992. In 1977 she became the guiding teacher of Zen centers in Chicago and Tallahassee, Florida. She helped found the Providence Zen Center and lived there for seventeen years, teaching and serving in a number of administrative capacities. A registered nurse since 1969, she works for Hospice Care of Rhode Island and lives in Providence with her daughter.

Furyu Nancy Schroeder is a Zen priest and longtime practitioner in the San Francisco Zen Center community, residing at Green Gulch Farm. She has held a number of monastic leadership positions and is currently vice president of San Francisco Zen Center.

Maylie Scott is a priest at the Berkeley Zen Center, and teacher for the Arcata Zen Group in Humboldt County, California. She began learning about social change during her career as a social worker, and since her retirement at age fifty she has pursued her social activism in various ways, including antinuclear protest at the Concord Naval Weapons Station, helping at the Center for AIDS and the Berkeley Men's Shelter, facilitating a meditation group at a women's jail, and, most recently, becoming a Buddhist Peace Fellowship Board member. What is Buddhist social action?

Joan Iten Sutherland is a teacher with the California Diamond Sangha, a Zen community in the Harada-Aitken lineage, located in Santa Rosa, California. Her Buddhist practice is informed by a longtime study of women's cross-cultural spiritual experiences and the indigenous religions of Old Europe. Joan is the editor of *Blind Donkey: Journal of the Diamond Sangha,* and a translator of Chinese. She is currently working on a book about women in the koan tradition of Chan and Zen.

Katherine Thanas started her Zen practice with Shunryu Suzuki Roshi in San Francisco in 1967. She was ordained by Richard Baker in 1975 and received Dharma transmission in 1988 from Tenshin Reb Anderson of the San Francisco Zen Center. She was resident teacher for several years at Tassajara Zen Mountain Center. Since 1988 she has been leading practice at the Monterey Bay Zen Center and at the Santa Cruz Zen Center. In addition to the teachers just mentioned, Dainin Katagiri Roshi was an important teacher for her. She lives in Santa Cruz, California.

Joan Tollifson is the author of *Bare Bones Meditation: Waking Up from the Story of My Life* (Bell Tower, 1996). Joan was on staff at Springwater Center for Meditative Inquiry and Retreat in Springwater, New York, for a number of years, and has recently returned to live in the San Francisco Bay area.

Fran Tribe began her Zen practice at the Berkeley Zendo in 1967 and was a student of Shunryu Suzuki Roshi before his death. She has also practiced at Tassajara, San Francisco Zen Center, and Koko An in Honolulu. She works as a psychotherapist and, together with her husband, leads a weekend zazen group at their home in Orinda, California.

Jisho Warner is the resident priest and Zen teacher at Stone Creek Zendo in Sebastopol, California. She was ordained as a Soto Zen priest by Reverend Tozen Akiyama of the Milwaukee Zen Center.

Ruth Zaporah is a San Francisco Bay Area performance artist, director, and teacher. In addition to creating set pieces which she performs solo or in collaboration with other artists, Ruth works within the improvisation, performance, and training process she calls Action Theater. She performs and leads trainings for dance and theater organizations throughout the United States, Canada, Europe, and Israel. In 1994, she performed with the Dove Tour in theaters and refugee camps in Serbia and Croatia. She teaches regularly at Naropa Institute, Esalen Institute, and Tassajara Zen Center in California, and is the author of *Action Theater, The Improvisation of Presence* (North Atlantic Books, 1995).

CREDITS